.CULINARY.
IMPROVISATION

....

Skill Building Beyond the Mystery Basket Exercise

**Jonathan Deutsch, Ph.D.
and Sarah Billingsley
with Cricket Azima**

Pearson Education

New York Boston San Francisco
London Toronto Sydney Tokyo Singapore Madrid
Mexico City Munich Paris Cape Town Hong Kong Montreal

Cover Art: Design by Landers Miller Design, LLC

Copyright © 2009 by Jonathan Deutsch and Sarah Billingsley
All rights reserved.

Permission in writing must be obtained from the publisher before any part of this work may be reproduced or transmitted in any form or by any means, electronic or mechanical, including photocopying and recording, or by any information storage or retrieval system.

All trademarks, service marks, registered trademarks, and registered service marks are the property of their respective owners and are used herein for identification purposes only.

Printed in the United States of America

10 9 8 7 6 5 4 3 2 1

2009800015

MP

www.pearsonhighered.com

ISBN 10: 0-558-33729-5
ISBN 13: 978-0-558-33729-2

CULINARY
IMPROVISATION

Skill Building Beyond the Mystery Basket Exercise

·CULINARY·
IMPROVISATION

Skill Building Beyond the Mystery Basket Exercise

Copyright © 2009 by Jonathan Deutsch and Sara Billingsley

All rights reserved.

No part of this book may be used or reproduced in any manner whatsoever without written permission.

Design by Landers Miller Design, LLC

ISBN 978-0-9824139-0-6

THE AUTHORS WOULD
LIKE TO THANK THE
FOLLOWING REVIEWERS:

Dr. Victor A.L. Gielisse

The Culinary Institute
of America

Hyde Park, NY

Michael Carmel

Culinary Institute of
Charleston

Charleston, SC

Abby Nash

Cornell University

Ithaca, NY

Joseph Wollinger

Blackhawk Technical
College

Janesville, WI

Michael Riggs

Bowling Green
Technical College

Bowling Green, KY

Wilfred Beriau

Southern Maine
Community College

Gray, ME

Joseph Schultz

Cabrillo College

Asptos, CA

About the Authors

Jonathan Deutsch

Jonathan Deutsch is a classically trained chef and is Assistant Professor and director of the Culinary Management Center at Kingsborough Community College, City University of New York. He earned his Ph.D. in food studies and food management at New York University and is Secretary of the Association for the Study of Food and Society and education editor of the journal *Food, Culture and Society*. He is the co-author of *Jewish American Food Culture* (Greenwood, 2008) and co-editor of *Gastropolis: New York at Table* (Columbia University Press, 2008). A graduate of Drexel University and the Culinary Institute of America, he has worked in a variety of foodservice settings including product development, catering, institutions, luxury inns, and restaurants, both in the US and abroad. He currently teaches, writes, and consults on food and foodservice and culinary arts and entrepreneurship education. For more information on the author and improvisation go to: culinaryimprovisation.com.

Sarah Billingsley

Sarah Billingsley is a cookbook editor, food writer and experimental home cook. She earned her masters degree in food studies and food management at New York University and is a member of San Francisco Professional Food Society. She worked at an editor on the 75th anniversary edition of *Joy of Cooking,* and was a dining critic and food writer at the Pittsburgh Post-Gazette. A graduate of the University of Pittsburgh, she has worked in publishing, public relations, product development and market research. Sarah currently lives and works in San Francisco, where she cultivates a backyard food garden during the endless California growing season.

table of contents/

UNIT II

1/
Introducing Culinary Improvisation

"The only real stumbling block is fear of failure. In cooking you've got to have a what-the-hell attitude."

– *Julia Child* (1912-2004)

"In the midst of researching flavor profiles and the words of chefs about putting potentially incongruous—even strange—flavors together, it was Valentine's Day, and I needed to make a dessert. My boyfriend adores chocolate, and I love fruit desserts, and I try, whenever possible, to create desserts for us that star both chocolate and fruit.

In the spirit of Valentine's Day, I bought blood oranges. Not only were they in season at the time, but their bright fuchsia hue is gorgeous and passionate. I see that color and I want to consume it.

I could have made a simple blood orange sorbet, since orange and chocolate is a classic pairing. But I wanted something more interesting, and personal, for my boyfriend. I was thinking spice and citrus, to cut the oozy richness of a molten chocolate cake, and we had a bottle of Lagavulin, a single malt scotch, which was a Hanukkah gift from my father. I'd just bought, for a stewed dish with an Asian flavor profile, some cinnamon sticks and some star anise.

Scotch. Spice. Blood orange. Hmmm. I started off by infusing the simple syrup for the sorbet with orange peel, star anise and cinnamon. When the mixture had gotten syrupy, I added a splash of scotch. I mixed this with the blood orange juice, froze a little for tasting, and—wow! The sorbet turned out to be a subtle masterpiece of contrasts, flame-colored but icy on the tongue, tart but sweet, with a haunting smoky/sharp/citrus finish.

Who needs a molten chocolate cake with that?"

– *Sarah Billingsley*

Why We Wrote this Book

The culinary arts is a creative field, where great ingenuity is rewarded; where problem-solving in a fast-paced environment is critical; and where the line between simply cooking tasty food and being a chef are worlds apart.

This book originated in a discussion with chefs. I (Jon) had just started to develop a new culinary program in a major city. I met with a group of chefs, foodservice managers and other hospitality employers to ask them what skills they wanted to be sure their students graduated with. My hope was that if the students had these skills, these chefs and managers would hire our graduates.

I expected the responses to be predominantly culinary skills—good knife techniques; soups, stocks and sauces; fish and meat butchery; pastry work. While these skills came up in conversation, I was shocked that they were very far down on the list and arose late in the discussion. What were the priorities for the employers?

- "A good palate."
- "Someone who shows up clean, on-time and ready to work."
- "Someone who will communicate if there's a problem."
- "Someone who can work well on our team."
- "Someone who doesn't need to be told every little thing—someone who sees a problem and fixes it."

We thought back to our own culinary educations. Were these skills we learned? Could these skills be taught?

We spoke with culinary instructors at other schools. Did they teach these kinds of skills? Did their employers demand these skills too?

This book arose out of those early conversations and many more over the past few years. Generally speaking, employers in our field want employees from culinary schools with strong knife and cooking skills, but also with some of the characteristics mentioned above—a professional work ethic, good problem solving, teamwork and communication and a strong palate. While there are many resources for culinary students to learn and practice excellent cooking techniques, how do they learn these other skills that chefs say are so important in their hiring decisions?

The cornerstone of much culinary education is replication. It's an important skill and was certainly the foundation of our culinary educations. Here's how it works. The instructor demonstrates a skill or dish—an onion brunoise, a sauce hollandaise, or a braised lamb shank. Then the students replicate the instructor's technique. If your hollandaise tastes, looks and smells like your teacher's, then you

did a great job! If it's lumpy, grey, oily, too salty, not acidic enough or otherwise "off," you did something wrong and need to keep practicing. This is an excellent way to develop culinary technique and is a good basis for culinary education.

Advanced cooking classes may also be founded on replication, but there's a new judge. Here's how that might work. The instructor demonstrates a dish such as a spinach salad with seared scallops and a cardamom cracker. The instructor provides instruction and recipes for the components. You replicate the dish. The instructor tastes a small amount or gives it a visual examination and then it goes out of the kitchen to be eaten by another student or a paying guest, who will judge whether it was done well. This is an excellent way to test your mastery of culinary technique and whether you could function in a professional environment where you're not just cooking for the instructor but for a guest.

This book offers another form of culinary education, one that forces you to apply the skills you learned throughout your education but not through replication. This is a culinary textbook with few recipes. It forces you to cook creatively, by improvisation, while building your culinary skills as well as four skills deemed essential by employers:

- Problem Solving
- Palate Development
- Teamwork
- Communication

When I (Jon) was in culinary school I wanted to get creative. One of my teachers told me that that's only the right of a chef; not a cook. A cook needs to build skills by replicating recipes until they are mastered.

A chef can then be creative with that recipe to create something new. I was impatient. I was creative while still learning to master techniques. And I turned out OK! While I can understand that instructor's point of view, I always wondered what he was afraid of. What if I did something really creative and it was awful? I would have to throw it out and try something else. So? Would it prevent the development of good culinary skills to try something new and be creative? To the contrary, I thought, it might enhance it.

actors, photographers—use studio space to practice. Why not chefs? These artists try things, discard some, refine others and invent new approaches in their studio. This book challenges culinary teachers and students to treat chefs as artists in the same way, with a kitchen as a studio to practice before debuting in the performance space of a restaurant, banquet or other foodservice operation.

The main inspiration for this book from the arts is the concept of "theater games"—creative, process-oriented activities used by

> *...many artists—musicians, painters, sculptors, actors, photographers—use studio space to practice. Why not chefs?*

Think of something in your life that you learned. Something where you can say, "Wow. That's something I really learned that will stay with me forever." In many cases, it's a mistake you made that you learned from. But in culinary school we don't like mistakes. Mistakes mean your food doesn't taste or look like the teacher's and that's bad replication. Further, we love food; that's why we're cooks! The worst thing is to make something poorly and have to throw it out. Isn't it?

This book challenges you to be creative, to take risks, to make mistakes but to learn from them, to try things and say to yourself, "I wonder what would happen if I..."

Culinary Improvisation teaches you how to practice your skills and build new ones in a studio environment. So many artists—musicians, painters, sculptors,

theater students and actors to hone their craft in studio. An acting class in the process of playing a theater game is a strange sight. Actors may pretend to be inanimate objects such as rocks or trees; they may be acting like animals or silently contorting their face to represent an emotion such as "anger" or "glee." Why are they doing those things? They are practicing their craft. Through theater games, they are challenging themselves to work on technique, try things out, be creative and refine their skills so that when they are performing for real, they can act with confidence. It may not be a realistic acting experience to express anger with no words. But that same angry face—practiced in studio—with some dialogue added will be a very convincing angry person.

So like these artists in studio, our hope for you is that you devote a bit of your culinary education to this type of creative cooking. We want you to engage with this text by having fun, practicing, learning, creating and being a better cook and better worker at the end of it.

How To Use This Book

This book is organized into two units.

UNIT I

Unit I is comprised of tools that will help you through the rest of the book and through your career. A key feature of Unit 1 are the platforms that will help in playing the games that follow. A platform is, in many ways, like a recipe. Like a recipe, a platform tells you how to cook something. But unlike a recipe, platforms are general guides for a dish in general; not for a specific preparation. To use the music example again, a platform is like a theme, the structure upon which you can build variations in tone, cadence, and so on. For example, a recipe for a vinaigrette may call for one tablespoon of minced garlic, two tablespoons of mustard, one cup of vinegar, two cups of oil, and so on. A platform draws the essential elements out of recipes and presents them as a blank canvas for improvisation. So a platform for the same vinaigrette might call for one part acid, two parts oil and list some ideas for flavoring components that could be added.

There are two ways to use Unit 1. Unit 1 could be formally taught chapter-by-chapter. Or it could be used as reference material to help with Unit 2. For beginning students, it is better to go chapter-by-chapter through Unit 1. More advanced students will want to use it as reference material to help with the games and to brush up on skills or knowledge that aren't as strong or that have been forgotten.

UNIT II

Unit II features Culinary Games arranged by those competencies that chefs and other foodservice employers tell us are critical and too-often underdeveloped in their new employees:

- Problem Solving
- Flavor and Palate Development
- Teamwork
- Communication

Of course these competencies interrelate. It is nearly impossible to complete one of these games without building culinary skills and multiple featured competencies. For example, since teamwork is so heavily dependent on communication, a game challenging a group to come together and perform as a team will simultaneously emphasize communication skills and, of course, culinary skills.

Beginning students can work through these games, focusing on the development of specific skills as well as gaining comfort in the kitchen. Advanced students can refine and integrate their skills, building creativity and testing their innovative ideas.

In addition to building knife skills and cooking technique, a successful outcome will require strong problem solving, knowledge of ingredients, an understanding and application of how the flavors will work together, working with your classmates and teammates and communicating with one another and with your instructor. The final chapter shows you some guidelines for creating your own games and assessing your performance.

The Games

Games, like simulations and other forms of problem-based and active learning, challenge you as a student to immerse yourself in your learning to work through a complex series of problems. The games in this text put you in complex situations that require a combination of skills—culinary, interpersonal, critical thinking, problem solving and others—in order to solve. Imagine, for example, that you are faced with developing an entrée that must meet the following criteria:

- Under $2 food cost
- Gluten-free
- Flavor principles from Korean cuisine
- Able to be hand-held when eaten

What sort of knowledge and skills would you need to draw from in order to successfully handle this challenge?

The games in this book range from realistic to far-fetched scenarios; and from easily mastered to challenging. But in all cases, they draw on your culinary, creativity and problem solving abilities to hone your skills.

Rubrics and How to Use Them

Each game (6–10) chapter provides an assessment rubric. Your instructor may provide her or his own as well. While individual results to the games will vary widely, the rubric will give you a sense of how you fared—how would a professional-level cook handle these scenarios as opposed to a beginning cook? And you can view these rubrics across a range of competency areas, from safety and sanitation to innovative flavor combinations. You should plot where

you think you will be on the rubric for each game and constantly strive to do better with each culinary improvisation exercise.

What is Culinary Improvisation?

Culinary improvisation is the ability to create dishes and menu concepts as needed. **Improvisation** is a creative process where, drawing on your knowledge and skills, you work creatively within given parameters.

Perhaps best known for their improvisational skills are jazz musicians. Jazz musicians often perform with no sheet music in front of them. How do they do it? They are skilled at playing their instrument. They have specific knowledge of tools like scales and chords. They have certain parameters in which to perform such as a variation on a standard tune or a certain rhythm. From there these elements are combined creatively so that no two performances are identical.

Cooks can use improvisation in much the same way. If you know basic preparations and cooking techniques, how flavors work together to contrast or reinforce one another, and how ingredients respond to various treatments, you can improvise within a given set of parameters. For example, if a cook is challenged to create a special dish for a guest with food allergies, she must combine her knowledge of ingredients, preparations and flavors in order to improvise an appropriate dish on the spot.

Good culinary improvisation is a skill that can separate a routine technician from a creative culinary artist. There is a place for both in the kitchen but a broader career ladder for the second.

The anecdote on page 2 epitomizes what this book is about: experimenting, creating, tasting, trying. Even burning, throwing away and re-trying are valuable experiences that will teach you what works and what doesn't. Honing skills, working in teams, stretching limits—all will make you a better cook.

observe the key, the tempo of the tune and the beat, but within that framework can use their skills to go in many different directions.

In the same way an improvisational cook can work within a set of parameters—

> *Good culinary improvisation is a skill that can separate a routine technician from a creative culinary artist. There is a place for both in the kitchen but a broader career ladder for the second.*

The culinary arts are much more than strictly a field of vocational study; they are also a creative enterprise synthesizing food science, visual arts, aesthetics of flavor, management and performance. This book helps you to apply your cooking skills in creative ways to build culinary mastery while concurrently building other skills that employers identify as critical in their culinary and foodservice employees.

Cooking by Improvisation

The heart of this book is the idea of cooking by culinary improvisation rather than by recipe. Following a recipe is an important skill for a cook. Cooking well without a recipe shows mastery of a variety of skills. This book will help you cook better through improvisation.

Cooking by improvisation is not much different from playing jazz, a largely improvisational form of American music. Jazz musicians have strong skills. They know their instruments well, can produce a wide range of sounds, and can use those skills to improvise within a given set of parameters. They can't play just anything. They need to

sweet, savory, main course, soup—and use her or his skills—knife skills, cooking techniques, palate, creativity—to create something as pleasing to the senses as visual art or music.

Molecular Gastronomy— Extreme Culinary Improvisation

The basic premise of a recent movement in the food world, dubbed **molecular gastronomy**, is that understanding the flavor components and chemical composition of an ingredient, using science and technology, will help you deconstruct it to create unique pairings and dishes. Many of the prominent chefs whose style and technique put them in the category of molecular gastronomists—Heston Blumenthal of Fat Duck in England; Wylie Dufresne of WD-50 in New York City; Fernan Adria of El Bulli in Spain; Thomas Keller of Per Se in New York City; Grant Achatz of Alinea in Chicago; and Will Goldfarb in New York City—began dreaming up new techniques and combinations in order to engage all the diner's senses, rather than focusing on taste alone. New techniques and concepts were needed to do this, to emphasize different characteristics of foods, like texture and temperature, to maximize fragrance. All the foams and spun sugars, flavored airs and jellies, edible papers, pop rocks and purees, powders, and fragile discs of dehydrated fruit achieved by utilizing a juicer, liquid

The merger of the scientific and the culinary is as old as cookery; better ways of distributing heat, treating plants or meat to make them edible, and applying spices are techniques that were concerns as long as Australopithecines have used tools and eaten. But the recent merger of serious

...if a significant number of flavor molecules in two foods are similar, they might complement one another, so the foods can be served together...

nitrogen, centrifuge, or maltodextrin to freeze, gel, aerate, smoke, and layer foods and flavors characterize the work of those adherents to the school of molecular gastronomy.

Over the past decade, it's become more common to not only know what the source of a food is, but to be able to explore its physiochemical properties: physical structure, temperature, texture. Chefs deconstruct the food, and then reconstruct it to play with textures and how its taste and texture are at different temperature. What do you end up with? Foams are the most commonly cited example of molecular gastronomy on the plate, but solid sauces, fried cubes of mayonnaise and all the savory cotton candies and lollipops that dissolve into your drink as you use them as a swizzle stick are the fruits of this scientific experimentation. Spraying a shot of gravy from an aerosol can into your mouth before taking a bite of whipped potato is an example, as is tableside service to present a food that turns to vapor when it meets the heat of your tongue.

science and cuisine is traced back to 1969, when Nicholas Kurti, a professor of atomic physics at Oxford University, gave a lecture at the Royal Institution titled "The Physicist in the Kitchen." Kurti is credited with coining the term "molecular gastronomy" as a way of winning academic funding for research into cookery. Herve This, a French scientist and author of "Molecular Gastronomy: Exploring the Science of Flavor" was first to hold a doctorate in molecular gastronomy and is attributed as the man who named the movement.

As for the molecular science of the movement, it goes something like this: if a significant number of flavor molecules in two foods are similar, they might complement one another, so the foods can be served together. This illustrates one principle of molecular gastronomy: unlikely matchings that work. Cooking no longer involves simply pairing things that traditionally go together because they grow together, during the same season, or come from the same part of the world. Instead, additional combinations are sought and explored; the basis for that exploration is imagination. Chefs who do this are playing on, or peeling away, the conventions of the food, separating it from traditional meanings and emotional resonance—or playing these up to such a degree that dinner feels like theater. In the mind of the diner, perhaps, it is transporting.

An effect of this experimentation on your plate, on your tongue, is that you're forced to think about what you're eating. Food engineered to touch every sense does this as well, which uncovers a second purpose of molecular gastronomy: it's meant to make your experience of eating different, and conscious.

This book explores other effects in cooking, such as proteins unfolding and binding, the effect of water in interstitial spaces, and what different degrees of temperature do to meat on a molecular level. A third principal is revealed: molecular gastronomy is about experimentation with sources of heat and cold (technology), and using scientific principles as the basis of the experimentation.

Lastly, many chefs are trying to find a chemical answer to why we taste, and what taste is. Molecular gastronomy explores flavor physiology—the connection of brain to palate.

Not only the food is subject to experimentation. Even tableware and cookware—the things we use to serve the food, and raise it to our mouths—is being tooled with, so to speak. How would you like a spoon with holes to let the milk drip through so your cornflakes stay crisp? Or to use a fork with a tiny clip on the handle to hold an herb spring, so you smell the fresh rosemary while you wrap your lips around a cube of grilled lamb?

What, you may ask, is the point of all this work and risk? Molecular gastronomy is employed to create an experience. To astonish, to surprise, to intrigue. To achieve showmanship, artistry, a gee-whiz moment for the diner. But most of all the purpose of molecular gastronomy is to eat.

Many of the prominent chefs who are now figureheads of the movement are rebelling against the label of "molecular gastronomists," saying it detracts from the truth of their craft. What chefs Blumenthal, Adria and Keller do, they say, isn't about the science, but about maximizing enjoyment of the food. Though these chefs embrace the technical wizardry that makes their dishes possible, it takes a back seat to their embrace of excellence, openness and integrity of craft, and in food. To disciples of the movement dubbed "molecular gastronomy," the scientific techniques should matter less than what they are trying to achieve: good food. It is in that same spirit that we encourage you to join us through this book. There is more about molecular gastronomy in Chapter Four.

Go Ahead—Play with Your Food!

CULINARY CREATIVITY BY LENNY DAVE

I have consumed many forgettable meals in my lifetime. But, it's the ones I can still vividly remember that we're talking about here. What made them memorable has nothing to do with the conversation across the table with family or friends. In this context, it's all about the food.

Whether you're in a five-star restaurant or at home, the kitchen is the quintessential, creative playground. Creativity involves playing with an idea, both literally and figuratively. This act of "playing" involves time, and time is a precious commodity these days. We're usually in such a hurry that we don't allow ourselves sufficient time for any of this necessary, creative experimentation to occur. At home, we pop a plastic package into the microwave and serve it up. And in many restaurants, the bottom line often depends on how fast they can turn the tables. Maybe that's why it's such a rare treat to enjoy a well-prepared meal at a leisurely pace—anywhere!

At its core, the preparation and presentation of any meal—no matter how elegant or simple—provides an opportunity for the culinary, creative spirit to "play" with some or all of the senses. How does it look? How does it smell? How does it taste? How does it feel? And, how does it sound? You heard me—how does it sound? More on that in a moment.

It is somewhat ironic that in teaching the fundamental concepts of creativity, I often use the analogy of a slow cooker or a crock pot, as if we were intent on preparing a hearty, beef stew. Faced with the challenge of preparing the stew or a special meal (with or without a recipe in mind), we actively search for and gather the ingredients. It is important to note here that we are looking for what already exists. We methodically navigate through the grocery store, gaze across our pantry shelves, and poke around the freezer or refrigerator for salvageable leftovers. We pick up a pound of this, a box of that, fill a produce bag with some of those, grab two cans of these, a new bottle of this, and then we sniff inside that plastic container from a week ago to see if its contents are still good.

Understand that the number one reason we fail to release our creativity is because we get frustrated too early in the process and we give up. We let ourselves be negatively influenced by others who say that our ideas are "half-baked."

We surrender before we've even mixed the ingredients and seen what it tastes like after it has finished cooking. Creativity requires patience, and persistence is paramount. Do not throw in the kitchen towel prematurely. Your culinary creation may, in fact, taste great—or it may need a pinch more of this or that—or it may be truly inedible and headed straight for the disposal. Change a variable. Try it again. Do not quit.

Now, let's go back to those five senses. It's time to play one of my favorite creative games, "I've Got a Question!" As we consider the senses of sight, smell, taste, touch and hearing, let's explore the culinary possibilities and look for some new ideas. Let's see what we can discover when we ask ourselves "What if we..." or "How might we..." or "How can we..." or "What would happen if we..."

In this game, try not to censor your thinking or be overly critical. Now is not the time to worry about whether our questions sound silly or our first answers make any sense. If you're working with a team, challenge each other to see how many ideas you can generate. If you're working alone, challenge yourself! Remember, these are just ideas. Later, you can evaluate, prioritize and decide which ones to try. I'll admit—the game is challenging at first, but it becomes fun and much easier once you get the hang of it. Always start simple and with the obvious solutions. Then, stretch and unleash your imagination and watch what happens!

Sight...

How might we change the appearance of the item—or the plate itself?

How might we add color to the presentation of this dish?

How might we give the food item an entirely different shape?

What would happen if we served this item on a unique type of plate or bowl?

What if we offered a smaller portion of this as an appetizer?

What if we offered a king-size portion of this item?

What would happen if we served this dish family-style?

What could we add to the presentation if we served it on a larger plate?

How might we literally give the food some personality (by adding a face to a kids item)?

What can we do to add some height to it?

How might we somehow stand it up on the plate?

What if we set it on top of another food item?

How might we make the item appear to shine, glisten or sparkle?

What can we sprinkle or drizzle on the plate for appearance sake?

What would happen if we made this dish upside down or inside out?

How might we add motion to this item—or the table itself?

How might we make it flow (like a chocolate fountain)?

How might we utilize flame to "sell" the dish (like Bananas Foster)?

Smell & Taste...

What aroma does the food item naturally give off when cooked? When raw?

What aroma fills the kitchen? The house? The restaurant? The parking lot?

What do we want the customer to smell as soon as they open the front door?

What would happen if we served the item chilled or frozen?

What would happen if we served the item hot?

What can we do to enhance the taste or smell?

How might we soften the taste or smell?

What unusual flavors might complement this item?

What side dish or entrée would complement this item?

What special beverage might complement this food item?

What special food item might complement this beverage?

Touch...

What sensation does the food item give the lips, tongue and mouth?

How might we modify the texture?

What would happen if we made it thicker?

What would happen if we added chips or chunks?

How might we make it thinner or smoother?

How can we increase the moistness?

What would happen if we dried it?

How might we present the item so it can be picked up by hand?

Into what might we roll the item?

Into what might we dip the item?

Hearing...

What sound does the dish make when prepared? When served?

Does it sizzle? Does it pop? Does it fizz? Does it bubble?

How might we somehow add sound to the presentation of the dish?

How might the server add sound to it at the table?

How might the customer add sound to it as they eat it?

What might make heads turn as the dish was brought out?

How might we "sell" the dish with a special presentation by staff?

Can we deliver the dish with a song? A band? Special piped in music?

And, as for the Preparation Process...

What ingredients might we prepare well ahead of time?

How might we combine some steps to simplify things?

What ingredients might we substitute for the health conscious eater?

What if an ingredient was heated and used as a liquid instead of a solid?

What if an ingredient was chilled and used as a solid instead of a liquid?

What if we chopped an ingredient instead of slicing it? Or vice versa?

What if we baked one item inside of another food item?

What if we hid a surprise flavor or ingredient deep inside?

How might we make many more of the item simultaneously?

What if we made a giant-sized version for large groups to share?

How might we make this item smaller? Petite?

What would happen if we prepared this dish in layers?

What if we prepared this dish at the table rather than in the kitchen?

How might we bottle it, package it, sell it or ship it?

Lenny Dave is a nationally recognized creative thinker, humorist and author. For over 25 years, Lenny has been helping the creatively challenged and idea-impaired who walk and work among us while suffering from a chronic case of "But We've Always Done It This Way!" Lenny knows there is always more than one right answer! As a veteran speaker and trainer, Lenny conveys the fundamental concepts of Creative Leadership to college, corporate and wellness audiences across North America. With information, energy and humor, Lenny's timely message helps individuals and organizations move forward—"Get Out of the Box or Get Out of the Way!"

Contact Lenny directly: www. creativity123.com

Creatively exploring and playfully answering these types of "what if..." questions will literally generate hundreds of new culinary possibilities for you and your kitchen staff to explore. As is the case with all creativity, some ideas heat up quickly—others need time to marinate. You may be perceived as a gourmet chef or a short order cook. You may be feeding the royal family or just your own hungry household on a school night. But, you always have the opportunity to make every meal memorable.

Go ahead—play with your food!

Chapter 1 Summary

This chapter introduced the ideas of culinary improvisation and creativity. The how and why of culinary improvisation provide the philosophical and practical underpinnings of the rest of this book. After exploring what culinary improvisation is—using improvisational music—jazz—as a reference point, we illustrated a compelling application of culinary improvisation: molecular gastronomy. Lenny Dave, creativity expert, concludes the chapter by offering suggestions for thinking and cooking more creatively. You will find it useful to return to these ideas throughout your work with this book.

Chapter 1 Assessment

❶ Name a technique or ingredient that epitomizes each of the five senses.

_____

_____

_____

_____

_____

❷ Define "molecular gastronomy" using your own words. Look at the statement you've written, and personalize it. Could this be a statement of your own cooking principles? Why or why not?

_____

_____

_____

_____

_____

❸ Chef Lenny mentions patience and persistence as being critical to creativity. What are some other qualities you can think of?

_____

_____

_____

_____

_____

_____

❹ What are some ways you can make time to be creative, or incorporate creative thinking into activities you perform on a daily basis?

_____

_____

_____

_____

_____

❺ Create a menu item that you feel embodies the spirit of molecular gastronomy

_____

_____

_____

_____

_____

_____

2/
The Basics

Knowledge of basic techniques is the necessary basis for all improvisation in the kitchen. Why? Because improvisation is all about judgment, and judgment is reliant on knowledge. Jazz musicians are great improvisers but also have their fundamental skills firmly in place—scales, articulation, tone, and pitch.

Without the basics covered, improvisation becomes a creative mess. When you master a series of basic kitchen skills, you have developed a set of tools pertaining to the elements of food, and these elements are the root of improvisation. They are the bass notes, the flavors that sing and the colors that pop. The elements add crunch, sweetness, richness and heat. When it hits your taste buds, food produces flavor. Flavor is, quite simply, what you taste. A popular theory is that the four basic tastes are detected by different parts of the tongue, but new research works to debunk that notion. On the tongue, in the world, flavor is a melding of chemical sensations.

Skills can be acquired through practice and dedication. Flavors can be learned through repeated tasting and cultural exploration. Then creativity can come into play.

Mise en place is all the preparation before the cooking is done. Having everything ready and organized—your equipment in place, ovens pre-heated, assembly of foods completed, and ingredients measured, cleaned, chopped—will help you produce a good-looking, delicious meal in a timely fashion. This chapter will teach the techniques and tools that help you assemble the mise en place that lets you cook like a jazz musician.

If you are using this textbook later in your culinary education, you will find this chapter most useful as a reference to remind yourself of the basics as needed. If you are relatively new to culinary education, read this chapter especially carefully as mastering these techniques will allow your improvisation later to flourish. The most important

---

CHAPTER OBJECTIVES

① To recap basic techniques and kitchen procedures.

② To develop a working knowledge of culinary terminology and mise en place.

③ To learn basic elements of food: flavor, texture, color, contrast, nutrition.

④ To provide recipe bases and establish a technical framework upon which competencies can be developed.

KEY TERMS

Mise en place

Pan-ready

Steel

Sharpening Stone

Whetstone

Chef's Knife (Cook's Knife)

Utility Knife

Paring Knife

Boning Knife

Filleting Knife

Cleaver

Serrated Knife

Tourne

Chevalier

Mirepoix

White Mirepoix

Matignon

Bouquet Garni

With a good chef's, paring and serrated knife, nearly any cut can be accomplished.

take-away from this chapter is that as a more advanced cook, you don't need to rely as much on exact recipes. Rather, once you know the general ratios and method, which we call platforms, you can use these platforms to build in nearly any direction.

Equipment (Batterie de Cuisine)

Matching equipment to task is an important part of mise en place, and specialized equipment will aid in achieving a superior product. This section will suggest what tools, small appliances, pots and other pieces of equipment are most commonly called upon in the kitchen.

Knives

Knives are the most personal of a chef's tools; their charm and utility are bound in a happy marriage of balance, weight and shape. Knowing the three main parts of the knife and how they work together is an important criterion for choosing knives, since all have an effect on the feel and cut of the tool. These parts are the blade, the tang and the handle.

Blades are typically stainless steel, carbon steel or high-carbon stainless steel. The tang is the portion of the blade that extends into the handle. A full tang extends the entire length of the handle; a knife with a full tang has a secure and balanced blade for heavy-duty chopping, through bones, thick pieces of meat or tough rinds. The handle should fit the hand comfortably.

Knives should be kept clean; for sanitary purposes they should be washed between uses. Knives that are properly stored and used will last longer and hold their edge better. Knives that are kept sharp perform better and are safer to use than blunt instru-

BASIC KNIVES IN A CHEF'S KIT:

CHEF'S KNIFE (ALSO CALLED COOK'S KNIFE)	This is the wide, sharply pointed all-purpose 6- to 14-inch blade. It has a slightly curved edge for slicing, chopping and mincing.
UTILITY KNIFE	Small, with a 5- to 7-inch blade, this narrow knife is lighter and smaller, for light cutting and peeling. Many chefs rarely use a utility knife.
PARING KNIFE	This short 2- to 4-inch blade, smallest of the knives, is shaped like a mini chef's knife, for paring and trimming fruits and vegetables.
BONING KNIFE	This thin, rigid blade, about 6 inches long, tapers to a sharp point, and is used for peeling meat from the bone.
FILLETING OR SLICING KNIFE	The blade is similar to the boning knife, but more flexible, for cutting fish into fillets.
CLEAVER	This large, rectangular blade is heavy enough to cut through bones and perform other multi-purpose, heavy chores.
SERRATED KNIFE	The fine teeth on this blade cut cleanly and neatly through tomatoes, cakes, breads and soft fish flesh.

ments. It is useful to have both a sharpening stone and a honing steel in your knife kit. The steel is a rod with a rough texture like sandpaper, used for honing, forming a temporary sharp edge on knife blades. A **sharpening stone**, or **whetstone**, is a flat, gritty surface, also used to grind or sharpen the edge of a blade.

To sharpen knives with a steel, hold the knife at a 30 to 45-degree angle to the steel. Run the steel along the blade lightly, with a gentle motion that takes the knife repeatedly and rhythmically away from the body. Repeat this motion on the other side of the blade, for an equal number of strokes, then perform a second pass on each side to smooth the blade.

More specialized knives include the **tourne**, a short knife with a small curved blade, useful for cutting vegetables into round shapes and forming garnishes; the **chevalier**, for cutting the sinews from meat; and various saws for cutting fish, meat and frozen foods.

Questions:

❶ Do you have a favorite knife in your kit? Why is it your favorite? What cuts do you enjoy performing?

_____

_____

_____

_____

❷ List three examples of how good knife skills can accentuate a chef's creativity.

1. _____

_____

2. _____

_____

3. _____

_____

Preparation and Cooking Equipment

This is a comprehensive list of general and specialized tools you are most likely to use in the kitchen:

Measuring spoons and cups, scales and liquid measuring cups

Cutting boards made of wood or polypropylene

Mixing bowls of stainless steel or ceramic

Kitchen scissors

Timers

Ladles

Offset spatulas

Parchment paper and aluminum foil

Whips and whisks

Peeler

Skimmers

Slotted spoons

Pitter

Zester

Reamer

Grater

Spiders

Pastry brushes

Pastry wheel

Piping bags and tips

Tasting spoons

Rolling pins

Scrub brush

Offset spatula

Wide and narrow spatulas and turners

Bulb baster

Bench scraper

Pepper mill

Mortar and pestle

Scoops and tongs

Thermometers: meat and candy

Tools to help you strain and texturize:

Chinois

Colander

Sifter

Strainer

Food mill (mouli)

Ricer

Held-held and table mixers

Blender

Ice cream maker

Grinder

Food processor

Tamis

Mandoline

Pots and pans...

should always fit the foods being cooked. They should be neither too large nor too small, otherwise the food will not brown, or will cook too quickly on a larger surface. Essential for stovetop use, in a variety of volumes and sizes:

Stock pots

Saucepans

Sauté pans

Frying pans

Skillets

A **double boiler** can double as a **bain marie**, or water bath. A **deep fryer** and **griddle** are useful, and you may want to dedicate a small, shallow pan for crepes only. Indispensable ovenware, made to withstand very high temperatures, include **roasting pans, racks, sheet pans, casseroles, ramekins,** and **gratin dishes. Oven mitts** come in handy. Bakeware includes **cake pans, ring molds, springform pans, baking sheets, loaf pans, pie pans, cookie, pastry** and **biscuit cutters.** You may also require various specialized equipment such as **molds, steamers** and **poachers.**

Questions:

❶ Can you think of other equipment you use in your home kitchen?
What are they?

_____

_____

_____

_____

_____

❷ Can you think of an unconventional tool for a kitchen, like pipe or a wrench,
that surprised you when you saw someone else using it in a kitchen? What
was it used for?

_____

_____

_____

_____

BOUQUET GARNI PLATFORM

1 celery stalk

sprigs of parsley

sprig of thyme

bay leaf

Tie with string, and add to simmering food.

SACHET D'EPICES PLATFORM

*A **sachet d'Epices** is also removed at the end of cooking, and contains dried spices bound in cheesecloth.*

dried parsley

dried thyme leaves

bay leaf

black peppercorns, smashed

garlic clove, crushed

Bind ingredients together in muslin and secure with twine. Adjust the amount of spices to the quantity of the main item (soup, sauce) being prepared and the flavor balance desired.

BASIC VINAIGRETTE PLATFORM

1 part acid such as vinegar or lemon juice

3 tablespoons oil

Pinch of salt

Pinch of freshly ground black pepper

A splash of water can cut the oily mouthfeel

Combine and whisk. The vinaigrette is a chameleon; other flavorings, such as minced garlic or shallot, citrus zest, mustard or herbs can be added. Specialty vinegars and oils add flavors as well.

Basic Flavoring Combinations

Classic recipes are reliant on classic combinations of flavors. Chapter Three will cover flavor principles, ethnic flavors and combining flavors in more depth, but this serves as a round-up of some classic combinations of vegetables, herbs and spices that enhance the flavors of a dish. They do not provide the main flavoring.

A **mirepoix**, often composed of two parts onion to one part carrot and one part celery, is used to flavors stocks, stews and braised dishes. The vegetables are chopped fine for a quick-cooking stock, like a fumet, or cut into larger pieces when added to slow-cooking dishes. Leeks, root vegetables, garlic, mushrooms and bacon can be included in a mirepoix, depending on the desired finished product.

The Philosophy of the PLATFORMS

Here is a convenient place to mention the philosophy behind the platforms used in this book. As culinary students we learned the following recipes for mirepoix: two parts onion, one part celery, one part carrots. Later in industry, I was making a glace de viande (meat glaze) made from heavily reduced brown veal stock. It was consistently too sweet for my taste and for the final application. I thought to replace most of the carrots in the mirepoix for the stock with other vegetables—mushrooms, leeks and scallion ends. The end result worked! The new glace was perfect.

While there are many classic recipes that can be followed, a cook should know when the ratios and recipes need to be honored completely and where they are suggestions.

A **white mirepoix** includes equal parts onion, leek, celery, parsnip, and a half-part mushroom. A **matignon** contains equal parts onion, carrot and celery, and uses half as much mushrooms and bacon.

A **bouquet garni** is typically composed of parsley, thyme, celery and bay leaf and is used to add aroma and herb flavor to a dish. The herbs and vegetables are bundled together, to be removed at the end of cooking.

Marinades and Rubs

In Chapter Three, we suggest flavor bases with various ethnic origins. Here we explore the traditional seasonings. Marinades and rubs are added as flavoring before foods are cooked. The food—meat, fish, poultry, vegetable—soaks in the mixture and takes on its flavors. A **liquid marinade** is often composed of oil mixed with vinegar, wine, beer or fruit juice and flavorings, such as vegetables and spices. A ratio of three parts oil to one part acid is most common. Again, the recipes are suggestions or platforms. A marinade for a lean fish to be grilled might be oilier than one for grilled pork belly. Vinaigrettes are often used as liquid marinades.

Vinaigrettes are a basic weak emulsion used for sauces and salad dressings. An acid is combined with an oil and herbs and spices, or mustard, honey or other nonsolid substances are added as flavor. A vinaigrette can be varied in so many ways, you may return to this platform again and again.

A dry marinade, or rub, is a mixture of spices rubbed all over the food, which is then refrigerated for a given period of time. The glory of the rub is that it is direct and intense. The dry marinade can form a crust on the food when cooked. The platform

DRY RUB PLATFORM

Remember that all sorts of dried and fresh herbs and spices as well as pungent ingredients such as garlic, ginger and shallot can be used to great effect in a dry rub.

A mixture using these proportions will coat 2 to 3 pounds of meat. This rub has a vaguely Mexican flavor profile. Keep in mind that salt will begin to cure the surface of the meat. Depending on the application you may want to salt the meat just before cooking or include it in the rub.

- 3 tablespoons brown sugar
- 2 tablespoons toasted cumin seeds
- 2 tablespoons crushed dried Mexican oregano
- 1 tablespoon kosher salt
- 1 tablespoons ground black pepper
- 1 tablespoon pimento, chili powder or sweet or hot paprika
- 2 teaspoons cayenne
- 2 cloves garlic, minced

Combine; rub into raw meat with your hands.

recipe has a Mexican flavor profile; refer to Chapter Three for more on flavor profiles to create something unusual and exciting.

Activity:

Write a recipe for vinaigrette, using flavored vinegars and spices, that accentuates a salad of apples, endive and walnuts. Explain why you chose your ingredients and how they flatter these specific elements.

_____

_____

_____

_____

_____

_____

Questions:

❶ What spices would you use in an East Asian-themed rub? A sweet rub? An Indian rub?

_____

_____

_____

_____

_____

_____

Making Stock

Never underestimate the power of stock. **Stock** is the flavorful liquid base for soups, stews and sauces, also used to cook vegetables, grains, meats and fish. A stock is made by simmering vegetables, bones and liquid to leach out and mingle their unique flavors. The flavor of the stock should accentuate the finished dish, not compete with it, and be rich and well-balanced. The meat, fish or poultry flavor—not the seasonings—should dominate, and stock should be clear.

For brown stocks, bones are roasted to lend a deep flavor, as well as color. For white stocks, blanched bones are added to the liquid, achieving a clearer, lighter flavor and clarity of appearance. Stocks are used in a variety of classical and contemporary kitchen applications: as a base for sauces and soups, as well as a cooking medium for meat or vegetables. Because of its prominence and versatility, its importance is emphasized here and in most professional culinary texts.

There are many variations on stock that are used as a cooking base. A **fumet** is a quick-cooked fish or mushroom stock which is reduced to enhance its body and flavor, a **court bouillon** includes wine or vinegar. Both are quick-cooking and used for poaching seafood. A **glaze** (glace in French) is stock reduced until it is thick and syrupy in texture, and very concentrated in flavor. Glaze is used to baste roasting meats, or to enrich a sauce.

An **essence** is somewhat different from both a stock and a glaze. Quite romantically, an essence is a characteristic that expresses something fundamental about a thing. So, in cooking, an essence is a reduction of cooking liquids, not always containing meat, and it provides the dominant flavor of a dish, rather than enhancing it.

The uses of stock and broth are similar. **Broth** is a cooking liquid made from simmering meat, and stock is made from simmering bones.

Stock-making is a classic technique, and there are "rules" that will result in a textbook-perfect product. Bones for stock should be uniform in size, and hacked to 3 inches in length to maximize flavor extraction. Vegetables should be cleaned of dirt, and peeled or trimmed if necessary. The liquid being added to the stock—most often water—should be cold.

For a meat or poultry **stock**, use a ratio of 8 pounds of bones to 6 quarts of water to one pound mirepoix. For a **fumet**, use 11 pounds of bones or shells to 5 quarts of water to 1 pound mirepoix. Sweat bones or shells so the fumet cooks quickly with maximum flavor. Lightly oil a round pan, then add fish bones or shellfish shells, along with mirepoix. Cook until the bones or shell release their moisture. For **white stocks**, blanch the bones by covering bones with cold water in a large stockpot, then bringing to boil over high heat. Once a boil is reached, drain the bones, discarding water. Rinse the bones and proceed with stock-making.

For **brown stocks**, brown bones and mirepoix in a 400°F oven or on the range top (some chefs burn the onion, alone, before browning the bones, then add it to the simmering liquid to achieve a dark amber hue). Rinse the bones, and dry them. Lightly oil pan and lay bones in a single layer. Roast, turning occasionally, until deep brown. Place in stockpot, then

DEGREASING STOCK

When stocks or sauces are simmering, the foamy scum that rises to the top of the pot should be skimmed off every 15 minutes or so. With a wide ladle or specially-designed skimmer, push the fat or scum to one side of the pan. With a flat spoon, capture it and discard.

BROWN STOCK PLATFORM

8 pounds chicken, beef or veal bones

2 tablespoons oil

1 gallon water

2 large onions, quartered

2 carrots, coarsely chopped

4 stalks celery, coarsely chopped

4 leeks, coarsely chopped

2 plum tomatoes, coarsely chopped

4 bay leaves

1 bunch parsley

2 sprigs thyme

In a large oiled stockpot over medium heat, or on a large oiled sheet pan in a 400°F oven, brown bones, turning, until golden brown. Place bones into a deep stockpot and cover with 1 gallon cold water. Bring to a simmer and cook for six to twelve hours, degreasing frequently (see below). Add vegetables and herbs, simmer for 20 to 30 minutes more, then strain. Return stock to pot and reduce liquid by ⅔. Use immediately, or chill and store.

WHITE STOCK PLATFORM

8 pounds chicken or veal bones

2 onions, quartered

2 carrots, coarsely chopped

4 stalks celery, coarsely chopped

4 leeks, coarsely chopped

1 bouquet garni

Place bones in a pot with water to cover. Bring to a boil for two minutes, then reduce to simmer. Simmer gently for four to eight hours, degreasing frequently (see below). Strain. Use immediately, or cool and store.

FISH STOCK PLATFORM

11 pounds fish bones or shellfish shells

6 quarts cold water

1 pound mirepoix

Combine all ingredients, bring the mixture to a simmer, and simmer 30 to 40 minutes, degreasing as necessary (see below). Strain, cool, and store.

VEGETABLE STOCK PLATFORM

½ pound mushrooms, chopped coarsely

1 pound leeks, chopped

1 pound carrots, cut into 2-inch pieces

1 cup chopped plum tomato

Bouquet garni

4 garlic cloves, smashed, skins on

2 tablespoons olive oil

5 quarts water

Toss together mushrooms, leeks, carrots, tomatoes, parsley and thyme sprigs, garlic, and oil in a large flameproof roasting pan. Roast at 425°F until vegetables are golden. Transfer to stockpot and add bay leaves and water. Bring to a simmer and cook 45 minutes, degreasing as necessary (see below). Strain, season, cool and store.

FUMET PLATFORM

6 pounds fish bones and trimmings

1 large onion or 2 large shallots, chopped

1 ½ cups quartered mushrooms

3 tablespoons fresh lemon juice

1 bunch parsley

2 sprigs thyme

1 bay leaf

1 teaspoon salt

Crush bones and trimmings, add to a hot oiled pan and sweat for 10 minutes. Add the remaining ingredients and 3 quarts water. Bring to a boil, boil 30 minutes. Strain and cool.

**WAYS TO DRESS UP/
GARNISH CLEAR SOUP:**

herb leaves or julienne: basil, chervil, cilantro, parsley, tarragon

sliced vegetables: carrots, celery, bean sprouts, peppers, fresh mushrooms

dried mushrooms: oyster, shiitake, wood ear, porcini

strips of chicken breast, beef, pork, or peeled, deveined shrimp

pour in a beaten egg, while stirring, so it forms threads

....

**SUGGESTED FRUITS AND
VEGETABLES TO PUREE
FOR SOUP:**

carrots, spinach, potato, pepper, mushrooms, tomato, artichokes, cauliflower, asparagus, celeriac, chestnuts, leeks, Brussels sprouts, sorrel, sour cherries, nectarines, berries, melon, mango, apples, pears, peaches, apricots, blueberries, rhubarb

....

GARNISHES:

fresh mint, fried sage or parsley, toasted nuts: hazelnuts, pecans, walnuts, almonds, pepitas, sunflower seeds, diced up vegetables or fruit that provide a good flavor and color contrast, croutons, cheese tuiles, crème fraiche, or flavored cream, cheese or yogurt

add mirepoix to pan. Brown, and add to stock in final hour. Deglaze pan, and pour deglazing liquid into stockpot.

Many different vegetables can be used to great advantage in a **vegetable stock**, which takes on the sweet or pungent character of the vegetables you choose to use. Begin with about 1 lb. of vegetables to every two quarts water. For a golden stock with a rich flavor, the vegetables can be roasted before simmering. For a clear stock with a light flavor, use sweet and pale vegetables, such as celery, white onions, turnip and parsnip.

Add mirepoix at the start of cooking for stocks that simmer for less than one hour. Otherwise, add mirepoix an hour before the end of cooking.

When the stock has finished simmering an hour or so for strong fish or vegetable stocks, up to twelve hours for brown stocks, strain it by ladling it through a strainer. The strainer can be lined with muslin, which traps even more of the silty particles that cloud the liquid. Cool the stock quickly with an ice paddle or in shallow pans in an ice bath, pour into storage containers, and don't neglect to label and date the stock before refrigerating. Stock is a protein-rich, pH neutral product which means that it is highly perishable. It can be stored for a few days in the refrigerator or for a few weeks in the freezer.

Soups

Though soups are traditionally grouped into two categories, clear and thick, there are many styles of soup that fall into these broad categories, such as vegetable purees, cream soups, bisques and veloute soups, richly thickened with egg, cream and but-

ter. Soups are a wonderful way to play with flavors and textures, and a great vehicle for experimentation.

Clear Soup

Broth is a clear stock-based soup, and can be made with chicken or meat. **Consomme** is broth that has been enriched with additional meat and vegetables and clarified with egg whites.

Pureed Soup

Pureed soups can be made from vegetables, fruits, or fish. A traditional bisque is a pureed lobster soup. Usually one fruit or vegetable is featured, with onion, leek, garlic or shallot and excellent stock added as flavoring. You can also add spices; star anise is an especially good seasoning for a pureed carrot soup, since it plays to the crisp sweetness of the carrot. Try combining fruits and vegetables in a soup. Some combinations include apple squash, cherry beet and mushroom rhubarb. Serve hot or cold.

Cream Soups

Cream soups are traditionally thickened with a roux, to which stock and milk and/or cream are added. Cream soups can also be thickened while cooking with flour, cornstarch or pureed root vegetables. A basic cream of vegetable soup has as many possibilities for creativity as pureed soup does, and you can use as wide a range of vegetables: cauliflower, spinach, potato, leek, asparagus, mushroom, celery, artichoke. Cream of beet soup turns a gorgeous magenta color. You can also make a cream soup of shrimp, chicken, crayfish or lobster by the same method.

CONSOMME PLATFORM

2 quarts stock

3 to 4 egg whites

½ pound ground meat or poultry

2 tablespoons lemon juice

2 cups mirepoix

Warm stock in a large stockpot. Whisk egg whites until frothy, and add lemon juice. Add egg mixture, meat and mirepoix to stock. Whisk for about 5 minutes, until a scum forms. Scoop out a window for the stock to simmer in, and simmer gently 1 hour. Ladle the stock out through the opening into a fine-mesh sieve lined with muslin or cheesecloth. Strain, and reheat before serving. Classic garnishes for consommé include julienne black truffle and chervil leaves or vegetable brunoise, but a good, clear consommé is a flavorful, beautiful base for anything you can imagine.

PUREED SOUP PLATFORM

1 pound diced vegetables

2 tablespoons butter

Stock or water

Cook vegetables in butter over moderate heat, stirring frequently until softened. Add stock or water to cover by 1 inch. Simmer until tender, 20 to 30 minutes. Puree in a blender or food processor, then reheat.

PUREED FRUIT SOUP PLATFORM

1 pound diced fruits

2 tablespoons butter

Fruit juice, milk or water

Soften fruit in butter over moderate heat, stirring frequently. Add juice, milk or water—depending on your main ingredient—to cover by 1 inch. Simmer until tender, 20 to 30 minutes. Puree in a blender or food processor, then reheat.

FISH PUREE PLATFORM

1 cup diced carrot

1 cup diced onion

1 cup diced potato

1 cup diced celery

2 pounds fish, crab or lobster, with shells

2 tablespoons flour

2 quarts fish stock

⅔ cup white wine

2 tablespoons tomato paste

Bouquet garni

2 to 4 garlic cloves, peeled

Sweat carrot, onion, potato and celery in a large pot. Add fish, crabs or lobster and cook until deep brown. Add flour, stir until the flour is blended in and starts to smell toasty. Add fish stock, white wine, tomato puree, bouquet garni, and garlic cloves. Simmer for 45 minutes, covered. Puree, discarding bouquet garni and shells. Strain through a fine sieve, lined with muslin if desired, reheat, and add cream.

CREAM SOUP PLATFORM

8 ounces chopped or shredded vegetable

4 tablespoons butter

2 tablespoons flour

1 c. milk or stock

¾ c. cream

Combine vegetable with butter and cook until just tender. Meanwhile, prepare a blond roux using butter and flour. Add milk to the roux, and cook, stirring, to thicken, then add the cooked vegetables. Simmer 10 to 15 minutes, until the vegetable is very tender. Puree the mixture in a blender or food processor. Strain if necessary, season to taste, and add cream. Heat through, then serve.

Activity:

You are making a lobster consommé. How do you make it unique? What type of stock do you use, and how do you flavor your mirepoix? What do you choose to use as garnish? Explain your choices.

_____

_____

_____

_____

_____

_____

Write a recipe for a pureed soup featuring a main item and a supporting complementary flavor.

_____

_____

_____

_____

_____

_____

EMULSION PLATFORM

Place some combination of acid, pasteurized egg yolk, and sweetener if you wish—such as lemon juice, vinegar or honey—in a medium bowl. Whisk until well combined. Whisking constantly, gradually incorporate oil in a steady stream. Once all the ingredients are combined, the emulsion should have the consistency of mayonnaise. If it is too thick, whisk in a little water; if it is too thin, add a little more oil. Season to taste with salt, pepper, and the herbs of your choice.

....

BEURRE BLANC PLATFORM

5-6 chopped shallots

1 c. white wine vinegar

1 ⅓ cups white wine or fish stock

16 tablespoons butter, chilled, cubed

Freshly ground pepper

Combine shallots, vinegar and wine or fish stock in a deep saucepan, reduce by two-thirds. Reduce heat to low and add butter gradually, whisking one piece at a time into the sauce until it is smooth. Season with salt and pepper, and keep warm until using.

The sauce can be **stabilized by adding cream** after the vinegar mixture has reduced, before butter is added.

....

CLARIFIED BUTTER

Melt butter in a heavy saucepan over medium heat. Carefully skim off the foam with a shallow spoon. When the white milk solids fall out to the bottom of the pan, tip the pan into another container and pour off the top liquid carefully. This clear butterfat is clarified butter.

Sauces

A sauce complements or contrasts the flavors of the foods it is served with, and adds moisture, color, texture, and flavor to a dish. A sauce can be used with raw food or cooked; it can be served hot or cold, served separately or have the food cooked into it, be smooth or chunky, viscous or thin. A good sauce will be rich in flavor and aroma.

There are many types of sauces, and those who monitor all things culinary group them differently. You may see sauces referred to as "mother" and small sauces, or broken into hot, great or cold sauces. Sometimes sauces are grouped according to how they are prepared, as in cold, roux-based, emulsions, and stock-based. An **emulsion** is a dispersal of tiny droplets of one liquid in another. The liquids in an emulsion do not easily combine, but by slowly adding one liquid to the other while mixing rapidly, enhanced by the use of an emulsifier like egg yolk, your mixture will combine. The result is smooth and thick; an example is oil and vinegar, which is an emulsion just after it has been stirred, and longer if an emulsifier such as egg is added, as for mayonnaise. There are also dessert sauces which are poured over the dessert, like a **coulis**, or used as the base for preparing a dessert, such as **crème anglaise** (which is also a stand-alone sauce).

Sauces can be grouped into two categories: **grand sauces** and **contemporary sauces**. By their definition, grand sauces include **demi-glace, veloute, béchamel, tomato** and **hollandaise**—the "mother" sauces many other traditional or "small" sauces are derived from. A **demiglace** is thick, glossy, and rich, and falls into the category of **brown sauce**, along with

espagnole, bordelaise, and chateaubriand. A **veloute** is a roux-thickened white sauce, based on a meat, poultry or fish stock, and allemande, andelouse and chaud-froid are derived from it. **Béchamel**, a milk-based sauce thickened with roux, is classified as a white sauce, along with Mornay and Soubise. A **hollandaise** is a warm emulsion of butter and egg; other emulsion sauces are béarnaise, **mayonnaise** (basis for aioli, remolaude and rouille) and **vinaigrette**.

Contemporary sauces, on the other hand, include compound butters, jus, salsa, and compotes. These sauces are typically lighter, not made with a thickener, and less complicated to prepare. **Beurre blanc** is considered a contemporary sauce, though it is also a classic sauce of butter stabilized by a liquid.

The mixture of egg yolks and cream used to thicken and smooth sauces is called a **liaison**. A small amount of hot liquid is added to the liaison, then that mixture is blended into the whole to prevent the eggs from scrambling. The ratio is three parts cream to one part egg yolk, measured by weight, therefore 3 ounces of egg yolk, or one yolk, would thicken 9 ounces of cream.

Clarified butter is sweet butter that has been heated until all the milk solids fall to the bottom of the pan and the water evaporates. The clear fat that rises to the top has been clarified, and has a higher smoke point than regular butter, so it can be used for sautéing at high heat without burning. Clarified butter is synonymous with **drawn butter**—this is when clarified butter is used as a sauce, as for lobster.

MAKING A ROUX

A **roux** is a cooked mixture of flour and fat. The technique is a classic French method of thickening a sauce, and espagnole, béchamel and veloute rely on roux for their texture. Be sure, if the liquid is hot, the roux is cold, or vice versa; this will prevent lumps from forming. Add the liquid gradually and whisk constantly.

A **white roux** cooks briefly, a **brown roux** is allowed to cook to a rich, chocolaty color and nutty fragrance. In between the two is the **blonde roux**, which is a golden hue. As the roux darkens in color, its flavor develops but its thickening power lessens.

A **slurry** is a starch dissolved in liquid, and used as a thickener. The starch—arrowroot, cornstarch, flour—is whisked into a liquid at a simmer or boil. The ratio is typically two times the volume of cold liquid, such as water, to starch, such as corn starch.

ROUX PLATFORM

Combine equal parts fat and flour and cook until desired color and aroma is achieved.

For a **white roux, add cold liquid (light stock or milk)** when the flour/fat mixture is barely colored. **Alternatively, allow the roux to cool and bring your liquid to a boil, then whisk them together. Whisk constantly to heat.**

For a **blonde roux, cook the butter and flour mixture a few minutes more, until it is golden, then add liquid in the manner described.**

For a **brown roux, cook the butter and flour mixture even longer, about 20 minutes, until it is brown, then add liquid.**

BEURRE MANIE

Unlike a roux, beurre manie, or kneaded butter, is uncooked. It is butter and flour, in equal proportions, creamed together with a fork or mixer. It is used for thickening as well.

For thickening 4 cups of sauce, combine 4 tablespoons softened butter with 1/4 cup flour. Work into a paste.

BÉCHAMEL SAUCE PLATFORM

Prepare a beurre manie (see above) with 1 tablespoon butter and 1 tablespoon flour, and heat 1 cup milk until it bubbles at the edges, then whisk in the beurre manie. Bring to a boil, whisking constantly, until thickened. This will produce a medium-thick sauce; adding more beurre manie to one cup milk will result in a thicker sauce.

Or, heat 1 cup milk with 1 bay leaf and one quarter of a small onion. When the milk bubbles at the edges, remove from heat and allow it to steep for 30 to 45 minutes. Strain milk. Prepare a beurre manie and melt it in a heavy saucepan, whisking constantly. Pour in the warm milk and bring to a boil, whisking steadily, until it is thick. Season with salt, pepper and freshly grated nutmeg, and serve immediately. A béchamel can also be traditionally flavored with ham and garlic, but this preparation is open to many flavor additions.

VELOUTE PLATFORM

Melt 3 tablespoons butter in a heavy saucepan over medium-low heat. Add 5 tablespoons flour. Stir to a blond roux (see above). Remove from heat. Add hot chicken, veal or beef stock, whisking constantly. Return to heat, bring to boil, whisking constantly. Lower heat and simmer 15 minutes.

You can flavor a veloute when you make the roux, or at the end; garlic, shallots, tomato paste, lemon or orange juice, toasted whole spices or fresh herbs are excellent additions.

ESPAGNOLE PLATFORM

Espagnole is based on basic brown sauce.

- 3 cups basic brown sauce
- 1 ½ cups chopped mushrooms
- 1 tablespoon tomato paste

Bring basic brown sauce to a simmer and add mushrooms and tomato paste. Simmer for 15 minutes. Strain or skim before serving.

HOLLANDAISE PLATFORM

- 3 eggs
- 3 tablespoons water
- ¾ cup warm clarified butter
- 3 tablespoons strained lemon juice

Whisk eggs and water together in a wide saucepan, over very low heat or a double boiler. When you draw the whisk through the mixture and see ribbons, add butter very slowly, whisking constantly. Add lemon juice and season to taste.

TOMATO SAUCE PLATFORM

Sweat finely chopped garlic and onion (and carrot, if you like) in olive oil until tender. Add chopped ripe tomatoes, salt, pepper, and, if the tomatoes have no sweetness, a bit of sugar. Cook until tomatoes are soft, 15 minutes. Use as a chunky sauce or put through food mill. You can also work the cooked sauce through a sieve to remove skins and seeds, resulting in a velvety, smooth sauce.

Activity:

What other vegetables or fruits could you prepare as for tomato sauce?

_____

_____

_____

Sweet Sauces and Cold Sauces

Crème anglaise is a basic custard sauce, thickened with egg yolks and flavored with vanilla. It is used as a base for mousses, ice creams and charlottes, and can be served hot or cold as a dessert sauce. Other custards and custard sauces are crème patisserie, sabayon, crème caramel and crème brulee.

A coulis is a puree of raw or cooked fruit.

Coulis can be made from all sorts of fruits: kiwi, berries, apricots, plums, mangos. Be sure the fruit is clean, and that you have removed any moldy or bruised spots. For sweeter fruits, use less sugar; for very tart fruits, use more. You can also add a dash of extract or liqueur to coulis, or very finely chopped herbs, such as lavender, mint or pineapple sage. Vegetables can be used, too: tomato coulis makes a fresh, savory sauce.

CRÈME ANGLAISE PLATFORM

> 1 cup superfine sugar
>
> Pinch of salt
>
> 8 egg yolks
>
> 2 cups milk

Whisk together sugar, salt and yolks. Scald 2 cups milk; you can infuse the milk with vanilla extract or bean, orange or lemon rind, caramel, liqueur, coffee or tea or other flavorings (see Flavors chapter). When the egg mixture thickens to ribbon stage (when lifted with a whisk, it falls back into "ribbons") gradually add the warm milk, whisking constantly. Stir until the mixture bubbles; it should be thick enough to coat a spoon. Strain through a fine sieve; serve hot or cool.

FRESH FRUIT COULIS PLATFORM

> 2 pounds fresh fruit, cleaned, pitted, peeled and chopped
>
> 1 cup sugar

Puree fruit in blender or food processor, and add the sugar gradually, tasting as you go.

COOKED TOMATO COULIS OR PUREE SAUCE PLATFORM

This method can be applied to fruits, too, and results in an intense flavor and a thicker consistency.

> 2 pounds peeled tomatoes, halved and seeded
>
> 1 tablespoon sugar
>
> Fresh lemon and salt

Puree the tomatoes with the sugar. Add a pinch of salt. Correct flavor with a squeeze of lemon juice. In a heavy pot, bring puree to a boil and cook until thick and fragrant, about 5 minutes. Strain, taste for seasoning, and cool.

MAYONNAISE

Mayonnaise, the classic suspension and cold sauce, can be made in the food processor or by hand, and flavored with a variety of seasonings such as finely chopped herbs—parsley, tarragon, chervil, basil—or garlic. It can be lightened with the addition of whipped cream.

Have all ingredients at room temperature.

> 1 egg yolk
>
> 1 tablespoon Dijon mustard
>
> ⅔ cup oil: vegetable or olive
>
> Salt and pepper
>
> 2 to 3 teaspoons white wine vinegar

By hand: Whisk egg, mustard, salt and pepper. Add oil in a very slow dribble, whisking continuously, until thickened. Whisk in the vinegar. Stores 3 to 4 days.

In food processor: Use the entire egg. Put egg and mustard in food processor and blend. With machine running, add 1 cup vegetable or olive oil in a thin stream. Season with salt, pepper and vinegar, and pulse to combine. Add 1 additional cup of oil with machine running until the mayonnaise is pale and full-bodied.

For aioli: Add 4 crushed garlic cloves and salt at the beginning of preparation.

For andalouse: Add 2 crushed garlic cloves and finely diced red and green pepper to your finished mayonnaise.

Activity:

What other ingredients, such as different oils, fruit juices, flavored vinegars, herbs and spices, could you use to flavor your mayonnaise? Create a mayonnaise to flavor the following dishes:

- A poached whole salmon
- A cold tofu salad
- A fruit salad

_____

_____

_____

_____

_____

_____

Cooking Methods

This section is about how to transform food. These techniques will change a raw thing to cooked and make inert elements dance on the palate. Flavorful fat will be distributed through the meat; soft, pale flesh will become crisp and golden. These techniques offer certain mastery of foods and flavors; the ability to apply these techniques in a skilled and creative manner are what set a chef's repertoire apart from a home cook's.

You have to know the food you're working with, and you have to know how to cook it. Matching a piece of meat with a method is the key to making it not only edible, but succulent. These techniques—roasting, braising, sweating, sautéing, blanching, steaming, grilling, poaching—all fall under the rubric of either dry-heat, moist-heat or combination-heat method.

Dry-heat cooking is for tender cuts of meat. By this method, the meat, poultry or fish is cooked by the hot air that surrounds it, and the techniques differ in the manner in which the heat is applied, and the direction it comes from. **Roasting**—in the oven, on a spit—is cooking foods with hot air from without, either from a flame or from radiant heat. This causes the natural juices within the meat to steam and cook the food from within. Roasted dishes are often begun with a high-heat sear on the stovetop for succulence, and to caramelize the outside for flavor. Meat that is pierced during roasting releases flavorful juices, which run off and go to waste. Don't spear roasting meat. But do **baste**, or moisten it. With a bulb baster, spoon, or brush, gather the cooking juices or melted fats in the cooking pan and spread them over the surface of the meat, to wet the outside layer, which dries out first. Do this repeatedly throughout roasting. When the meat has cooked, let it rest for at least 15 minutes before serving, so the juices will redistribute. Remember that the temperature of the meat rises while it is resting, so plan for this if you are cooking to a certain temperature.

In **grilling**, the heat comes from below, from hot coals, wood, or a gas or electric source. Similar to the roasting method, the high heat forms a crust on the exterior of the meal, sealing in the juices. This is also true of **broiling**; when broiling, the heat comes from above, as in an oven broiler or professional salamander.

Grilling can be done on an open fire, in a hearth, over hot rocks, on a spit, on a hibachi or other type of backyard grid, and on a range top in a pan. The food should be lightly oiled, so it doesn't adhere to the hot metal grill. Cooking on an outdoor grill

DRY MEAT / MOIST HEAT COMBO FOODS

DRY HEAT	seafood, young poultry, pork except shoulder and hocks, lamb except breast and shank, veal roasts, beef steaks form young steers, rib roasts, short loins, sirloins, some round cuts
MOIST HEAT	some seafood, stewing cuts of poultry, pork shoulder cuts and hocks, lamb breast and shank, veal chops, cutlets, streaks, shoulder, round roasts, shank and breasts cuts, Beef chuck, round, fore shank, brisket, short plate, flank and tip cuts

FORMING A PAPILLOTE PACKAGE

Cut a large sheet of parchment into a heart shape large enough to contain the food. Place food in the center of one half of the heart, close to the center fold. Fold the empty half over and twist the sealed edge. Place on a baking sheet and into the oven.

....

BAIN MARIE

A water bath, or **bain marie**, is used for even, gentle cooking of delicate foods, for keeping foods warm, or for melting chocolate. The water is never brought to a boil. There are professional bain maries, but a hotel pan holding ramekins or a gratin pan also qualifies as a bain marie. Assembling a bain marie requires a deep pan into which your baking dish fits. For baking in a bain marie, place the deep pan in the oven, and fit the baking pan into it. Pour hot, even boiling water two-thirds up the sides of the dish.

allows for the use of flavored woods, which impart a smoky flavor to the food that varies with the wood type used, and you may want to marinate meats to flavor them before grilling. Though the word **barbecue** often refers to the event of cooking foods over high heat outdoors, by definition barbecued foods differ from grilled in that they are cooked slowly using indirect heat. Fast-cooking dry heat methods, such as grilling, broiling and roasting, can be done with minimal oil, as can sautéing and pan-frying.

Sautéing, a rapid, high-heat method, is for small, tender foods. The foods are browned in fat, the pan is hot enough that the food "jumps." Do not crowd the pan when sautéing; the food will release too much moisture at once and will steam rather than brown. It is good for some cooking juices to gather in the pan while sautéing; these become the base of a sauce that carries the prominent flavors of the food and reintroduces moisture lost in cooking. **Sweating**, on the other hand, is done over low heat over a long time, so the foods turn up their flavors without browning. Sweating is often done in the first stages of sauce- or stock-making.

Moist-heat cooking is done in or over liquid, and includes blanching, steaming, poaching, simmering, and cooking en papillote. **Poaching**, or gently simmering in liquid, is an excellent method for tender foods, such as whole fish, as the not-quite-boiling liquid helps keep the delicate flesh intact. Simmering is a slow and steady bubbling of the cooking liquid over gentle heat.

Blanching, or lightly cooking in boiling water, serves many methods and encapsulates many purposes. Blanching firms, purifies, and removes salt or bitterness from foods. **Parboiling** lightly cooks foods prior to the completion of cooking by a different method. When is food is fried twice, the initial frying, to partially cook, is a form of blanching. Blanching is also a brief soak in boiling water for foods that need to be peeled or skinned, such as peaches or filberts.

Steaming cooks the food with vapors, and the foods are not touching the cooking liquid, but suspended in a basket above boiling liquid. Moistened food can also be steamed in packages, as in the **en papillote** cooking method, in which food is wrapped in parchment and baked in a hot oven. Juices from the food and flavorings in the packet release steam, which cooks them.

Braising and **stewing** are both known as combination methods. Typically foods are seared, then cooked in a little liquid, being simmered and steamed in tandem. Through these methods, tough cuts become tender, and all flavor and nutrients are retained in the cooking liquor, and flavors are beautifully integrated.

Stewing, cooking in liquid over a long term, can be done on the stove top or in the oven. Stewed foods are cut into bite-sized pieces, as are vegetables, browned, then covered with liquid, such as water or stock, which is kept at a low simmer. Stewing allows for flavors to combine slowly and intensely, for meat to be falling-apart tender and for the cooking liquids to reduce to a rich, thick sauce. The same qualities are true of braising, which is different from stewing in that it uses little liquid and is done with larger cuts of meat. Braising is done over a very low heat over

CARAMELIZED ONIONS

4 tablespoons oil or butter

4 onions, peeled and sliced thinly

Salt and ground black pepper

Heat the oil in a heavy pan over medium heat. Add onions and salt, then reduce heat to low. Cook, stirring occasionally, until all liquid evaporates from the pan and the onions have turned a deep brown.

a long period of time, with aromatic spices and vegetables.

Other methods, used in tandem with the methods described above, will help you achieve deep, rich flavors in your dishes. **A reduction** is cooking a liquid until a percentage of it has evaporated. This serves to concentrate flavors and to thicken the liquid. Reductions made excellent sauces, and are often made from the cooking liquids produced by braising, poaching, sautéing, or stewing.

Caramelizing, or **glazing**, is when vegetables such as onions, tomatoes or carrots are heated with fat and a pinch of sugar and slowly browned. This treatment

farm-raised game, such as venison, elk, boar, rabbit, bison, and bear. We eat many kinds of poultry, including duck, turkey, chicken, quail, goose and squab. The toughness or tenderness of different cuts of meat is dependent on the type of tissue the cut is composed of. Cuts with lots of connective tissue, such as those that come from muscles the animal exercises most, like shanks or cheeks, are toughest, though very flavorful. These rely on gentle, moist-heat methods to make them tender.

Fat flavors meat. Meat that is marbled contains fat in the muscle, and this fat tenders the meat as it cooks. Marbling various by cut, the diet and breed of the animal,

MASHED POTATO PLATFORM

Different kinds of potatoes need more or less milk or butter to make them creamy, so know what you're working with. You can use other liquids, such as stock or juices from cooking, or add other root vegetables to mashed potatoes, such as sweet potatoes, squash, parsnips, turnips and beets. Roasted garlic or shallots are classic, as are roasted artichokes. Herbs, spices, flavored oils: mashed potatoes are a blank palette for all your creative impulses.

2 pounds potatoes, peeled and cut into 1 to 2-inch chunks

Salt

Pepper

1 cup milk, sour cream, buttermilk, stock or heavy cream, warm or at room temperature

¼ c. butter, softened or melted

Place potatoes in a large saucepan and cover with cold water. Stir in salt. Bring to a boil and cook until tender. Drain and immediately rice or, using a stand mixer, mash. Add liquid, combine well, and then add butter. Whip, season to taste, and serve.

intensifies the flavors of the vegetables, which can then be used to add deep flavor to soups, stews, sauces, even salads, mashed potatoes or polenta.

Choosing and Storing Meats

We all know that meat is the flesh of beasts. In the United States, we consume beef, pork, lamb, mutton, veal and wild and

how old it was when slaughtered, and how active a lifestyle it led. Old, active animals have tougher meat; young, sedentary beasts yield softer meat. Meat that is evenly marbled with fat generally denotes good quality. The fat should be white, the flesh should be deep red and moist in appearance. Familiarize yourself with different meat cuts and how to prepare them to

TRUSSING A BIRD

Position the bird breast side up. With a long piece of string, bind the legs together, drawing the string into an X and pulling the legs together. Bring the string toward the neck opening, running it between the legs and the body. Flip the bird, then make an X over the center of the bird, and bind the wings to the body by wrapping the string around them, and pulling them together. Tie the string in a strong knot.

....

ROASTING A BIRD

Many a chef has a built a reputation on their special roasting method. This is a basic method.

Wipe inside and out, season. You can add to the cavity a stuffing, a halved lemon, an herb bundle, whatever aromatic ingredient you desire. Truss if desired. Place bird on a rack in a roasting pan in a 400° oven, breast side up. Place slices of butter on the breast or under the skin. Baste frequently, and turn the bird after 20 minutes, then turn back to breast-side up until the end of roasting. To check for doneness, pierce with a fork at a thick point, or lift from the pan. The juices should run clear.

....

CARVING A BIRD

Cut off the legs at the joint. Made a horizontal cut to the bone just above the wing, into the breast. Carve slices, repeat on other side of the breast.

their best advantage. Hindquarter cuts are typically used for quick cooking; these include the round and rump steaks and roasts. The forequarter is best cooked with slow, moist methods; these are the chuck, shanks and ribs.

Meat quality relies on several factors: color, tenderness, flavor and succulence. All meats should have a moist surface. Beef should be deep red; pork and veal pale pink, lamb a magenta tone.

Knowing primary cuts and basic fabrication techniques enable you to cut meats to specification and control portion quality and size, as well as achieving consistency in cooking time and appearance. Meat cut or pounded to uniform thickness cooks evenly, as do roasts tied into an even cylinder. Storing meat properly is very important: meats should be refrigerated and loosely wrapped, separated into type to prevent cross-contamination. Store meats separate from other foods. Meat can be frozen for several months.

Trimming meat for dry-heat platform

Remove only fat, gristle and the silver membrane called the silver skin. With your fingers, begin to pull the fat away from the meat. Run a sharp knife along the edge where the meat and fat separate. Work the tip of the sharp knife under the silver skin. Pull the silver skin taut, and run the knife underneath it, severing it so no meat is cut away.

Butterflying meat

With the blade parallel to your cutting surface, make a cut through the meat's center, leaving one edge intact. Open the meat so it is flat and of even thickness throughout.

To cut into **medallions**, rounds of meat 3 to 7 ounces, simply cut the trimmed tenderloin into round portions. You can mold the medallions into rounds for even cooking and a neat appearance.

Poultry

The category of poultry applies to all birds that are raised on a farm: chicken, duck, goose, turkey, guinea hen, quail. Whole poultry can be roasted, boiled, steamed, barbecued and braised. Poultry cut into parts can be poached, sautéed and grilled as well. Never serve poultry raw. Although the idea of a chicken-mango milkshake may seem revolutionary to you, it's a bacterial disaster waiting to happen. When purchasing poultry, look for moist, intact skin. Flesh should be plump and firm, with a fresh smell. Frozen poultry must be completely defrosted before cooking.

A NOTE ON BUYING MEAT AND POULTRY

In recent years, consumers have begun to take an interest in the meat and birds they eat. Prompted by books such as *Fast Food Nation* and animal welfare groups such as the Humane Society of the United States and People for the Ethical Treatment of Animals, consumers want to know where their animal came form, and how it was raised. Be aware of this interest in choosing your purveyors. Know that there's a big difference in flavor and texture when you compare grass-fed beef and corn-raised beef. A free-range chicken is more yellow than a chicken raised in battery cages. These differences are relevant to you if you can taste or see them, if your customers demand them, or if you're interested in supporting a different sort of food system than the one we have now.

Trussed poultry has had its wings and legs bound up by twine. A trussed bird is easier to handle; it sits nicely in the pan, and can be turned and basted with ease. Sometimes birds are trussed by stitching up the legs and wings with a trussing needle.

Activity:

Imagine what techniques or flavors you could apply to a roasting a chicken that would make it unique to you. List them.

_____

_____

_____

_____

_____

Fish

There are tens of thousands of species of fish and probably as many ways to prepare them. All the cooking methods can be applied to different varieties of fish. Fish are grouped into many categories, including cartilaginous versus bony, or saltwater or fresh, and by body type. All these factors are important to consider when buying and preparing fish. When purchasing whole fresh fish, eyes should be moist, bulging and bright. Gills should not be slimy, and the body should be firm, not floppy. Flesh should be firm and springy, and smell of the water but not overpoweringly fishy. It is best to buy a whole fish, or large chunk of fish and cut fillets or steaks yourself. When buying fish that is cut, look for firm flesh with good, even color. We include preparations specific to round fish and flat fish. Round fish is usually firm and meaty-- trout, perch, salmon, bass, bream, eel, hake, bream, snapper, swordfish, tuna—and flat fish usually have a more subtle flavor and delicate texture--- sole, flounder, grouper, halibut, john dory, turbot. There are also cartilaginous fish, which some-times must be handled differently; these are shark, ray, monkfish, and skate. Fish should not be stored for more than a few days as it deteriorates quickly, and it should be stored in ice on perforated pans, not in water, in the coldest part of the refrigerator or walk-in cooler.

Shellfish should be active and intact, with a fresh smell. Avoid very dirty mussels and clams. Some varieties of clam, such as cherrystone or littleneck, are served on the half-shell. Others are poached briefly or stewed for a long time—these two treatments yield tender clams. Oysters should be tightly closed (raw on the half shell with a mignonette sauce or

---

A NOTE ABOUT SOURCING SEAFOOD

A 2006 report by the journal Science stated that by 2050 the oceans would be overfished and polluted to the extent that our children will not be able to eat the fish we do today. Already, we hear about endrangered species: redfish, Chilean sea bass (aka Patagonian toothfish), and bluefin tuna.

Be an informed seafood buyer. Find out what fish are plentiful and fished in a sustainable manner. It is also possible to source sustainably-raised seafood if you do your homework. Ask where your fish came from and how it is caught. The Monterey Bay Aquarium and other conservation and marine life groups publish a list of consumer guidelines to buying seafood that may make your choice a whole lot easier.

Many consumers are concerned about the provenance of seafood because farm-raised seafood has a bad rap. There are sustainable, clean aquaculture operations, but there are also giant industrial operations with overstocked ponds to which pesticides, disinfectants and antibiotics are added. Traces of these chemicals show up in fish and in human bodies, and your customers may have tough questions about the fish on your menu. Be prepared to answer them.

---

squeeze of lemon), and should not be washed once opened, as you wash away the flavorful brine. Oysters are cooked when their edges curl and turn white. Scallops should smell briny and have a faint gray cast. Perfectly white scallops have been treated with chemicals. Shrimp in the shell should be firm and gray; black spots indicate deterioration.

Cleaning Fish

Cut away fins and tail with a sharp knife or scissors. If the fish is to be served whole, cut away most of the tail, leaving a V shape. You may do this under running water to contain the flying scales. Using a fish scaler or other thin, flat surface, such as a spoon handle or blunt edge of a knife blade, scrape lightly against the fish, from the head toward the tail.

On a flat fish, starting at the tail end, scrape the skin away from the tail to loosen it from the flesh. Using a kitchen towel for leverage, get a firm hold on the skin and tail, and pull the skin away, all the way to the head, and detach completely.

If the fish has not been gutted:

For a flat fish, make an incision in the fish's belly, reach in and pull out the soft guts and discard.

For a round fish, cut a v around the fish's face, cutting through the fish. Pull the head away, and the guts will trail out as well.

A fish is **pan-ready** when it has been scaled, trimmed, gutted and rinsed.

To fillet a round fish, beginning just behind the gills, cut toward the tail with a sharp knife. The knife should press against the backbone, and the flesh should peel away from them under the steady pressure of the blade. Turn the fish over and repeat. Cut away any belly bones. To skin: place skin-side down on a cutting board, and position the blade of the knife at the edge of flesh and skin at the tail end. Using a gentle sawing motion, run the knife along the skin so it shaves off.

To fillet a flat fish, cut all around the fish, detaching where the fins and flesh meet. Make a cut along the backbone, angled toward the edge of the fish. Starting at the head end, run the knife along the bones to make a fillet. Turn the fish so the head is toward you. Cut away the second fillet on this side. Flip the fish over and remove the other two fillets.

Peeling and deveining shrimp

Gently wiggle the thumb in under the legs and under the shell. Pull the shell away carefully, so the tail does not break off. With a short blade, make a small cut along the curve of the shrimp and peel out the gray intestinal vein.

Cleaning and debearding mussels

Scrub the mussel with a brush to remove all grit from shell. Take hold of the little bristly beard and pull gently.

Vegetables

So many vegetables are available these days, it's as though there's a new one to experiment with every day. Vegetables are a main dish or an accompaniment, and add color and texture to meal, as well as their own particular flavors. Some vegetables are integral to classic technique, such as the onions and celery used in a mirepoix. Without the aromatic onion or the acidic tomato, so many soups and sauces would be dull. Vegetables should be cooked and served when they are as fresh as possible, so it is ideal to purchase them as frequently as possible. Some vegetables keep for a very long time, such a root vegetables, whereas others are highly perishable, such as tender microgreens. Store vegetables in the least-cold part of the refrigerator or walk-in.

Before cooking, vegetables must be pre-pared in many ways; this is a considerable part of mise en place. Wash, clean and core. Peel and shape. Snap the woody ends from asparagus. Destring the peas and beans.

Remember that root vegetables, when boiled, must be cooked through to their core. Green vegetables, when boiled just until tender, should go straight to the table or into an ice water bath to retain color and crunch. Steaming cooks vegetables while preserving many of their nutrients. And roasted vegetables acquire intense flavor. Roasted garlic and shallots become mellow, but intense, peppers becomes sweet and smoky, and beets sweeten.

Peeling and chopping garlic or shallots

Separate the cloves from the head. Cut off the clove's root end, then press the flat side of a knife on the clove to crack the skin. Peel the clove from the skin, discard the skin, then crush the clove, and chop.

Garlic which has been roasted has a milder, sweeter flavor, and garlic that has been cooked into a dish for a long time will lose pungency. Burnt garlic becomes acrid and unpleasant.

Peeling and seeding tomatoes

This method works for tomatoes of any size and shape.

Bring a pot of water to a boil. Cut an X in the stem end of the tomatoes. Immerse completely in the boiling water for about 30 seconds, until the skin loosens. Remove from boiling water to cold water. Peel with your fingers when cool. Halve tomatoes, not from stem end, but through the wide middle. Run your thumb into the pockets, dragging out the seeds, or turn the tomato upside down over a bowl to let liquid seeds run out.

Tomato concasse is peeled, seeded, chopped tomato.

Roasting and peeling peppers

Peppers can be peeled with a swivel peeler. Cut the pepper into sections at the folds, remove the seeds and ribs, and peel off the skin.

To roast a pepper, hold over an open flame with tongs until the skin is blackened. Turn, so every side of the pepper is charred evenly. The peppers can also be broiled until black. Steam by closing in a paper or plastic bag. When cool, peel off the black skin with your fingers.

Mincing an onion

Peel the onion, and cut it into halves. Place half-onion with the flat side on the cutting surface, and cut vertical slices into, not through, the half. Turn the knife and cut horizontal slices into the onion from top to bottom, again not cutting through the onion. The root end should hold the onion together.

Cut across the slashes you have made so the onion falls away in tiny squares.

Chopping herbs

Use a chef's knife. Gather the herb into a tight bundle and slice into strips, sliding the knife down the fingers. Then, holding the handle of the knife loosely, and touching the tip of the knife softly with the opposite hand to direct the blade, rock the knife front to back over the sliced herb to chop more finely.

Washing Greens

Cut out the tough stem end. Remove the outside leaves, then cut into halves and wash in cold water. Break up the head, drying leaves gently in a towel or spinning them.

Grating citrus rind

The rind of citrus fruits contains the most oil and flavor, so it lends a vibrant citrus flavor when used. Make sure, when grating, not to go into the white pith below the bright skin, which is bitter. With a grater or Microplane zester held firmly in one hand, run the fruit lightly along the teeth, so tiny strips of skin come off. Bang the tool against the cutting board to release all zest. Julienne strips of rind, sans pith, is wonderful for candying.

Sectioning citrus fruits

Cut off both ends of the fruit so the bright flesh is visible. With a sharp knife, cut into the flesh just under the thick white pith, preserving as much flesh as possible, and cut off the skin in strips. Cut out each section, working the knife between the membranes, and discarding seeds. Or, from top to bottom, cut the fruit into round slices.

Pastry

Pastry is, in essence, flour and fat bound by water, which takes on marvelous forms! From flaky pastries to layered, these doughs can carry sweet or savory foods, and it is important to master them. The higher the fat content, the flakier the pastry will be, and fat need not be restricted to butter or shortening. Lard, nut butters, olive and other oils, and suet, alone or in combination, make fine fat for pastry. You can vary the type of flour used, as well as season the dough with a multitude of dried spices, extracts, zests and cocoa.

Plastic-lined pastry bags are made to contain heavier stuff, and can be washed and reused. Metal tips are fit inside the pastry bag to provide different piping

PATE BRISEE PLATFORM (ONE 9-INCH PIE)

This dough is good for both sweet and savory tarts. The sugar is optional, and you can experiment with different types of sugar and fats for an unconventional pate brisee.

Place in a bowl 2 cups flour, 6 ounces unsalted butter, chilled and cut into cubes, a pinch of salt and ½ teaspoon sugar. Mix with your fingers to coat the butter with the flour. Drizzle in approximately ⅓ cup ice water and use your hands to form a ball, working it as little as possible but bringing it together.

Turn out onto a floured surface and roll to ⅛-inch thickness. To transfer dough to a mold or pie plate, roll it onto the rolling pin, and unroll over the pan. Push the dough into the pan with your fingers, and form a lip of crust with your fingertips. Cut off excess dough. Now you can prick with the tines of a fork or your fingers. To precook, line with pie weights or beans and bake.

PATE SUCREE

This is a sweet dough with a cookie-like crispness.

Make a heap of 2 ¼ cups flour, a pinch of salt and ⅓ cup sugar on a clean surface. Form a well in the flour, and break into it 1 large egg and 8 tablespoons softened butter. Draw the flour into the egg with your fingers, then knead the dough, working all the ingredients together to form a soft ball. Cover and keep cool until you use the dough.

PATE A CHOUX PLATFORM

A paste, not a dough, this becomes the classic cream puff, the éclair, or, as a savory dough with the addition of pepper, cheese and herbs, gougeres.

Place in a heavy saucepan over high heat 1 cup water, 4 tablespoons butter, ¼ teaspoon salt. Bring to a boil. When the butter is melted, remove from the heat and dump in 1 cup of flour. Mix vigorously with a wooden spoon. turn the heat to low, then put the pan back on the heat, stirring occasionally, until the dough has dried and a white crust appears on the bottom of the pan. Place this mixture in a mixing bowl, let cool slightly, then beat in 4 large eggs, one at a time, until the dough is smooth and shiny

CLASSIC PUFF PASTRY

Puff pastry preparation is a long and complicated process, but the golden, flaky finish is achieved by the continual folding and rolling of the dough and butter. This process creates layers of fat and air; the air "puffs" the pastry, the fat crisps it. The butter and basic dough should be at the same temperature to start, and the quality of the butter you use will have a definite effect on the flavor of your puff pastry. Puff pastry is baked at high heat and can be deep-fried. It can be flavored with zests, extracts, and cocoa, mixed in with the butter.

On a clean working surface, make a pile of 4 ½ cups flour. Make a well in the flour, and add 1 ½ teaspoons salt and approximately 1 ¼ cup water. Knead until smooth and elastic. Let rest for 30 minutes.

Roll the dough into a rough square, then cut a crisscross on the top of the dough. Roll the dough out so it forms a rough cross. Place, in the center of the cross, 2 ¼ cups softened butter. Spread the butter in an even layer in the center of the cross, fold the ends of dough over it, and rest in a cold place, 10 minutes.

Roll the dough out on a lightly floured surface to a 2-foot by 8-inch rectangle. Fold he rectangle into thirds, as you would fold a letter, turn it 45 degrees, and roll the dough out into a 2-foot by 8-inch rectangle again. Fold into thirds again and let rest if necessary, in a cool place, 15 minutes to firm the dough. Repeat the rolling and folding process 4 times more, letting dough rest in a cool place for 15 minutes after reach rolling. After the sixth turn, the dough is ready to shape and bake, or freeze to keep. Refrigerated puff pastry turns grayish, so it is better to freeze the dough, and thaw before using.

patterns. These can also be washed and re-used. To use, fold down the sides of the bag before scooping in your filling, and only fill the bag halfway, otherwise your filling could leak out onto the outside of the bag or the surface you are piping onto. Gather the top and twist it, pulling it between your thumb and forefinger so the pad of your palm is against the bag. Push with the palm and the tips of the fingers, working the filling through the bag from the top.

Whipped egg whites and cream are often used to lighten mixtures, such as mousses and frostings, so they are of a soft consistency, which can be piped. Both form a base for many creative products.

To Separate Eggs

Set out two clean bowls. Working over one, crack the egg and open gently, holding the egg upright, not sideways, to contain the yolk. The white will run out, into the bowl. Transfer the yolk to the empty half for the shell, letting more white run off into the bowl. Pour the yolk into a separate bowl.

Whipping Egg Whites

A trace of grease on your bowl's surface will inhibit the foaming of the eggs. Make sure your bowl and whisk are scrupulously clean. In a wide bowl, whip whites at medium speed, by hand or in a mixer, until they are foamy. Then increase the speed until you have reached the stage you desire. Overbeaten eggs look dry, and are useless, as the proteins are clumped together.

Soft peak whites are glossy, but when the beater is removed, the peak droops to the side.

Medium peak whites form a rounded peak. Sugar and flavorings can be added at medium peak stage.

Stiff peaks stand up without rounding over.

Whipping Cream

The cream, bowl and beaters should be cold before it is whipped. Proceed as for whipping egg whites, achieving foam and then various stages of peak. Sugar and flavorings should be added after soft peak is reached. If overbeaten, cream forms curds and turns into butter.

To Fold Whipped Egg or Cream Into a Base

Use a folding motion and a spatula to preserve the airiness of the whipped stuff. Add one-third of the whipped substance to the base and incorporate, then add the remainder and fold in only until just blended.

To Summarize...

With these basic techniques mastered, you will possess the foundations of culinary technique. You will be able to tackle all the exercises in this book, which will help you put technique to creative and unique uses. Use this chapter as a reference when faced with challenges in the games that follow later in the book.

Chapter 2 Assessment Questions

❶ Define mise en place and discuss its importance.

❷ When would you use a white mirepoix versus a standard mirepoix? A matignon versus a bouquet garni? What changes could you make to these classic platforms to achieve different flavors?

❸ Describe how you care for your knives in daily usage.

❹ What is the difference between a vinaigrette and a rub? Define essence versus stock, emulsion versus coulis.

_____

_____

_____

_____

_____

❺ What cooking method would you use on a flatiron cut of beef? Explain.

_____

_____

_____

_____

_____

3/
Expanding The Basics

Chapter Two provided reference and basic platforms to build on. This chapter introduces different techniques and gets into the art of balancing flavors and composing menus.

Chapter Two was about mastering the essentials; Chapter Three is about enhancement and artistry, using a different set of tools and acting from a different set of impulses: to preserve, to present, to contrast. We think of these skills as advanced, insomuch as they advance the dish from basic and good to exciting and unique. We need the platforms and ideas to facilitate the pairing of foods and carry the marriage of flavors. Skills can be acquired through practice and dedication. Flavors can be learned through repeated tasting and cultural exploration. Then creativity can come into play.

This chapter is also about finishing touches, from special knife cuts that can shape a radish into a rose, to serving seared scallops on a beet chip instead of a plate, to the dollop of sweetened cream or chutney that elevates the flavor and texture of each bite. **Garnish** is not only that sprig of parsley positioned on the edge of the plate, an addition to the plate that adds visual interest; garnish encapsulates all the daubs and flourishes that enhance the presentation, texture and flavor of a dish. You develop the basics for doing this by tasting, touching, smelling—familiarizing yourself with ingredients, knowing what works together by complementing or offsetting.

This chapter offers a cross section of salads, sauces, relishes and pickles that are used as standalone foods, or make standard foods more intriguing, for instance spiking a white bean puree with basil pesto and toasted pistachios. Different presentations, surprising flavor combinations and solid production methods provide you with an opportunity to showcase a truly unique product.

CHAPTER OBJECTIVES

① To build on techniques described in the Basics Chapter.

② To provide an overview of pantry staples, basic charcuterie and cheeses.

③ To outline menu composition, presentation and garde manger.

④ To introduce specific skills and recipe platforms from diverse culinary traditions.

⑤ To inspire the student to begin imagining flavor and texture combinations by presenting a number of hors d'oeuvres, appetizers and amuses, as well as recipes for pickles, compotes and condiments.

⑥ To provide differentiation between different terms and products used in commercial kitchens, including types of salts and oils.

KEY TERMS

A la Greque

Amuse

Canapé

Charcuterie

Chiffonade

Coagulation

Confit

Cornets

Crème fraiche

Creme anglaise

Crudite

Duxelles

Flavor wheel

Forcemeats

Galantine

Ganache

Garde manger

Garnish

Julienne

Macedoine

Mince

Pate

Pate en croute

Phyllo

Render

Rondelle

Terrine

Truffles

Vol-au-vent

Menu Composition

A menu is, quite simply, a list of dishes to be served in the order they are to be served in. This list establishes what is to be served, how, and in what order. It's a guideline for both the diner and the kitchen. It's a statement of intention and establishes expectations.

A good menu is all about contrast. The menu you create should feature a series of light to complex dishes, starting simply and getting gradually richer, constructed in an order to excite the palate, a progression food writer Richard Olney described as being guided by a "gastronomic aesthetic."

To hone your gastronomic aesthetic, think of how you experience food, with your eyes, your mouth, even your ears. If you have just sipped at creamy chowder, do you want to fill your mouth next with a rich fettuccine Alfredo? Or does a crunchy salad of watercress and tart apples appeal more? We don't want to eat course after course served atop mashed potatoes, or a succession of salty fried foods. A parade of noodles covered in spicy marinara sauce, even if they are different noodle shapes, bores the palate because the same flavors—acidic tomato, pungent garlic, sweet basil—are repeated, as is the same starchy, semi-soft texture of the noodles.

Offer Variety

Repetition of flavor, texture, temperature and color makes for a dull menu, to the eye, to the teeth, to the tongue. Follow a chilled food with a hot food, a smooth soup with a crunchy vegetable, a mellow flavor with a sharp, a chewy meat with a crumbly cheese. If you serve a course of brown meat and pale potatoes, precede it with a bright beety soup, and follow it with a scoop of

jade green tea sorbet. Even on an a la carte menu, have a variety of complementary choices and servers trained to steer a guest into menu combinations that you think work well. The same principles apply to a buffet, or passing hors d'oeuvres: the flavors, textures and colors should complement and contrast each other. Often, parties that feature a buffet or passing hors d'oeuvres are organized around a theme: a happy event such as a birthday or wedding, a holiday, a season. Your menu should echo this theme, with both ingredients and presentation. Your presentation must be both appealing and accessible for the guests, and remember that people want to know what they are eating. When organizing a menu, don't pile on the spices, course after course, dish after dish. You increase the excitement and intensity of a spicy dish if you serve it after a simple flavor.

These tenets apply to plate composition, too. If serving a duck breast with cherry compote, consider what else would work on the plate. A bitter green would add contrasting color, texture and flavor. Fanning slices of the brown meat over orange smashed sweet potatoes is a nice color contrast, and the tartness of cherries and meaty duck flavor are offset by the soft, sweet tuber. It's for contrast of texture and flavor that strawberry ice cream is served with a cracked pepper tuile. You have, in that combination, sweet versus spicy, soft versus crisp, and very different temperatures of the cookie and the frozen cream.

Flavor

Four basic tastes—salty, sweet, sour and bitter—and an ambiguous fifth savory taste, called umami. These tastes, in an infinite number of combinations with each other, create all the different flavors of everything we eat. Flavors are often represented on a **flavor wheel (see chapter 4, page 98)**. A flavor wheel is somewhat like the color wheel: a way of visually organizing the broadest flavors you may encounter in food. The flavors, or sensations, are laid out as a circular arrangement of sensations experienced by the taste buds on most flavor wheels, and include many more sensations than these five, sensations such as sharp, flabby, fatty, and lean. The wheel illustrates opposites, or contrasts, and can serve as guide when composing a plate. On a menu or a plate, you'd balance the tender with the crisp, the spicy with the cool by offering both, at different times, on different sides of the plate.

Perfumer and Flavorist Magazine offers an arrangement of distinctive and stable aromas, which also relate to food. Their wheel is ordered into ranges which overlap to form four broad categories: sweet/ fresh, sweet/savory/cooked, savory/cooked, savory/fresh. Within these categories are a wealth of aromas that may help you think about balance, when you contract them: green, grassy, herbaceous, spicy, fruity, tropical, blackcurrant/cassis, vegetable, nutty, caramel, smoky, burnt/roasted, beefy, pork/lamb/chicken, savory/bouillon, fatty, rancid/cheesy, mushroom/earthy, truffle, garlic, onion.

Balance

The concept of balance is helpful not only to flavors, but to presentation as well. When composing a plate or a platter, allow different parts of the plate to offset each other. Arrange tall stacked items on one side, and low, flat items on the other. Insert a line of brightly-colored vegetable or tangle of greens between a mound of shaved smoked salmon and mound of crème fraiche. Arrange geometric shapes— canapés cut into squares or triangles—in parallel lines to form a pattern. Offset this with bright carrot rondelles or curls, long chives that draw the eye in a different direction, or squiggles of a vivid condiment.

Composition and Design

The techniques of Chapter Two were the basic tools of production to outfit the hot kitchen. **Garde manger** is a specialization which covers the chefs and foods of the cold kitchen, including curing, preserving, assembling a cheese plate and preparing charcuterie, salads and cold soups. Yet many of the Chapter Two's techniques show up at the garde manger station: pea pods are blanched for a salad, a compote of dried apricots is reduced during a slow simmer. In addition to building on basic techniques and platforms, the products of the garde manger are well-considered starters, pauses and polishes: the house-made sausage and duck confit that elevate a cassoulet, the lacquer of fruit jam on a tart, the perfect mesclun salad full of snipped herbs and flowers. Garde manger products are fun to experiment with, and contribute to the beauty of a bite.

Balance is a key word when applied to both food flavor and to design. When composing a plate or a platter, garnishes should be interesting visually and flavorful, and add to the meaning of the dish or platter. Microsprouts punctuate a platter with green and their delicate, curving shape; they look good enough to eat, so they should

Activity

Consider the following menu:

- ● Beef and Red Pepper Fajitas
- ✳ Guacamole
- ■ Chipotle Tomatillo Salsa
- ▲ Chips

Map this dish on the flavor and composition graphics reproduced below. Guacamole has been completed as an example. How is the balance of flavors and textures? How might it be improved?

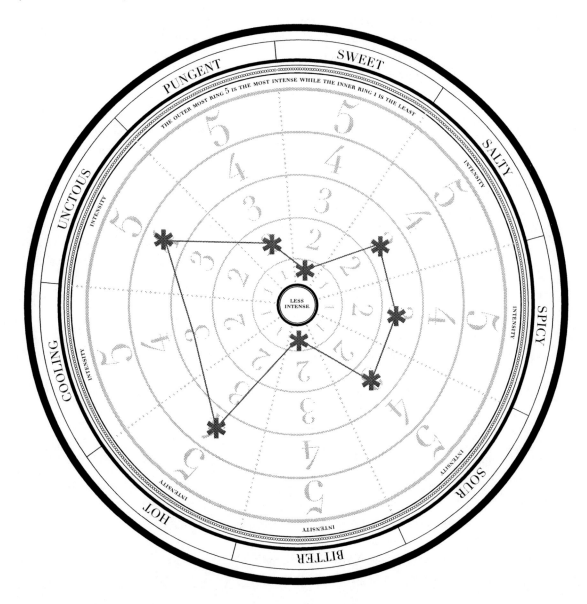

be! As often as possible, try to integrate the elements you are presenting. For example, choose peppery microgreens, dress them with a sweet vinaigrette, and serve them as a base for a taste of soft chevre.

Remember these basic tenets of design when presenting food: spacing, symmetry, and contrasting elements of color and shape. **Spacing** is a distance between things that makes each thing stand out. **Symmetry** is formal balance: two identical forms, one on each side of a dividing axis, that correspond in size, shape and position. **Contrast** is a comparison of differences.

These tenets—spacing, symmetry and contrast—draw the eye in specific ways, and it is through experimenting and moving shapes around that you develop an eye for presentation. You must also watch the world around you, be in touch with pop culture, trends and graphic design on book covers, in magazines, even furniture stores, textiles, and the fashionable shades and patterns you see in street clothing. Design is ubiquitous, and the world around you is your greatest reference tool.

Don't crowd your tray or plate with one color; provide some pop. Food can be round, square, rectangular, and peaked or flat. Foods can be piled for height, and one focal point food, the element you want to star on the plate, can take up the most space. Playful, creative food presentation is fun for the chef and the guest, but don't get carried away. The food being eaten should be recognizable.

An example is a visit to a restaurant where the plate was unidentifiable.

We ordered a simple entrée, roast breast of chicken. Wedged into the mashed potatoes was a waffled tuile. There were yellow squash moons and zucchini tournes on the plate, which was drizzled and splashed with sauces in three different colors: yellow squiggles, red lines, green circles. The strangest and tallest element of this wildly garnished plate were the three fried strands of spaghetti, fanned and stabbed into the chicken breast so they stood straight up from the plate. The chef was very creative with plate decoration, but had too much garnish. The plate looked ridiculous, and inedible.

In this example, elements of the garnish don't complement the main foods on the plate. There are too many garnishes on the plate. Too many colors, too much height, too many fried things stuck into piles of food—the result was a plate that looked like a page from Dr. Seuss' *If I Ran the Circus*.

Adding height and excitement does not require adding fried noodles, stabbing chives into a plop of hummus, or piling food on top of food. Use your judgment. If the stack looks precarious, don't send it to the table. You're asking for a mishap there. No one wants to be served a teetering stack.

Question:

❶ What other strategies can you use to add height and excitement to your presentation?

_____

_____

_____

_____

❷ What can you do to add color to your plate without relying on sauces?

_____

_____

_____

_____

❸ Name a garnish you've seen that struck you as clever. Name one that struck you as too cute, ineffective, or tasted bad. How can you learn from the experience of these foods?

_____

_____

_____

_____

Activity

Consider the following menu:
- Sautéed Supreme of Chicken
- Mashed Potatoes garnished with Fried Shallots
- Pan Steamed Haricot Verts

Diagram this dish on the square and round plate in a way that you think is visually appealing.

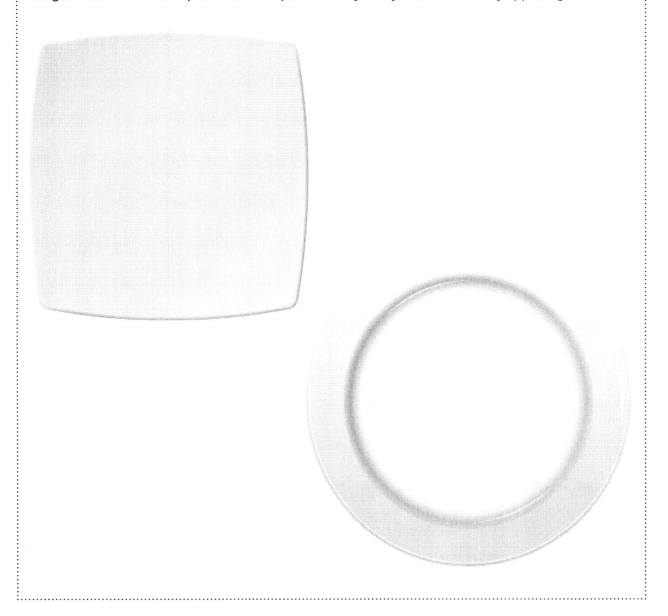

Knife Skills

You have assembled the perfect knife kit and should develop a skill with these crucial tools so they act as an extension of your own limbs. The knife skills of a great chef create art, as a sculptor does with an awl, as a pianist does with fingertips.

There are two basic knife holds, which facilitate control and agility. In the first, wrap all four fingers under the blade and press the thumb to the top of the blade. The second involves wrapping all fingers around the side and top blade, and resting the index finger against the side of the blade perpendicular to the handle. Press your thumb against the other side of the blade.

Knife Cuts

The item to be cut—say, an onion—should be held by a hand with fingertips tucked under, so the blade of the knife rests against and is guided by the flat part of the knuckle. The knife, while cutting the onion, should slide up and down against the knuckles, which provide a guide for where the blade will land. With the knife hand, use a rocking or down and back motion while cutting. The speed and precision of your cuts is relative to the speed at which you move your knuckles back, and how quickly you rock your blade. The faster your knuckles retreat and the faster you rock the blade, the quicker you will make your cuts.

Many platforms in Chapter Two suggested the ideal size of vegetable cuts, but here is a guide:

Coarse chopping is for foods that are not part of a presentation, such as vegetables going into a stock. Trim the root and stem ends, then slice the vegetable so that all the pieces are approximately the same size.

A **mince** is a very fine, even cut. The vegetable should be roughly chopped to begin. If it is an herb, stems should be removed before chopping. Then gather the pieces into a pile. With the tip of the knife blade against the cutting board, repeatedly lower the knife to chop through the item being cut. Guide the blade with your free hand. Go over the item until it is chopped to the fineness you desire. In all cases, the vegetable is cut through at even intervals.

Dicing produces an even cube of varying fineness. Slice the vegetable lengthwise into slices. Stack the slices and make parallel cuts to firm strips. Then cut across so the vegetable falls away in cubes of the size you have chosen.

Julienne is a fine, rectangular cut, slices of the vegetable cut into sticks. A **chiffonade**, which translates from the French to "made of rags," is a julienne-style cut of leaves, the slim shreds of a basil leaf cut into 40 slices, for example. **Batonnet** is slightly wider than a julienne. **Rondelles** are small rounds, like those from a carrot cut crosswise. **Macedoine** is a small dice of not one vegetable, but a mixture of various vegetables, traditionally carrot and turnip.

Once you have decent knife skills, you can begin to attempt your own sculptures and graphic flourishes made of food. You can cut slices of beet, carrot or other bright vegetable, then, from those slices, cut shapes to assemble a central pattern or decorative border on the surface of a terrine, cake or any other flat food surface. When you were a kid, did you ever play with ColorForms, combining flat, colorful shapes into flowers, trees, funny faces? The same principle applies when using shapes cut neatly from thinly-sliced and colorful foods.

You can also create three-dimensional garnishes from tomatoes, radishes and other fruits and vegetables, which can be used with flat decoration. Some people see these as fussy, others as charming. If a vegetable design is well integrated with your plate design, they will not annoy, but may delight. Children love funny, whimsical shapes and for many of us, they tap the child inside.

To shape a vegetable into a flower:
First, cut a thin disc from the item to act as the flower base, leaving a thin strip that is still bound to the fruit. Work this strip, ½-inch to 1 inch thick, depending on what fruit or vegetable you are working with, cutting close to the surface so you have a thin ribbon from the surface of the fruit. Cut a second strip. Form the first strip, which is attached to the base, into a loose spiral. Roll the second strip, then place it inside the first, and you will have a "rose" *(see sidebar illustration).*

Or you can make neat, even triangular cuts along the sides of a round fruit or vegetable, each going to the middle, so that when you have worked your way all the way around, it will open easily, revealing a center design as shown in the sidebar.

In general garnishes such as rose tomatoes are considered "non-functional" garnishes. They may add visual appeal to a dish but contribute nothing to flavor or texture. They are best used on platters for buffets or passed hors d'oeuvres rather than individual plates.

Softer foods, such as butter, mousse, icing and melted chocolate can be piped into rosettes and other shapes with a pastry bag or **cornet**, a cone made of paper. Such garnishes are typically functional. Unlike a tomato rose, a rosette of lemon butter along side a plate of broiled scallops will add flavor and mouthfeel to the finished dish when added.

To make a cornet:
Cut a large square of parchment paper in half, to form a triangle. Holding two corners of the paper triangle, curl one under the other, forming a cone shape. Pull smoothly at the seam, while holding the cone shape, to form a sharp tip at the opening. Holding the seam tightly, fold the edges over to secure the taut sides of the cone. Fill with the soft substance you are piping. Fold one edge of the open side of the cone to the center of the cone, then the opposite side, so the cone is now folded closed. Fold the center over to secure it, cut the tip from the cone so the filling comes out smoothly.

Salads

The act of making a salad offers endless opportunities to riff with colors, flavors, textures and ingredients. Salads, of course, are a wonderful tool for showcasing both produce at its peak and classic and unique flavor combinations. A simple green salad, composed only of lettuces and vinaigrettes can contain flavors from delicate to bitter to robust. Vinaigrettes can be made from a seemingly-endless array of oils and acids: grapeseed and grapefruit juice; curried sunflower oil and white balsamic vinegar;

flower cut 1

flower cut 2

As a general rule, rinse greens thoroughly in cold water, then dry completely in a spinner or basket.

smoked olive oil, black pepper and red wine vinegar.

Salads are not only made from vegetables; there are noodle salads, grain salads, bread salads, and composed salads, which take all sorts of complementary ingredients and arrange them enticingly.

Starting with the basic green salad, it is important to familiarize yourself with types of greens. Mild lettuces include butter, iceberg, red leaf, oak leaf, romaine, mache and most types of baby green. Arugula, sorrel, mizuna, amaranth, watercress, and tat soi are all spicy greens. Bitter greens include endives, chicories, dandelion, mustard, beet, carrot, chard, kale, escarole, curly endive, frisee, and radicchio. All these bitter greens can be braised and served warm. Beyond lettuce, there are mung bean and broccoli sprouts, and pea and sunflower shoots, all of which make a crunchy salad base.

You can add edible flowers, such as chive and garlic blossoms, blossoms of fruit trees, bee balm, day lilies, gladiolas, jasmine, hyssop, angelica, bachelor's buttons, nasturtium, pansies, calendula, fuchsia, geraniums, violets, marigolds, primroses, linden, Queen Anne's lace, snap dragons, squash blossoms, sweet woodruff, hybrid begonias, water lotus, sunflowers, roses, leaves from herbs, such as borage, lavender, mustard and sage. Be sure that the blossoms you serve have not been treated with pesticides, and serve in small quantities. Always be positive that the variety of flower you are serving is edible, and that it is a food crop, not treated for florists or nurseries. Many varieties of edible flower lend themselves to different preparations; they can be candied, stuffed, pickled or fried.

Salads can be built or garnished with an equally wide range of ingredients: wedges, slices or shreds of tomatoes, cucumbers, carrots, radishes, jicama, beet, olives, peppers, cheese crisps, nuts, pomegranate seeds, segments of citrus, poached eggs, slices of pineapple, apples, cooked grains, torn bits of bread or croutons, pasta shapes or noodles, poppy or sesame seeds, beans, corn, pickled vegetables, crab meat or shrimp, baked cheese, roasted vegetables or fruits, duck or tuna confit, and so on. They can be flavored with all manner of foams, emulsions, spiced yogurts, snipped herbs and juices.

As a general rule, rinse greens thoroughly in cold water, then dry completely in a spinner or basket. Dressing will not adhere properly to wet leaves, and the taste of your dressing may be diluted. Don't stack lettuces or cram them into a small container. You don't want them to bruise. See the section on hors d'oeuvres further along in the chapter for more salad composition inspiration.

FRIED HERBS PLATFORM

Fried herbs make a beautiful garnish and contribute unusual and intense flavor to dishes. Frying will not only change the texture of the herb by crisping the leaves, but it will change the flavor. Even a common herb, like parsley, becomes tangier—it's flavor more "green"—when it is fried.

You can fry the individual leaves of herbs, or gather the herbs into small bunches or clusters. Make sure the leaves are washed and totally dry. You can fry them plain in very hot oil (365°F to 375°F), dust the herbs with flour, or batter-dip them; experiment with technique to see what you end up with.

A simple batter for herb garnish might be egg white whisked with flour and a pinch of salt.

Batter-dipped or plain, lower herbs into hot oil for 10 to 30 seconds, until crisp. Drain on paper towels before using.

Activity

Compose a salad of at least five ingredients that will show balance and variety of flavors, textures and colors. Then explain what each ingredient contributes to the finished dish.

_____

_____

_____

_____

_____

The key to a working vinaigrette is the balance of flavor, acidity and oiliness. Vinaigrettes are not only for dressing greens; they can be used as marinade and dressing on vegetables, grains and pasta. Choices for your acid component include vinegars, the juice of grapefruit, lemon, orange, blood orange, tangerine, satsuma, Meyer lemons, pineapple, or apple cider. The mixture can be stabilized with prepared mayonnaise, mustard, fruit or vegetable puree, or pasteurized egg yolk. Minced vegetable or aromatic—garlic, shallots, peppers, tomatoes, or beets, for example—can be added, as well as herbs, liquors, and spices.

Activity

Using the vinaigrette platform from Chapter 2, imagine and write a delicate and robust vinaigrette that could be used for salad.

_____

_____

_____

_____

_____

_____

BEAN COOKING PLATFORM

First soak overnight. Drain, and pick out any shriveled or broken beans. Rinse, and then bring to a boil in unsalted water to cover by an inch or two. Reduce heat, and simmer the beans until they are tender, two to three hours, depending on the size of the beans. Beans can be seasoned when they are cooked, or seasonings such as salt, pepper, bay leaves, onion, garlic, pancetta, ham hocks or a rind of Parmigianino can be added while they cook. Do not add acidic ingredients such as tomato or vinegar to cooking beans; the acid will toughen the skins.

LENTIL COOKING PLATFORM

Bring water to a boil, and then add lentils that have been rinsed and picked over for discolored or broken lentils or stones. Simmer in water until tender, then drain.

Remember that acids, such as tomato, vinegar and lemon, toughen legumes, so it is best to dress lentils at the last minute and not to cook with acidic ingredients.

Beans and Legumes

From black to cannellini, beans offer a number of sizes, textures and colors, and a basic but earthy flavor that plays well with others. Cook beans until they have a soft give to the tooth and delight in the texture that results not only from the individual bean, but from the collection of small, al dente forms. Beans can also be roughly or smoothly mashed, and that paste used to carry other flavors.

Lentils are versatile little legumes commonly associated with the Mediterranean diet. They come in a variety of colors—yellow, orange, red, green, beige, brown—and shapes, from flat discs to pebbles to a round like a clamshell. Lentils soak up flavor and can be cooked to different textures. They can star as the basis for a dish, or make a colorful garnish, side or starch.

Rice is a staple for a large portion of the world's population, and there are as many ways to cook and season it as there are people to eat it. Use your imagination! Use rice in entrees, appetizers, desserts or drinks; form it into balls, float it in soups, get it crusty in a cast iron pan and serve it in a wedge.

There are many types of rice—white, brown, red, jasmine, basmati, Arborio, black—and seemingly endless varieties to experiment with, which come in many

TABLE OF RICE AND GRAIN RATIOS AND COOKING TIMES

GRAIN	GRAIN: WATER RATIO	COOKING TIME (APPROX)
White Rice	1:2	15 min
Brown Rice	1:3	45 min
Basmati Rice	1:1.75	15 min
Arborio Rice	1:2.5	18 min
Wheat Berries	1:3	80 min
Bulgur Wheat	1:2	12 min
Wild Rice	1:4	50 min
Pearl Barley	1:3	50 min
Steel Cut Oats	1:4	20 min
Rolled Oats	1:2	8 min
Rye Berries	1:3	100 min
Buckwheat Groats	1:3	20 min

Note: These are general guidelines and not a substitute for package directions or tasting for doneness.

RICE COOKING PLATFORM

There are several different methods to cook rice, and a general proportion of rice to water is 1 cup rice to 2 cups water.

For the steamed rice method, bring water, rice and salt to a boil. Stir, cover pan, lower heat to low. Cook 15 minutes, then turn off heat and let stand 15 minutes. Fluff before serving. Brown rice requires more water and more time.

For boiled rice, bring a pan of water to a boil. Add salt, then rice. Simmer uncovered until tender, then drain.

Either of these methods can be used for grains such as barley, farro, amaranth, quinoa, couscous, teff, and wheat berries.

shapes, sizes, colors and flavors. Thai sticky rice makes a wonderful dessert topped with mango. Louisiana popcorn rice tastes and smells just like its name. Bangladeshi Kalijira tastes like Basmati but has tiny grains.

Cooked beans and legumes form the base for many spreads, which can go far in assembling appetizer platters and individual hors d'oeuvres, as well as sparking a salad, sandwich, or main dish. Traditional hummus is a paste made from cooked drained chick-peas, tahini, lemon juice, olive oil, garlic cloves and salt. Many spices and seasonings can be added to this basic recipe, and the proportions altered, as some like hummus with a strong lemon flavor, or leave out the tahini altogether. The same formula can be prepared with cooked drained white beans, fava beans or black beans, and any number of herbs: cilantro, mint, tarragon, basil. Toasted nuts or roasted vegetables, such as peppers or eggplant, can be added to hummus, as well as hot peppers, olives, or capers. Hummus-like spreads can be made from fresh peas and fresh garbanzo beans, as well as other mashed fruits and vegetables. You can change make the consistency of your mixture more mousselike and unctuous by adding more olive oil as the mixture blends, or go for a tighter, starchier spread by adding few liquids.

Activity

Imagine a bean type and flavor that is uncommon but could be delicious in a bean spread.

_____

_____

_____

_____

Charcuterie

We can't underestimate the power of meat, both as a starring ingredient, and as an accent to other foods and flavors. Sometimes within one meat product—sausages, pates, and terrines—is the opportunity to develop flavor, texture and color combinations that please the eye and the mouth.

Sausages are ground meats, vegetables and spices, formed or stuffed into casings. They can be fresh, cooked or cured by smoking or drying, and made from pork, poultry, fish, beef, lamb, tofu or seitan, and game. As a method of preserving meat and utilizing all the edible parts of the animal, the craft of sausage-making is age-old and global. Mexican or Spanish

SAUSAGE MAKING PLATFORM

All tools and machines—grinder, blades, knives, and receptacles—must be sanitized and spotless. Trim meat—beef, pork, turkey, bison, whatever you choose—of gristle, connective tissue and sinew, as these will cause chewiness in the sausage (though some cultures relish this and treasure the tendon). Make sure to mix the meat with the seasonings and fat until it is well-blended, so the flavors are distributed. Grind and form into patties or enclose in casings. To taste test the sausage, cook a small portion: do not taste raw sausage mixture.

PATE PLATFORM

Trim the meat as for sausage, then dice it. Begin with well-chilled ingredients. Forcemeats are often bound with egg, dry milk or pate a choux or other starch and enriched with heavy cream. Garnish such as nuts, vegetables, herbs or contrasting cuts of meat can be folded in or used to decorate the exterior of the terrine or pate.

Vegetarian terrines are often bound with cheese, but if you are using aspic choose one with a hue that offsets your vegetable, or flavor your aspic with complementary spices. If you are leaving vegetables whole for their dramatic shape when cut, make sure they are uniform in size. Vegetables should be blanched, enough so they cut without resistance, but not so much that they lose their shape.

PATE EN CROUTE PLATFORM

For cooking pate en croute, select a flavorful dough, and roll it out so it can line a hinged mold with overhang enough to fold over and seal, to a thickness of ¼-inch. Lower gently into the mold, cutting away the excess dough at the corners of the mold, if you are using a rectangular mold. Spread with forcement and any other ingredients, fold the dough over this filling, and seal with egg wash. Cover the whole with a separate, neat piece of dough, tucked into the pan. Vent the pate en croute by cutting through the dough layers and inserting a "chimney" made of foil, which funnels the steam out so the pate does not explode.

COUNTRY PATE PLATFORM

¼ lb chicken livers

1 lb pork shoulder

½ lb pork fat back

¼ lb skinless chicken breast

¼ lb ham, cut into ½ inch dice

½ cup pistachio nuts

6 cloves garlic, chopped fine

2 shallots or 1 small onion, diced

1 tablespoon chopped fresh marjoram

1 tablespoon chopped fresh thyme

1 tablespoon salt

2 teaspoons fresh ground pepper

½ cup cognac

½ cup port

½ bunch flat leaf parsley, finely chopped

cheese cloth

bay leaves

Keeping meat separate, finely grind chicken livers, ½ pound pork shoulder, chicken breast and ¼ pound pork fat back. Coarsely shop remaining pork shoulder. Finely chop remaining fat back.

Sauté chicken livers in oil over high heat. Remove livers from pan and add aromatics and herbs; cook until softened. Mix this, and livers, with other finely ground meats and grind once more. Stir in cognac, port, salt, pepper, Coarsely chopped pork shoulder, diced pork fat back and ham, pistachio, and parsley. Mix to distribute all ingredients evenly.

Line a terrine with cheese cloth and fill with the meat mixture. Wrap with additional cheesecloth. Cook gently in water that is hot but not boiling, with optional bay leaves. Your pate should reach an internal temperature of 140° to 150°F; then cool. Weight the top of the terrine and refrigerate for at least 12 hours.

TERRINE OF ROASTED VEGETABLES PLATFORM

The bulk of the work on a vegetable terrine is cleaning, trimming and cooking the vegetables.

Use some combination, equaling 3 pounds, of:

Eggplant, sliced into strips or rounds and roasted

Zucchini, sliced into thin rounds or strips, and roasted or sauteed

Spinach, chard, mustard, beet or other green, washed and wilted or steamed

Small golden beets, cleaned and roasted until tender, then sliced into wedges or rounds

Haricots verts, fava beans, wax beans or runner beans, trimmed and blanched

Green peas, blanched until tender

Asparagus, blanched until tender, or grilled

3 cups vegetable stock

½ cup chopped fresh herbs, such as basil, thyme, oregano, chives, rosemary and mint

4 ½ teaspoons gelatin

Bring stock to a simmer. Stir gelatin into ¼ cup cold water and let stand 1 minute to soften, then add to hot stock, stirring until dissolved.

Oil terrine lightly, and line with plastic wrap, leaving 2 inches of overhang on each side. Pour about ½ cup gelatin mixture into terrine and freeze for 10 minutes, until set. Layer in the vegetables, alternating varieties and cheeses, sprinkling with herbs between layers. Remember that you are serving the terrine in slices, and layer for maximum visual impact of contrasting colors and textures. Pour 1 ½ cups gelatin mixture over the layered vegetables and chill until top is set, 1 ½ to 2 hours. Gloss chilled terrine with remaining gelatin mixture, and chill until firm.

CHICKEN LIVER MOUSSE PLATFORM

Mousse, in French, is "foam." This rich mixture achieves its lightness of texture through beating, and a liberal use of fat, which smooths out the grainy, sometimes bitter quality of the liver. You can add an apple to the onion mixture for an extra layer of flavor.

- 2 tablespoons butter
- 2 cups chopped onion
- 1 clove garlic
- 1 teaspoon chopped fresh thyme leaves
- 1 pound chicken livers, cleaned and stripped of sinew
- 2 tablespoons chilled butter
- ¼ teaspoon ground white pepper
- ½ teaspoon salt
- ¼ cup brandy, Cognac or Scotch whisky
- 1 cup heavy cream, whipped to stiff peaks

Melt butter over low heat in a heavy saute pan. Add onion and thyme and cook, covered, until onions soften. Remove lid, increase heat to medium, and add the livers. Saute until firm and still pink inside. Add the garlic clove in the last minute of cooking. Cool the mixture. Pulse in a food processor, adding pepper, salt, and spirits. Add the chilled butter piece by piece. Fold the whipped cream into the pureed liver mixture until it is creamy and smooth.

ASPIC PLATFORM

Aspic is a clear jelly thickened with gelatin. It is used to bind or decorate foods, and rarely serves as a standalone food. It is basically a jam, and like jam, aspic is wildly variable, and can contribute a wide range of vibrant colors and flavors to your repertoire. Cubed or otherwise shaped, it can serve as a garnish. Aspic can be prepared in many savory flavors, from sherry to tomato to beet, and sweet, such as apple, cranberry or grape.

As a general rule, aspic requires 1 tablespoon of gelatin for every 2 cups of liquid.

- 2 cups chicken or beef broth, fish stock, fumet or fruit or vegetable juice
- 1 envelope (1 tablespoon) unflavored gelatin

You can add additional seasonings, such as spices, onions, port or other liqueurs. If you are adding more liquid, you can add up to ¼ cup. A crushed egg shell and an egg white added at the start will clarify the aspic.

Combine liquid, seasoning, egg white and crushed shell, if using, in a large saucepan. Simmer for 10 minutes then let stand at room temperature for 15 minutes. Strain through a sieve lined with cheesecloth.

Combine gelatin with ¼ cup liquid and let rest for 5 minutes to soften. Heat this mixture over simmering water, stirring, until gelatin dissolves. Add to liquid. Cool to room temperature, then pour into your mold and chill until firm.

---

chorizo contains garlic, paprika, cinnamon, oregano, thyme, cumin, sage, pepper, and chili. North African merguez is spicy with red peppers, orange zest, and harissa; German bratwurst sweet with mace, sage, celery seed and lemon zest. Chinese sausages often contain white pepper, 5-spice powder and soy sauce, and Cajun andouille is seasoned with cayenne, allspice, cloves, garlic and thyme.

As well as offering a wide range of spice combinations, sausages come in many textures, from crumbly Italian sausage to the chewy Chinese and the bologna-like Vietnamese sausage, or mortadella of Emiglia-Romana. To experiment with your own flavors and textures, begin with this basic platform.

Forcemeats, the English name for pates, are characterized by their rich mouthfeel and come in many textures: smooth, coarse, mousse, light and heavy. The formal French definition of **pate** is of a savory pie or preparation of meat, poultry or fish packed into a lined mold and served cold. In contemporary cooking, the term has come to encompass

BRINE AND BRINING METHOD PLATFORM

1 ½ pounds salt

¾ pound sweetener (sugar)

Seasoning of choice

3 gallons warm water

Stir until sugar is dissolved in water. Cool brine. Place the food you are brining in deep stainless steel or plastic container and submerge in brine, weighed down with a plate or other heavy item. Brine 2 to 3 days. Remove, rinse, blot dry and cook by your preferred method, often roasting.

....

DUCK CONFIT

6 pounds duck legs

6 tablespoons kosher salt

4 tablespoons brown sugar

1 tablespoon dried thyme

2 garlic cloves

10 peppercorns

8 cups duck fat

2 cups water

Prepare a cure of the salt, sugar, spices and garlic, cover the legs, and refrigerate for several days. Rinse, dry. Bring fat and water to a simmer, add legs and simmer 3 hours, until tender. Allow legs to cool in fat. Refrigerate.

Fish can be made into a type of confit by poaching in flavored oil, which is then strained, poured over the fish and stored.

molded foods made from vegetables and fruits, as well, or fruits and chocolate, for a dessert. A terrine is a pate. **Terrines** are baked in a ceramic, lidded mold; **mousseline** can be formed into quenelles and poached, layered together, or used as a filling in pasta. **Galantines** are bound in skin, as in a chicken mousse poached in chicken skin, and **roulades** are rolled for cooking in plastic wrap or cheesecloth.

Like sausage, pates are made from a variety of meats: fish, pork, scallops, poultry, livers, game, rabbit, which are poached or baked en croute. Sometimes terrines are formed from cooked meats and vegetables bound with aspic, cheese or custard.

Cures and Brines

Cures and brines are used to preserve and to flavor meats and to add moisture as well. In some cultures, brining is used as a preservative. Dry cures are made of salt, sweetener and flavorings. Wet cures, or brine, are made of the same ingredients as dry cures, but the food soaks, submerged, or is injected with the mixture. Some cheeses are brined during the ripening process, which affects the flavor of the cheese.

Cure or brine mixes contain salt and sugar (or honey, molasses) in equal proportion, or slightly less sugar, depending on the food. They can also contain seasonings such as black pepper, fresh herbs, dill, horseradish, cilantro, parsley, shallots, garlic, peppers or cayenne, bay leaves, coriander, cumin, oregano, zaatar, harissa, lemon juice or zest, cloves, allspice, mustard, ginger, nutmeg, paprika, tequila and wine. There are so many seasoning that complement various brines meats and

poultry—brining and dry rubs are excellent for culinary improvisation!

Smoking

Smoking meats serves to flavor them and to dry them out, for keeping. This is most often done in a smokehouse or smoker, not in the kitchen, using hickory, cherry, oak, chestnut, mesquite, alder, cedar or other woods, from which aromatics are transferred into the meat via the smoke. Teas, herb bundles, such as dried sage, gravevines, corn husks, and dried orange peels can also be used to smoke food and add rich aromatic qualities. To add smoke flavor to a dish in the kitchen, an improvised smoker of a hotel pan, wire rack and lid can be used on a range and used to burn some tea or wood chips.

Preserving in fat

Another method of preservation which is common in kitchens is preserving in fat, as for rilletes and confit. This is one of the oldest methods of food preservation, and are now a specialty of many cultures. Think confit d'oie of Gascony, the oil-cured tuna of Siciliy—even Morroccan oil-cured olives! The result is a luscious, flavorsome addition to any composed salad, cassoulet or pasta. By this method, the meat or fish is simmered in rendered fat, and then stored covered in fat, which seals out contaminants and seals in flavor. The meat that results is rich and tender, with deep flavor.

Jams, Preserves, Jellies, Fruit Butters and Curd

What would the world be like without PB&J? It's the J in that equation—oh

FRUIT JAM PLATFORM

4 cups crushed strawberries, raspberries, blueberries, peaches or other fruit

4 cups sugar

Wash the fruit, remove stems, leaves or pits, then crush. Mix fruit and sugar in a large saucepan over medium-high heat, stirring well. Boil until the mixture reaches 220°-222°F. You will see it thicken, and it will coat a spoon. Remove from heat and strain, if desired

....

TOMATO PRESERVES PLATFORM

2 lbs. small tomatoes, peeled and seeded

1 ½ cups water

½ lemon, sliced into thin rings

3 cups sugar

Bring water and sugar to a simmer in a large saucepan, simmer 5 minutes until the sugar dissolves and you have a syrup. Add tomatoes and lemon. Boil until tomatoes are clear and syrup thickens. Fish out lemon.

....

CHILI JAM PLATFORM

Green chilis, red chilis—there are all sorts of peppers to experiment with when making this. Realize, of course, that the heat varies from pepper to pepper, and certainly some varieties are far hotter than others. Scotch bonnets are hot! But they have a lovely sweetish flavor. Poblanos are mild, mellow and full-flavored. The combination of spice and sweet creates interesting flavor potential.

wonderful jelly!—that sweetens, tartens, spices up or mellows out so many foods.

Throughout human history, we've preserved seasonal foods in honey and sugar. It's similar to suspending decay by curing in oil or fat. Canning preserves, jams and jellies is a somewhat more modern process, by which we heat foods to a temperature at which all dangerous bacteria are killed, then storing the hot food in an air-tight environment. Traditionally, pectin, essentially a colloidal carbohydrate found in plant cell walls, therefore a thickener that occurs naturally in fruits, was used to thicken jams and preserves. Pectin makes jelly gel. Pectin is commercially available, in powder or liquid form. Some fruits have a high level of pectin, which is naturally-occurring. Apples, plums, cranberries and citrus are high in pectin; berries—strawberries, cherries, raspberries, blueberries—are not.

Jams, preserves and jellies, as we have seen, can be sweet and savory. Larousse Gastronomique draws the distinction between **jams** and **preserves** in the following manner: for jam the ingredients are pureed, in preserves they are left chunky. In **jellies**, the fruit pulp is filtered out, resulting in a clear, sweet spread. Curds contain butter and egg to enrich them. **Fruit butters** are made differently from the above; instead of stewing the ingredients together, you cook the fruit to a stewed consistency, then add sweeteners. **Marmalade** is fruit and/or peel suspended in a jelly. **Conserves** are made form a mixture of fruits, such as apricots and plums, or peach and raspberry. Nuts, coconut flakes or other additions are commonly mixed in as well.

Canning is a serious procedure involving sterilization, heat processing and other scary terms. Jam can also be made by the freezer method, in which you use cold temperatures instead of high heat to arrest the spread of microorganisms. Freezer jams also have a fresher fruit flavor, whereas cooked jams, jellies and preserves are intense. You may have to experiment with the amount of sugar you use. Also try adding liqueurs and spices, as well as combining fruits and using unusual varieties of fruit for a wide-range of flavors. Try savory ingredients, experiment, and think of how many wonderful complementary flavors you can create.

Cheese

Cheese is made from the drained, coagulated milk of cows, sheep, goats and more exotic beasts—such as water buffalo and yak—which has been fermented into curds, drained, and aged. The basic cheesemaking process includes **coagulation**, during which rennet or some other coagulant is added to the milk, and curds form. The curds are separated from the whey, then cut and drained, perhaps pressed, salted, or cooked, and packed into moulds for storage. Unless it is a fresh cheese, such as ricotta, the cheese is ripened for some length of time in a cave or other storage area, where it develops texture, flavor and appearance.

There are endless methods for making simple ingredients into wildly divergent varieties of cheese. Different types of cheese are made by altering the curd, the type of milk it is made from, the starter, where it's stored, how it's stored, how it's shaped, whether the rind is washed or the cheese is wrapped in leaves, wax, ashes, or rubbed

MARMALADE PLATFORM

Use oranges, grapefruit, lemon or combinations of citrus fruits.

4 whole oranges, washed and thinly sliced

3 whole lemons, washed and thinly sliced

6 cups water

sugar

Combine fruit and water. Simmer until tender, about 30 minutes. Measure this mixture and add 1 cup sugar for each cup of fruit and liquid. Cook, stirring, over medium-high heat, until the mixture thickens and reaches a temperature of 220°F.

....

FREEZER JAM PLATFORM

2 cups prepared fruit

4 cups sugar

¾ cup water

1 tablespoon powdered fruit pectin

Crush the fruit. Add sugar and mix well. Meanwhile, mix water and pectin in a small saucepan. Bring to a boil and boil 1 minute, stirring constantly. Stir into fruit, stirring for several minutes until the sugar is mostly dissolved. Pour into freezer containers and let rest until the mixture sets, then transfer to freezer.

with salt or spices. Cheeses also differ because of the bacteria that is present in them, and all these differences add up to cheese being categorized with words such as: Spanish, stinky, funky, goat, Wisconsin, fresh, rind-ripened, semisoft, blue, hard, very hard. Processed cheeses are made from cooking several cheeses together, and adding flavors, which may be artificial.

Soft, or fresh, cheeses are unripened. Microorganisms coagulate the milk, which is drained gently. These creamy, perishable cheeses include: cottage cheese, ricotta, queso blanco, mascarpone, cream cheese, crème fraiche and chevre.

Pasta filata, or shaped-curd, cheeses are also aged little. They are formed from a spun paste made from a mixture of curds and whey that is heated, stretched and shaped. These have an elastic texture; Mozzarella, Scamorza and Provolone are examples.

Soft-ripened, or "bloomy" cheeses are dusted with mold and ripened. If they are ripe for eating, they will ooze when cut; if they smell of ammonia they are too old. These are: Brie, Camembert, Pyramids, Perail, soft Tomme, Neufchatel and St. Marcellin.

The surfaces of **washed-rind cheeses** are brushed with salt water, wine, beer, brine or oil while they ripen. These soft cheeses include: Muenster, Limburger, Reblochon, Epoisses, Pont l'Eveque, Feta, and Livarot.

Blue, or veined, cheeses, are produced when bacteria is introduced via holes that are made in the cheese to allow mold growth within the cheese while it ripens, or otherwise cultured with bacteria. These

include: Maytag, Roquefort, Stilton, Gorgonzola and Queso Cabrales.

Both soft and hard cheeses are made from curds that are cut, stirred, pressed, or cooked, and can be broken down into other categories. **Dry-rind cheeses** form a rind naturally while ripening; examples are Bel Paese, Havarti and Crottin. **Waxed-rind cheeses** are sealed in wax prior to aging, like Gouda and Edam. Semi-soft cheeses include Fontina, Port-Salut, Morbier and Saint-Nectaire. Harder cheeses are produced when, in the initial stages of cheesemaking, the slabs of pressed curd are stacked or weighted so more whey runs out of them, resulting in a firm cheese such as: Cheddar, Cantal, Emmenthaler, Manchego, Colby, Monterey Jack, Gruyere, Jarlsberg, Comte, Beaufort, Tomme de Savoie or Petit Basque. Very hard cheeses, such as Romano, Parmigiano, dry Jack and Mimolette are aged for a long time, sometimes years.

Like fruits and vegetables, the quality of cheese changes with the season. Many cheeses are made from milk taken from animals in a particular season, and all cheeses are at the height of their glory at a particular time of the year, or in a set amount of time after they began ripening. See Chapter 5, Cooking Seasonally, for a seasonal guide to cheese.

Store cheeses at 50 to 60 degrees, wrapped in parchment paper or waxed paper, as plastic wrap smothers cheese, causing it to age rapidly.

Cheese can add rich texture and flavor to many platforms, as well as be formed into crisps, tuiles and fried, frazzled garnishes. A good cheese plate reflects many different textures, colors, shapes and flavors. The cheese course can be slanted toward a

CRÈME FRAICHE PLATFORM

Used in many recipes and as a garnish, crème fraiche flatters both sweet and savory foods. Comercially prepared crème fraiche is also available.

    4 cups heavy cream

    1 cup buttermilk

Heat heavy cream to 70°F. Mix with buttermilk. Cool, cover, and rest, 12 to 24 hours, in a warm spot, until thickened.

CRÈME ANGLAISE PLATFORM

While not formally a cheese, crème anglaise belongs with its versatile neighbor, crème fraiche. Crème anglaise forms a basis for ice cream or many baked custards, and is a gorgeous sauce to which there are hundreds of variations, by adding different speces, extracts, flavorings or infusions. To infuse is to flavor a liquid by steeping—a spice, bark, peel, vanilla bean—which is left in the liquid and removed before serving. Sometimes infusing involves heat, sometimes not.

    3 egg yolks

    ¾ cup sugar

    Pinch of salt

    1 ½ cups heavy cream

    ½ vanilla bean, split or 1 teaspoon vanilla extract

Whisk together egg yolks, sugar and salt. Bring cream and vanilla being to a boil in a saucepan. Slowly whisk the warm cream into the egg mixture. Return the mixture to saucepan, and cook, stirring constantly, over very low heat, until it thickens. Cool, then strain and refrigerate.

CHEESE WAFER PLATFORM

Many recipes recommend freezing your cookie sheets before baking these wafer.

On sheets, sprinkle finely grated hard cheese such as Parmigiano-Reggiano, Asiago or Pecorino Romano into thin rounds. You can use cookie cutters for guidance in making shapes, or create free-form wafers with jagged edges. Spread each pile of cheese so it makes a very thin layer on the cookie sheet, and press with your fingers to adhere the cheese strands to one another. Bake 2 to 3 minutes. Do not let these wafers brown. You can sprinkle with freshly ground pepper, chopped herbs or many ground spices, such as cayenne pepper. Incorporate slivered nuts if you wish.

TUILE PLATFORM

Tuile means "tile" in French because the food imitates the shape of slate roof tiles. Thin, crisp—even brittle—a tuile can be sweet or savory. They do not keep longer than a day, but the batter can be kept for several days to make fresh batches of tuiles for service. Tuiles can be shaped when they are still warm—folded into pockets or triangles, or rolled around a rolling pin or handle to form a crisp tube. You can vary the amount of sugar, below. Add nuts: sliced almonds, hazelnuts, pecans, pine nuts. Other excellent tuile combinations are: pepper and parmesan, lavender or rosemary, olive oil and sea salt, lemon, orange or grapefruit rind. Some recipes incorporate liquor. Go forth and experiment!

For tuile batter:

    ⅓ cup flour

    ½ cup plus 2 tablespoons sugar

    ⅛ teaspoon salt

    3 egg whites

    2 ½ teaspoons melted butter

Whisk flour, sugar and salt together. Add egg, butter and other seasonings. Stir until just combined. Let batter rest one hour to overnight.

On a cookie sheet lined with a Silpat or parchment paper, drop batter by teaspoonfuls. With a moist fork or wetted spatula, press the batter into a thin round. Bake 7 to 9 minutes at 350°F. Cool 30 seconds before peeling from the sheet and shaping as you choose. If tuiles on the sheet harden while you shape, put them back in the oven for a minute or two to soften.

Well-stocked Pantry

The better stocked your pantry, the more capable you are to change a dish rapidly. You offer a special of osso bucco, and the risotto that was to have been served with it is scorched and ruined. Luckily, you have a sack of orzo, a quick-cooking, grain-shaped pasta, which can be substituted.

Here is a general list of the items that comprise a well-stocked pantry:

Dry goods: Grains, legumes, coffee and tea, for service and for seasoning. Pasta, sugars and syrups, canned foods, such as artichoke hearts, cornmeal, flours, nuts, seeds, oils, spices, condiments, wine and liqueur for cooking, chocolate, extracts, leaveners, such as baking powder, and thickeners, such as cornstarch.

These are perishable, and should be stored away from light, heat and dampness, and not stored on the floor. You may also want to stock frozen doughs, such as puff pastry.

For the games in the following chapters, a well-stocked pantry will be helpful in allowing for maximum flexibility and creativity.

category, grouped by type of milk or region of cheese production. Cheeses should be served at room temperature, with bread, crackers, or fruits, dried fruits, preserves and pastes—and wine, of course. In Britain and the United States, the cheese course is served after dessert; in France it is served between the salad and the dessert. Cheeses are often served as appetizers as well.

Cheese pairings

Two or three well-chosen cheeses are usually ample for a post-meal cheese plate, when an eater's capacity and sensory appreciation is nearing its limit. For offsetting the cheese, simplest is best. A handful of toasted nuts, a condiment or a fruit that works with the texture, flavor and fragrance of the cheese is ideal. The more aromatic the fruit, the more it's likely to clash with the cheese, unless the cheese is fresh and sweet, such as ricotta.

with: romance, luxury, passion. Chocolate is used as a solid, a liquid, and a powder. It is used in pastries, confections, as flavoring for ice creams, mousses and, to sauce, coat and rub into savory foods. Chocolate is an integral addition to your pantry; it should be stored well-wrapped between 54° and 68°F.

The long process of chocolate production has never received as much attention as it has recently. Customers are curious about the entire chocolate system, from where the beans are grown and who picks them, from how they are dried and get to market, and who buys them. This is all pre-production; then the beans are heated and crushed to extract the cacao, which is mixed with sugar, and tempered, and hardened into bars that can differ wildly in flavor and texture. A chocolate's flavor and quality are dependent on many factors: the type of bean it was made from (there are three, forastero, criollo and trinitario), the

Here are some classic pairings:

PARMESAN	dates
GRUYERE OR CHEDDAR	walnuts, hazelnuts, or pecans, and cherries or tart apples, like Pippins
MANCHEGO	almonds and membrillo (quince paste)
DRY JACK	prunes or figs
GORGONZOLA	with honey, walnuts, ripe pears
STILTON	black walnuts and brandied raisins
REBLOCHON, BRIE OR ROBIOLA	pistachios and fennel
EPOISSES	ripe pearr
WARM CROTTIN	dandelion greens

Chocolate

Ah, chocolate. It is as universally loved as it is versatile, for all the meanings it is rich

handling of the beans, and its manufacture, from roasting to mixing.

CHOCOLATE TEMPERING PLATFORM

Place a double-boiler or metal bowl so it is over—not touching the surface of—a saucepan filled half-way with water. Turn the heat to medium-low. Place ¾ pound chopped chocolate into the top bowl and melt, stirring occasionally. Measure with a candy thermometer; when the melted chocolate reaches 100°F, remove the bowl from the heat. Add ¼ pound chocolate, chopped, and stir until the chocolate cools to 85°F. Place the bowl back on to the saucepan, and when the chocolate reaches 88° to 90°F, it is ready to use.

GANACHE PLATFORM

Ganache is a combination of chocolate and cream used to make truffles, as a cake or tart filling, or to pipe decoratively. It can be glossy and thick, or whipped to a lighter shade and consistency to spread more easily. Melt chocolate in a double boiler with cream, stirring to combine. Remove from heat and allow to cool to a spreading consistency. For 10 ounces of chocolate, melt ¾ to 1 cup of heavy cream. Up to 6 tablespoons of butter can be added for a richer ganache.

It's a good idea to experiment with different types, brands and cocoa contents of chocolate, not only because it can be used in so many ways in the kitchen, and you want to find one to suit your specific needs and tastes. As more customers become knowledgeable about chocolate, and many restaurants and food stores specialize in chocolate tastings and unique chocolate products, you may find it necessary or useful to justify your own chocolate choices. Using free-trade, or specific brands of chocolate, is to some customers as important as the use of organic or local products. As a chef, not only color, taste and cost matter; more often it is how foods are grown, harvested, and processed that count to a customer as well.

There are three types of chocolate, and each definition categorizes a wide range of qualities. **Bittersweet or dark chocolate** contains less sugar and is darker in color than milk chocolate. Its cocoa content, or the amount of cocoa liquor or cocoa solids—the raw material that is the essence distilled from beans—used in the making of it, ranges from 35 to 99 percent (99 percent bars or pastilles are almost pure chocolate; only one percent of the bar's weight is sweetener, or sugar). Bittersweet chocolate has recently been touted for health benefits to blood vessel function due to the flavonids present in raw cacao. This is only true of chocolate that is more than 60 percent cocoa liquor. Bittersweet chocolate has an intense, rich flavor, with a bitter edge. It is sometimes labeled as **semisweet**, though semisweet, at a minimum, contains 35 percent cocoa solids, often less, and therefore has more sugar than true bittersweet.

MAKING CHOCOLATE SHAVINGS

Spread chocolate in a thin layer on a marble slab or other clean, firm, cool surface. Allow to firm, then use a knife to shave up large, thin chips. For smaller shavings, use a vegetable peeler or knife scraped across a large block of chocolate.

Milk chocolate contains milk solids, powdered milk, condensed milk, milk or cream, and is usually made of around 10 percent cocoa liquor. It is lighter in color and sweeter than bittersweet chocolate, with a less intense chocolate flavor. Its flavor is creamy, mild and sweet. This is the variety of chocolate preferred by most Americans.

White chocolate is sweetened cocoa butter. It's not really chocolate, but a combination of sugar, milk, and vanilla or vanillan. Unsweetened chocolate has no sugar in it; it contains half cocoa butter and half cocoa solids. This is chocolate in its least refined form.

Quality chocolate has a shiny sheen to it and snaps cleanly when pressed. It has a pure flavor that is unmuddled by a buttery taste or acrid, burnt flavor. The "flavor" of chocolate, like that of wine, is a complicated bouquet. Chocolate can be smoky, flowery, fruity, herby—it can even taste like raisins, toasted nuts or tobacco.

In the commercial kitchen, you will find cocoa powder, which is a highly concentrated powder of ground cocoa butter from which the fat has been removed, leaving pure cocoa solids. It is a by-product of chocolate production. **Couverture** is high-quality tempered chocolate, used to coat and cover cakes, truffles and fruits. **Tempering** chocolate is a process of heating and cooling chocolate to spread and homogenize the fat molecules. This is usually done in a bain marie to achieve a smooth and glossy finish which retains its shine and shape when used to coat or decorate foods.

Activity

Flavor truffles with a favorite element. Next, add a second complementary or contrasting flavor element.

_____

_____

_____

_____

Olive Oil and Other Oils

Olive oil is obtained by pressing the fruit of the olive tree. There are many varieties of olive used in olive oil making, and many countries of the world produce olive oil: Greece, France, Spain, Italy, Turkey, Morocco, the United States. Within these countries, even, the oil is labeled to originate in different regions, where different techniques and olives are used in production. As you can imagine, every brand of olive oil has a unique flavor!

Olive oils fall into different levels of classification. **Extra virgin olive oil**—fruity and aromatic—is extracted from the first cold pressing of the olives. (Heat is often used in the grinding and pressing of the olives because it speeds the oil extraction, but it also affects flavor.) Extra virgin olive oil has the lowest acidity of all olive oil classifications. It's meant to be used as a flavoring, in a dressing, in ice cream. Slurp it from a spoon, which many do for health.

Virgin olive oil is nicely balanced, has low acidity as well—2 percent or less—and can contain no refined oil. **Ordinary or pure virgin olive oil** has an acidity level of up to 3.3

CHOCOLATE TRUFFLES PLATFORM

A steady increase in unusually-spiced truffles has proved what a fine platform they are for experimenting with flavors. Spices, liquors, fresh herbs, cream infused with fresh herbs, tea, and coffee can be added to the ganache, or the truffles can be rolled in spices, crushed nibs or nuts.

Over, not touching, simmering water, melt together 1 tablespoon heavy cream and 9 ounces bittersweet chocolate. Allow to cool, then refrigerate for at least two hours, until you can form the mixture into balls with your hands. Coat as desired. Truffle centers can also be piped, or formed with spoons.

OTHER FLAVORFUL COOKING OILS INCLUDE:

GRAPESEED OIL	Made from the seeds of grapes, this vegetable oil has a very high smoke point, and can be used for frying. High quality grapeseed oil has a lightness and toasty, nutty flavor that is lovely in salads.
PISTACHIO OIL	Pressed from pistachio nuts and used primarily for dressings, pistachio oil is very expensive and very flavorful. Bright green in color, it also makes a beautiful drizzle on the plate.
SUNFLOWER OIL	From sunflower seeds, this is most commonly a frying oil and has a fatty flavor that makes it not so great for dressing, but a healthful alternative to frying in lard.
WALNUT OIL	Pressed from walnuts, this has a lovely, soft flavor and odor that makes it ideal for dressing salads and vegetables.
SESAME OIL	The distinctive odor and flavor of this oil make it a wonderful addition to dressings and drizzles. Don't apply it to anything you don't want to take on a sesame flavor! Pressed from sesame seeds.

NOTE* Because oils are volatile, they should be stored in a tightly-closed container, away from light and heat. It's best to buy oils in small quantities.

percent, and can contain some refined oil. Use for sautéing and frying; this is not recommended for dressings. **Plain olive oil** is a mixture of refined and virgin oil, and **refined olive oil** has been processed to lower acidity and mask defects. **Pomace oil** is made from ground olive flesh and olive pits; it is industrial grade and commonly used in soap-making.

Ideas for Appetizers and Hors d'Oeuvres

Hors d'oeuvres, literally "outside the menu," are served before the meal; on restaurant menus in the United States, the first course is often considered the appetizer, but the formal definition of appetizer is to stimulate the appetite before the meal commences. An **amuse**—also known as the amuse bouche or amuse-gueule—is much

the same thing: a small bite presented by the chef to amuse the mouth, raise the diner's interest in the meal, or set the theme for the dining experience. All should stimulate the palate in many ways: by taste, by texture, by concept, by look. They should be small portions, well-plated and perfectly executed. Hot or cold, always whimsical, always enticing, these small bites are a big way to have fun with food.

Exquisitely rendered, beautifully presented, these small tastes that come before the meal, amuses, hors d'oeuvres and appetizers, present an opportunity for cleverness and fun, as they can relay a big message and intense flavor in a small package. Because portions are tiny, you can use such high-end ingredients as caviar, quail eggs, aged balsamic vinegar, o-toro. This is where, if you have a particularly excel-

Since amuses are typically offered for free and are only a bite, it is a good opportunity to showcase the creativity of the chef.

lent ingredient—tiny wild strawberries, farm-fresh eggs—but not very much of it, you can spread it around while celebrating its glory. These should always be visually stimulating, as well as compelling in taste.

Since amuses are typically offered for free and are only a bite, it is a good opportunity to showcase the creativity of the chef.

Simple items, such as nuts, olives, dips, spreads, and hard-boiled eggs can be made as interesting as composed hors d' oeuvres, appetizers or amuses that involve several elements. Composed appetizers feature a base, a vegetable or meat, a sauce, foam, spread or jam, cheese—there are endless combinations that encourage a rich imaginative effort to create them. In addition, kebabs, soups, salads of all kinds, including pasta and grain, charcuterie, and filled pastries and dumplings can be used as hors d'oeuvres. The sky's the limit!

There is also a wide range of possibilities of how hors d'oeuvres can be served. They can be served in any form of utensil or vessel, such as shot glasses, ramekins, demitasse cups, fingerbowls and saucers, long-handled iced tea stirring spoons, tiny cappuccino spoons, wound around a fork, or in cleaned, dried egg shells. The service vessel can be edible, and a crucial part of the flavor. Try hollowed, sliced or cubed fruits or vegetables, such as daikon, radish, apples, watermelon, potatoes, cherry tomatoes or avocado. **Crudités**—or raw

vegetables and fruits cut into sticks, slices or florets—can carry other elements of the hors d'oeuvres, as can leaves of endive, cabbage, or radicchio. Also try: phyllo cups or purses, or nests made of baked, shredded phyllo; sheets of crisp bread, blinis, toast rounds, bread that has been soaked and seared as for French toast, grilled bread that has been rubbed with garlic or compound butter, crackers, tuiles, puff pastry formed into **vol-au-vent**—a small pastry container, with a lid—gougeres or shapes made from flavored pate a choux, cheese crisps, on pork rinds, in tart shells (bouchees), or in scrubbed oyster, mussel or clam shells. Elements can be wrapped up in sheets of seaweed, soft, thin breads, such as crepes, lavash or tortillas, or thinly-sliced vegetables such as potatoes, beets, or celeriac. The wrapped foods can be sliced. Or, foods can be stacked between thin layers, and then the item is cut into wedges, slices or triangles that show the layers, as for slices of black pumpernickel layered with smoked salmon, cream cheese and chives, then sliced to reveal stripes of black, pink, white, and fine dots of green. Amuse the eye as well as the mouth! Layers of phyllo or puff pastry can be rolled around savory or sweet fillings, cut into shapes and baked.

Any raw, edible vegetable can be used for crudite. Try fennel, tomatoes, carrots, celeriac, celery, cucumber, peppers, cabbage, endive, radicchio, broccoli, asparagus, cauliflower, mushrooms, radishes, artichokes, avocado—or fruits, such as grapefruit, orange, apple, watermelon, and berries. Crostini can be built in layers, first topped with compound butters (suggestions below), tapenade, mayonnaise or aioli, then with caramelized, grilled or pickled vegetables, ripe tomatoes and infused oil, white beans and tuna confit, fresh sardines or anchovies. **Canapés**—open-faced sandwiches—are similarly versatile, and can be built of flavored butter and duck confit, pepper puree and mashed chickpeas, seafood mousse and chive garnish, to name a few. Stuff an empanada with braised pork and pineapple, or a wonton with leftover brisket and barbecue sauce.

Activity

Design a canapé that will have high flavor impact.

_____

_____

_____

_____

HERE ARE SOME OTHER CLASSIC COMBINATIONS OR RIFFS FOR APPETIZERS, HORS D'OEUVRES OR AMUSES

Inside a gougere: Fill with savory mousse, pate or spread made from duck, salmon, or vegetables, or with layers of greens, pickled vegetable and pancetta or prosciutto.

Serve grilled or filled dates and figs with cured meat, blue, goat or hard cheese, and balsamic or honey. Fill them with almonds, flavored whipped cream or mascarpone.

Rounds of sausage or charcuterie can be topped with compote, cheese, or a foamy sauce.

Raw, caramelized vegetables or vegetables a la greque—a Mediterranean-inspired preparation served cold in an olive oil and lemon marinade—and herbs or cheese, on top of a vinaigrette or flavored béchamel.

Frittata, omelet or torta can be cut into small pieces and served with flavored aioli. Quiches can be built from any meat, cheese, vegetable or combination of these, and made large and sliced, or in tiny individual shells. Tiny savory custards such as soufflés or savory flans, made from shallot, garlic, herb, cheese or vegetables such as fennel, asparagus, or carrot.

A whirl of pasta, soba or rice noodles, or shaved vegetables, twirled around the tines of a fork or wound on a spoon, and sauced.

Sushi or sashimi, or any number of combinations of meat, vegetable, pickled foods and grain rolled as for sushi. Or any combination of things rolled up as for a spring roll and served with creative dipping sauces.

Clams, mussels, cockles or oysters can be steamed in a fragrant liquid—wine, Pernod, stock, infused cream—and flavored with herbs, shallots, diced apples, or thinly-sliced merguez, chorizo or linguica.

Serve seafood with dipping sauces, such as mignonette, ginger-soy, sriracha, cocktail sauce, Russian dressing or aioli. Top with savory granite, such as salty grapefruit, habanero or bloody mary.

Feature a pickled product, meat or cheese on top of a dollop of grits, polenta, mashed potatoes, risotto, quinoa, farro, amaranth, or sticky rice. Also form into balls or cakes.

Cakes made of grains, risotto, polenta, potatoes, crab, or meatballs—spiced as for many ethnic traditions, like kefta, keftedes, fleischlaberl (Austrian meatballs) or kottbullar (Swedish meatballs)—chicken, ground lamb or beef. For vegetables, make fritters from zucchini, pumpkin, corn, onion or eggplant; spicing and saucing combinations are infinite.

Chilled pureed soups can be topped with: crème fraiche, infused oil, scoop of savory sorbet, deep-fried herbs or thinly-sliced vegetables, pickled vegetables, fruit or ginger, microgreens or sprouts, caviar, small bits of cooked meat, chicken or seafood, cubed, cooked pancetta or bacon, toasted spices or seeds, cubed aspic, mousse.

Serve a warm broth in a shot glass with a poached scallop, tortellini, wonton, or seviche, or oysters and mignonette, or vegetable or fruit juices that have been spiked with fresh herbs or spices, and made from combinations of interesting fruits and vegetables, such as grapefruit, passion fruit, pomegranate and carrot.

Tiny salads of thinly and finely sliced vegetables, pickled vegetables and fruits, microgreens, edible flowers, foraged foods, such as fiddlehead ferns

Or warm salads of sautéed greens—kale, chard, rapini, escarole—and a contrasting vinaigrette.

Sweet/savory pairing of fruit with cheese, balsamic vinegar, or fennel with cherry jam and cheese

Play with your dehydrator: beet chips with goat cheese, apple chips with Stilton and toasted walnuts

Basic Recipes for Creating Hors d'Oeuvres

The following are a collection of recipes and techniques that will go far in allowing you to freestyle appetizers and amuses.

INFUSED OIL PLATFORM

Start with olive oil, grapeseed or another mildly flavored oil. Warm in a saucepan, and add your seasoning—citrus peel, herbs, spices, seeds. Turn off heat, and let it steep for several hours.

PICKLED VEGETABLES PLATFORM

A basic pickling technique is a great platform for spices and extending the life of vegetables with a short season, such as ramps. Onions, garlic, ginger, beets, fennel, celery—the sky's the limit on what you can pickle, and how you can season it. Add bay leaves, peppercorns, star anise, cumin seeds, citrus peels, herb bundles. Use flavored vinegars and combine vegetables and fruits.

You may want to bundle the herbs or spices you are using in cheesecloth. Make a simple syrup, add vinegar and spice sachet. Bring to a boil, then reduce to a simmer. At this point, you can take out the sachet or leave it in for more intense spicing. Pour the liquid over your thinly-sliced vegetable, and cool and marinate at least 2 hours.

With harder vegetables or those cut into larger pieces, you can simmer vegetable in water to cover until tender. Make a solution of 1.5 parts vinegar to 2 parts sugar and 1 ½ tablespoons salt. Combine and boil to thicken. Place the tender vegetable in a bowl or a jar and pour the pickling solution over it. Or boil thinly sliced vegetable in pickling solution for as long as it requires to become tender, cool and store in pickling liquid.

FLAVORED BUTTERS PLATFORM

First cream the butter. Then mix in your flavoring: ground almonds, hazelnuts, walnuts, pistachios, smashed anchovies, grated horseradish, minced spinach, watercress, arugula, herbs, caviar, herbs, roasted or raw garlic, minced roasted or raw sweet or hot peppers, cooked and minced crab, crayfish, lobster or shrimp, parsley, lemon juice, mustard, blue cheese, minced raw or caramelized shallots, onions, leeks, green garlic, minced dried cherries or sun-dried tomatoes, tapenade, or pesto—even finely diced apples or peaches. This list is as long as your imagination is expansive.

SALSA PLATFORM

In the United States, the term "salsa" has come to mean a chunky mixture of tomatoes and onions, but in Spanish it is literally "sauce"—so feel free to improvise with fresh and cooked ingredients. This recipe can be varied with other fruits, vegetables, aromatics, herbs, and spices—even beans in lieu of tomatoes. Try roasting or grilling the fruits or vegetables for salsa for intense flavor.

> Tomatoes, diced
>
> minced onion
>
> cilantro
>
> fresh lime juice
>
> minced jalapeno

Combine ingredients in a bowl. Season with salt and pepper.

PESTO PLATFORM

Pesto, or "paste," is a thick puree. This is a basic platform for traditional pesto, which can be varied with different spices, nuts, herbs and oils, or make a paste of sun-dried tomatoes, arugula or other vegetables.

   ¾ cup pine nuts

   2 cloves garlic, crushed

   1 ½ cups basil leaves

   ¾ cup grated Parmesan

   1 ½ cups olive oil

   Salt and pepper

Combine all pine nuts, garlic, basil, and Parmesan in food processor. Pulse until it forms a paste, then add oil in a thin, steady stream with the motor running. Taste for seasoning.

TAPENADE PLATFORM

Although it won't be a "traditional" tapenade, you can experiment with different olive types, black or green, brine-cured, capers only, oil-packed dried vegetables, and other seasonings.

   5 to 10 anchovy fillets (can be soaked to remove salt)

   2 cups pitted black olives

   1 tablespoon capers

   1 teaspoon Dijon mustard

   1 clove garlic, peeled

   2 sprigs thyme or lemon thyme

   6 tablespoons olive oil

In food processor, grind anchovies, olives, capers, mustard, garlic, and thyme into a paste. With the motor running, add oil in a slow stream. Taste for seasoning.

Granita and sorbet

Granita and sorbet are used as a dessert or palate cleanser, and can also be garnish or condiment. They can be made from fresh juices of fruits or vegetables, such as beets, strawberries, watermelon or corn, cucumber, lemon, celery, herbs, or other liquids, such as coffee.

For both granita and sorbet, begin by washing the fruit, then puree or juice it. Strain the liquid. Don't assume equal parts water and juice; the amount of water you add depends on the fruit you use, so values below are approximate. Remember, for both sorbet and granita, taste at every phase of preparation, as the flavors change with the temperature of the mixture.

GRANITA PLATFORM

Combine liquid with a sweetener such as sugar or honey. For savory granite, add a splash of vinegar, and salt and pepper.

   2 cups pureed strained fruit

   Sugar, salt and vinegar as necessary to adjust the flavor.

   2 cups water, or a mixture of water and wine to thin puree

Add water to juice or puree and freeze the mixture in a hotel pan, so there is lots of surface area. Stir frequently to keep ingredients homogenized. You want the mixture to become a slush, then allow it to harden slightly. Chop or coax the crystals apart with a blunt tool or fork. Long shards make for an interesting texture.

SORBET PLATFORM

Sorbet is much smoother than granita, and contains finer crystals. The proportion of water to juice and sugar is different from granita, and also varies according to the fruit you use. Berries require more liquid, and peaches less sugar. The best sorbet results from liquid that is chilled before it is frozen. The simple syrup can be infused with herbs or spices for a more complex flavor.

Prepare a simple syrup. Mix with your juice or puree, and chill the mixture. Freeze in an ice cream maker which churns the mixture. If the sorbet isn't firm enough, place in the freezer for an hour or two to firm it up.

SIMPLE SYRUP PLATFORM

A solution of sugar and water that is used to carry flavor in all sort of preparations: brushed over pastries, as a base for a quick, sweet dipping sauce, for a sweet sauce, in the preparation of sorbet and jams, and as a base for mixed drinks. For a heavy syrup, use equal parts sugar and water; for lighter syrup use less sugar to water. When the sugar has dissolved, you can add your flavoring: a liquor, juice or extract, fresh or dried herbs, cinnamon stick, cardamom, citrus zest, vanilla bean, fresh diced fruit, or flower petals.

In a large saucepan, combine 1 cup sugar and 3 cups water. Heat, stirring, until all sugar granules have dissolved, and bring to a boil for two minutes to thicken. Add flavorings when warm, allow to infuse as the syrup cools, then strain it before using.

Spring Rolls

We include a recipe for spring rolls as they can be sweet or savory, and a wide array of foods can be combined inside them, and served in these neat bundles. Using two sheets to wrap will make the rolls easier to slice, and will hold together better. You can add garlic, other vegetables such as daikon, radish, garlic, red onion, asparagus and sliced snow peas to this mixture, or invent your own of shredded vegetables or fruits such as mangos, or use other types of thin noodle. Meats, such as whole shrimp, sliced chicken or pork, or ground lamb or pork can be added.

SPRING ROLLS PLATFORM

  3 ounces bean thread vermicelli

  1 shallot, minced

  1 carrot, shredded into long strings lengthwise

  4 scallions, finely sliced lengthwise

  1 bunch cilantro, washed, trimmed

  2 tablespoons soy sauce

  4 tablespoons sugar

  pepper

  12 ounces spring roll wrappers

Soak the noodles in warm water until they are soft. Drain and chop into manageable shreds. Mix with shallots, carrots, scallions, cilantro, soy sauce, sugar. Use this filling raw or stir-fry briefly.

Stack two spring roll wrappers. Place 2 to 3 tablespoons filling in wrapper and fold the wrapper up and over the filling. Fold in the sides, then moisten the remaining edge, bind tightly, and seal. At this point, these can be deep fried or sliced and served fresh.

Phyllo

Phyllo, or filo, dough is paper-thin dough used in layers, which crisp from the hot air that gets between them when the dough is baked or fried, resulting in a flaky pastry. Phyllo is made from flour and water, and works equally well for sweet or savory preparations. Making it by hand takes enormous patience and skill; phyllo is available fresh or frozen in sheets. It must be used quickly, for the sheets get dried and crumbly if left uncovered. Brush the sheets with oil or butter, and layer them, for it takes several layers of phyllo baked together to support food and hold a shape. Phyllo layers can be formed to the shape of the pan or mold you are using, folded into triangles or squares, cut into shapes or folded into tulip-shaped purses with the food inside.

Forming Filled Pastas and Doughs

Cultures the world over offer lovely filled pastries and pastas, all of which can be mined for inspiration. These three result in different shapes and thicknesses of the dough.

Empanadas, tiny pastries usually filled with spicy meat fillings, are formed by rolling dough into 6-inch rounds. The filling is placed in the middle of the round, then the edges of the dough are moistened, drawn into a half-moon shape, and pinched to seal. The tines of a fork can also made a decorative border that will crisp when baked or fried.

For wontons, you can buy thin dough from Chinese stores or many grocery stores. The dough, square in shape, can be moistened at the edges and folded into triangles or rectangles. An egg wash is usually more effective than water to hold these thin dough layers together tightly.

Ravioli are made from fresh egg dough, which has a tensile strength that holds up to the sometimes runny fillings. Form the dough, with a rolling pin or pasta machine, into long, thin sheets. Place drops of filling, about 1 teaspoon's worth, spaced 1 inch apart along one side of the sheet. Moisten the edge of dough above the filling, then fold the other half of the dough sheet over the fillings, tamping down the dough between mounds. Use a pastry wheel or pizza cutter to seal and cut the dough into squares, pinching together if necessary.

Most simply, pasta dough is the mixture of flour and moisture.

PASTA DOUGH PLATFORM

> 3 to 4 cups flour
>
> 5 eggs
>
> ¼ teaspoon salt
>
> ½ teaspoon olive oil

Make a heap of 3 cups flour in the center of a clean counter or cutting board. Use your fingers to make a well in the heap, then break the eggs into this indentation. Add salt and oil. Using a fork, beat together wet ingredients. Using your (clean!) hand, begin incorporating flour into the wet mixture, using your other hand to hold the outside of the well, so the mixture doesn't run all over the counter. Work the flour in until you have a stiff ball, adding more flour is necessary. You may need ot add more flour or a little water, to get your dough ball to a pliant, supple texture.

Knead the dough. On a lightly floured surface, press and fold the dough, over and over, until the dough becomes elastic, and had a slight sheen to it. This may take up to 10 minutes. Cover with a clean towel or plastic wrap and let the glutens relax, at room temperature, for at least 30 minutes or an hour.

DIPPING SAUCE FOR DUMPLINGS PLATFORM

A very basic **dipping sauce** can be made by combining sugar syrup with sriracha. You could also add: chopped chilis or garlic, hot bean paste, minced shallots or green scallions, shrimp paste, soy sauce, chopped nuts, hot mustard, sesame seeds or rice wine for flavor and texture.

Chutney

Chutney is a savory relish—and there the formal definition ends. Chutneys can be made of raw or cooked ingredients, including but not limited to mango, tamarind, tomotoes (and green tomatoes!), cauliflower and peppers. These are spiced and cooked in vinegar until the mixture is jammy.

Start by heating oil in a large saucepan, and add your aromatics (onion, shallot, garlic, pepper, ginger) and cook until softened. Add main fruit or vegetable and spices, stir until the spices are fragrant. Then add 1 cup vinegar for every 2 pounds of fruit or vegetable, and any fresh herbs you are using. Cook over low heat until the mixture is thickened to the consistency of jam. Taste for seasoning.

Compote

Compote is fresh or dried fruit or vegetables poached in sugar syrup. The syrup not only exaggerates the flavor of the fruit or vegetable and lends a rich moist texture to whatever it is poured over, it is also an excellent platform for carrying flavors: vanilla, citrus zest, star anise, cinnamon, peppercorns. Apricots, figs, dried cherries and onions are examples of foods that lend themselves well to compote, but anything goes. Try kiwi, nuts, rhubarb

COMPOTE PLATFORM

For 2 pounds of fruit, make a simple syrup of 2 cups sugar in ¾ cup water, adding the seasonings when the syrup is formed, before it boils. Bring the syrup to a boil, and add fruit that has been washed, pitted, peeled and cut into cubes or slices. Poach until tender.

DUXELLES

Duxelles, a mixture of chopped mushrooms, shallots and white wine, are a classic addition to many meat dishes, and used to stuff pastas, meats, and would be good atop crostini. Other vegetables prepared this way are also often referred to as duxelles. Some chefs add cream at the end for a richer duxelle.

Finely chop about 12 ounces of mushrooms and ½ tablespoon shallots. Heat in a saucepan ½ ounce butter, then add shallots and cook until translucent. Add mushrooms and cook until they give up their juices, then allow them to brown. Add parsley and season to taste with salt and pepper.

or quince, alone or in combination. You may want to soak dried fruit until it has regained some moisture, or poach dry for a chewier consistency. Nuts, crystallized fruits and dried coconut are classic additions as well, but anything that strikes your fancy for spiking the flavor and texture is worth experimenting with. Figs, red wine, orange peel and toasted pistachios? Why not! Remember that you can use different types of sugar—superfine, rock, Demerrara—other sweeteners, such as honey or molasses, and fruit or vegetable juices, or liquers, for the syrup.

Salt

There are so many different kinds of salt; there are books about salt. The importance of this ingredient cannot be overstated. You should understand the various kinds of salt you may encounter in your kitchen, because they vary in intensity and purpose.

Rock salt is a naturally-occurring salt mined from the earth. It can be white, gray or brown and comes in very chunky crystals that are typically too big for cooking. Rock salt makes a great bed to serve oysters on or to prop up other protected foods—in a shot glass or a spoon—if making a tray of passing hors d'oeuvres. **Kosher salt** is refined rock salt. The crystals are largish, but it's often used for cooking. It won't cloud liquids, because it contains no magnesium carbonate, and it's clean, bright flavor is because it doesn't contain iodine. Kosher salt is "kosher" because it was used in "kosherizing" meats; the large grains sopped up blood from the meat but the large crystals didn't dissolve into the meat, rendering it inedibly salty. Because of its large particle size, never replace kosher salt

with an equal amount of table salt; you will have oversalted.

Table salt is a refined salt with additives that keep it from clumping. Iodized salt has iodine and will cloud liquids. This is the most common form of salt in most kitchens.

Sea salt comes from areas where saltwater was trapped and evaporated, leaving behind the salt. Sea salt is flavored by trace minerals. Appearing in all colors of the rainbow and sizes of grain, sea salt is a beautiful addition to many foods, and can even be used judiciously as a garnish. Sea salt is often sought for its mouthfeel. **Fleur de sel** is a particular variety of sea salt from France. **Smoked salt** is sea salt that has been smoked in a wood smoker or mixed with a smoke flavoring. It is typically used as a spice, not a salt. It adds a smoky depth to food but must be used carefully.

To Summarize...

In this chapter, we learned to marry the chemical and the philosophical to explore taste and flavor. The techniques and concepts outlined here allow you to apply artistic principles to food, to contrast and balance flavors and textures, to use symmetry, spacing, color and shape to enhance presentation. Curing, preserving, and possessing a deep understanding of specific types of food, such as cheese, will go far in making your plates unique.

Chapter 3 Assessment Questions

❶ List three important qualities of a menu.

1. _____

_____

2. _____

_____

3. _____

_____

❷ Describe balance.

_____

_____

_____

_____

_____

_____

❸   What meats would you smoke, versus using a confit preparation?

_____

_____

_____

_____

_____

_____

❹   Name three factors that differentiate varieties of cheese from one another.

1. _____

_____

2. _____

_____

3. _____

_____

❺   Create a menu item drawing from the flavor ideas presented in this chapter.

_____

_____

_____

_____

_____

_____

4/
Flavors

"The world's culinary traditions are collective, cumulative inventions, a heritage created by hundreds of generations of cooks. Tradition is a base which all cooks who aspire to exellence must know and master."

– The International Agenda for Great Cooking

Have you ever asked yourself this existential question: What is flavor? If someone asked this of you, what would you say to them? Flavor is what happens when what you put in your mouth meets your taste buds. In his book, *On Food and Cooking*, Food Scientist Harold McGee refers to "many hundreds of volatile molecules that are small and chemically repelled by water, and therefore fly out of the food and into the air in our mouth." This, my friend, is a scientific explanation of how flavor happens.

CHAPTER OBJECTIVES

① To develop a working knowledge of flavor principles

② To recognize individual characteristics of foods and use those characteristics to develop flavor concepts

③ To learn food affinities, food families, and other ways in which foods are grouped according to flavor and origin

④ To learn from how to taste, and how to use tasting in your culinary work

⑤ To build confidence and knowledge to improvise using flavor principles

⑥ To learn ethnic techniques and preparations of foods

⑦ To have a basic and growing understanding of molecular gastronomy and other innovative culinary movements

When it hits your taste buds, food produces flavor. Flavor is, quite simply, what you taste. A popular theory is that the four basic tastes are detected by different parts of the tongue, but new research works to debunk that notion. On the tongue, in the world, flavor is a melding of chemical sensations.

Flavors are complicated, as they contain certain aspects of all tastes— salty, sweet, sour and bitter. The "flavor" you experience is the dominant taste. Flavors and certain notes of all tastes—salty, sweet, sour and bitter— are complicated, but the "flavor" of a thing is the predominant taste. If that thing is endive, and the prominent taste is bitter, we say, "Endive is a bitter flavor." If it is potato chips and the prominent flavor is salty, we say, "potato chips are a salty food."

Some factors, like temperature and texture, work against taste. Both extremely hot and extremely cold foods numb the taste buds. Some flavors, such as salty, obliterate all others when used in excess. The texture, consistency, color and temperature of foods will affect how the flavor is experienced.

Working in tandem, flavors accent each other, like how a dash of salt in a sweet dessert tempers the cloying sweetness (think salted caramel). Sugar brings out the deep savoriness of a marinara sauce; goat cheese eaten with watermelon makes it taste so sweet, and accentuates both the crunchiness of the

KEY TERMS

Flavor principles

Umami

Concept

Inspiration

Essential oils

Recado rojo

Picada

Tunisian five-spice
powder

Chinese five-spice
powder

Garam masala

Zaatar

Chermoula

Adobo

Mouthfeel

Tandoor

Wok

melon and the creaminess of the goat cheese. See further along in the chapter for an explanation of the science of taste.

When cooking and experimenting in the kitchen, it is important to understand flavors and the distinctions of each ingredient. With this knowledge, one can better understand, explore and adapt recipes to suit personal preferences and/or specific needs. Each herb, spice, starch, protein, and so on has its own set of characteristics, whether crunchy, chewy, musky, tangy, hot or cold—not only what they taste and smell like, but how they feel in the mouth. While cooking, try using new combinations of flavor and texture to find the personality, style and charisma of your cuisine.

Flavor is not just about taste, and an entire chapter dedicated to knowing and experiencing flavor requires that you use all of your senses. Smell is intricately tied to flavor. A familiar aroma can make us crave a food, whereas we may find an unfamiliar odor off-putting. Touch and hearing come into play with the textures of the food, and texture is crucial to how flavors are presented. The overall presentation or look

our preconceptions of what we "should" taste—sometimes what you see is not what you get!

For example, contrast the cinnamon taste you sense when the spice is presented as a crisp wafer cookie, compared to a cold, sweet cinnamon ice cream that melts into spicy cream on the tongue. What about the cinnamon flavor in a hot turkey mole? How does this cinnamon flavor compare to that of the ice cream? What if you're served a tiny cone filled with a scoop of spiced ground lamb, which contains cinnamon. What do you expect it to taste like? Part of developing your ability to try new flavor combinations is to think about how to play with these expectations, because contrasts are exciting.

Even a simple meal can bring all the senses into play; take the experience of slurping a noodle. Drawing flavors into your mouth, you are collecting molecules that hit the smell receptors in your mouth and nose. You smell pungent garlic, acidic tomato, wheaty pasta, sweet basil. You feel the texture of the smooth, long noodle against your lips, coil it inside the mouth

The mind, body and senses are all engaged in the process of eating. Maximum flavor, therefore, comes from reaching all of the senses at once, engaging the mind, memory and body in one bite.

of a dish contributes to our imagination of what it will taste like, and therefore influences what we taste. Sight helps us know what we're eating, or to introduce the element of surprise by working against

with the tongue, and bite it with your teeth. Is it lukewarm? Or very hot? You produce a slurpy sound as you suck it up to your lips, and, if you listen carefully, hear the tiny boom of your teeth sinking into the noodle.

You see a plate of noodles, and before you start to eat them, you know noodles can be slurped, be picked up with fingers and lowered into the mouth, coiled around the tines of a fork, or cut into tiny bits and spooned into the mouth. You expect the noodle will taste starchy; your expectation of "noodle" may be egg fettuccine in a creamy sauce of cheese and milk, because that's the type of noodles mom served. What about a cold noodle dish involving soba, ginger and soy, or spaghettini, red pepper, anchovy, and tomato? These dishes embody very different flavors, textures, smells, sounds, and were developed by different cultures.

"Mouthfeel"—quite literally how the food feels in the mouth—will affect the flavor of food, too. For example, fats not only carry flavor, but lend a pleasing unctuousness, in terms of mouthfeel, to the food. A crisp apple, which breaks open and spurts juice when bitten, contributes a very different experience of "mouthfeel."

The mind, body and senses are all engaged in the process of eating. Maximum flavor, therefore, comes from reaching all of the senses at once, engaging the mind, memory and body in one bite. When this happens, and all these parts of the taste experience are stimulated, it is a rare occasion of food functioning at the highest level. The important takeaway is that all the features of food—texture, temperature, appearance, and aroma—as well as the cultural pathways that food has traveled to end up on our plate, or its back story—communicate to the eater. The way you handle these variables, through every step of the cooking process, is what gives your food personality, and makes your cuisine unique.

HOW DID
I GET HERE?

Culinary Backstory

Remember that both preparation—frying, steaming, braising, preserving—and seasoning—fresh herbs, pungents, ground spices—affect flavor. Often these methods and seasonings are culturally different, because they come from different people, with access to different foods, spices and fuels for cooking.

Every dish comes from a place, somewhere, and every ingredient comes from a person. People eat food; people make food. The backstory of food is the collection of stories that makes it resonant. A food doesn't merely exist, fully formed, on the ground under a tree. Years, decades, centuries, millennium of invention and experimentation are contained in that fruit, vegetable, slab of meat, or stirfry.

Here's an illustration. The history of the tomato stretches back to the seed that turned into a tomato, and encapsulates the journey of the tomato from South America to Southern Italy, the Italian culture of scarcity that encouraged the development of a technique: fashioning thousands of unique shapes from a paste of flour and water to make dinner a little different every night (pasta). The tomato, which grew well in various regions of Italy, came to be a classic with these pasta shapes. Fresh or cooked, it softened and coated the pasta, lent juices and flesh to the dish, contributed a richness and a tanginess of flavor.

Now, you have a tomato in your kitchen. Did that tomato come into your kitchen on a flat from Sysco, or did you go to the local farmers market and buy it after talking to the people who grew it, about the varieties of tomato that thrive in the shady versus sunlit parts of their garden? Or are these tomatoes dropped off on your doorstep by a small farmer who comes every week with the variety of Roma tomato he's experimenting with, because it's been grown in the United States since the 1930s? How different are these methods of acquiring a tomato?

A trend in restaurants today is to tell this story on the menu. Your customers may find it interesting or irritating; what we're suggesting is a deep familiarity with your ingredients, how they are used in other cultures, what they potentially mean to your customers. Being a great chef is about more than being able to saute' and season—it's about playing to customer expectations.

Taste includes sensory properties that are both cultural, as in the acceptance or rejection of the tomato, and physiological, as in the physical description of flavor in the previous passage. Our expectations, formed by culture, of smell, color and texture, do in fact affect the way we taste.

Developing Flavor Concepts

Chefs that are capable of combining incongruous foods in delicious and surprising ways may seem like they're working magic, but when a dish that is "thrown together" works, you can be sure that a deep knowledge of flavor concepts and culinary techniques is behind it. Even when you're forced into improvising in the kitchen, some thought goes into what you reach for from the spice rack, and what you gather from the cooler. How do you know what to do when called upon to improvise? What skill sets can a chef develop to make improvisation a process?

Architects, builders and performers of all kinds begin projects with a plan. Without a plan, they don't know what materials to use, what time to show up, what notes to play, or who their audience is. The first imaginative step in coming up with a plan is developing a concept. A concept is an articulation of an idea, something you've worked out in your head. It is particular to you, but it is developed enough to be grasped, used and executed; it is an idea, with shape. A concept can be well-developed or it can be a starting point; it can be simple or it can work on different levels of complexity and rely on multiple relationships. Most of all, your concept relies on what you know.

Many disciplines offer step-by-step guides to developing concepts. Any culinary program teaches you how to plan your menu, weigh its cost and feasibility, prep your mise en place, organize your line, and execute a final product—these important steps echo the "concept implementation" you find in boardrooms and design shops. But we focus less on how you put your concepts into action, and more on how you begin the process of conceptualizing. Conceptualizing involves the imagination, and it's an ongoing process.

To develop a food concept, the first step is to get inspired. Inspiration is simply stimulation, a thought, sight, sound or feeling that leads to emotion, creation, energy. The imagination can be triggered by any occurrence: a road-trip or vacation, eating, a passage in a novel, magazine or newspaper, watching a documentary about the pyramids on PBS, the weather, painting your bathroom, overhearing a conversation, smelling a delicious fragrance that reminds you of something in your past, going to a farm, walking through a market, finally understanding the lyrics to an 80s pop song, passing someone on the street who has an interesting look. Everything in your life has the potential to inspire you and translate into interesting food concepts.

Sometimes multiple experiences or thoughts will crystallize into one food concept. For instance, you're driving down the road on a sunny day, listening to Puccini, craving pasta, and you spot a farm stand. You pull over, and the woman running the stand is eating from a bag of microwave popcorn, which smells delicious. You look at what she's selling, and see sage, corn, and mini sugar pumpkins. You take these home, where you have a box of orecchette, and your vision gels. Before you boil it, you toast the pasta so it takes on a nuttiness not unlike popcorn. You sauté small cubes of pumpkin and the corn, sliced from the cob, in butter. Finally, you deep-fry the sage leaves, mellowing their flavor, and crumble them into the finished pasta dish, adding crunch. Voila! Many elements of your day: the farm products, the popcorn, the pumpkin's sunshine color, and your craving for pasta, all combined in one bowl into one delicious food concept.

More abstractly, you're catering an event at an avant garde gallery. The artist, whom you've encountered only once, has a wild fashion sense and his photographs are of rebellious teenagers on mean streets in war-torn cities. How can your buffet fit into this scene and deepen the experience of visitors to his show, beyond featuring foods people can eat while standing and talking? You think, "I could feature street foods" and "What do punks eat?" Will preparations

based on these questions resonate with gallery goers? What about common foods, arranged artfully? The long table of finger foods you envision for the event begins to take shape in your mind: spiky tortilla chips standing up in a deep swoosh of guacamole like a Mohawk, tempura green beans arranged in a criss-cross pattern like a zipper. The preparations are common, but the displays are unexpected.

A popular business saying is that a good businessperson never ignores the innovations or successes of the competition. You can imitate another chef's innovation or play on a food trend—something you've tasted, read about, or talked about—and make it your own by adding a subtle or obvious spin: changing ingredients, technique, or the way the food is served. The exciting work of others can provoke or inspire great work from you—this is why creative people, like chefs and artists, hang together. Later in this chapter, we'll examine the flavors and techniques of various cultures, which can be mined and provide inspiration as well.

Once you've thought of a concept, write it out and see if it makes sense. Prepare it, taste it and get some other people to taste it and weigh in. At any point in this process, adjust the concept: change the seasoning, swap out an ingredient, reconsider the service temperature or plating. Ask yourself: is what you imagined what you taste? What's working, and what isn't? Is your concept strongly articulated through the execution of the dish? Later in this chapter you'll learn about regional flavor principles, as well as balancing tastes such as spicy, sour, bitter and sweet. All of these factors serve as both criteria for judgment of your dish, and inspiration for your concept.

Remember that what you are conceptualizing is one dish or menu, with many components, and you must stick to your overall theme, flavor, or guiding principle. No one wants a plate piled with confusion or a mouthful of spices that war. And, throughout this chapter about flavors, we're not only talking about using herbs and spices. This is about combining foods in unusual ways and playing with contrasting materials: cooking a vegetable we're used to seeing raw, serving raw and cooked together.

Take something as basic as a carrot. You boil, then puree that carrot. You serve your puree with more carrot, raw, and sliced very thinly. You add parsley, dill and fennel, because they're all in the same family (we'll get to food families later in the chapter), and add a splash of almond oil, because it echoes the sweetness of the carrot. You've layered flavors, textures and applied multiple flavor principles—all in one carrot dish.

Questions:

❶ Can you think of an occurrence in your life that inspired a food concept?

_____

_____

_____

_____

❷ Can you imagine being in a situation that might lead you to find food inspiration? Describe.

_____

_____

_____

_____

_____

❸ Name a few contrasts you'd like to employ in a food concept.

_____

_____

_____

_____

❹ Can you think of a culinary backstory for a favorite food or dish?

_____

_____

_____

_____

_____

❺ What famous dish or invention of a well-known chef would you like to imitate, and how would you make it your own? Explain.

_____

_____

_____

_____

_____

How to taste

Flavor is a composite of aroma, taste, texture and neural stimulation. How is it that our bodies taste? There's a complicated chemistry to taste, involving taste buds and receptors in our nose. This is a simplistic explanation: taste buds sense the salts, sugars, sour acids, savory amino acids, and bitter alkaloids present in foods, and receptors react to the odor molecules. Nerves in our mouth are aggravated by hotness and astringency. Taste buds know when you've added too much pepper by registering its pungency, and nerves react with puckering and tingling of the mouth.

Noses collect molecules. Aroma is the product of molecules unique to a substance, and there are thousands of molecules and thousands of odors at work in every bite, which is why taste and smell are so complicated. There are infinite combinations of odor molecules, resulting in different odors. In fact, affinities between foods, explained later in this chapter, often result when two foods share similar aroma molecules.

Aroma molecules in foods are activated by exposure to air and to heat. When you cut into a peach, you begin a chain of chemical reactions in that peach, changing the chemical composition and releasing the smell of the fruit by exposing molecules to the air. It is a change in chemical composition that makes toasted nuts smell so much richer than raw nuts, and the interaction of banana flesh and air that makes a banana smell sweet when the skin is peeled away.

There are five basic tastes: **sweet, sour, salty, bitter, savory** and **umami**, which is a bit tricky to explain. In Japanese, umami means "delicious," and sensing it is a savory sensation of the kind experienced when seaweed or MSG is eaten. Umami is the tongue's experience of glutamate, an amino acid and, some scientists say, a measure of determining the protein content of a food. Some say umami is an attempt to capture a description of something indescribable, an experience of flavor that is fleeting and nebulous because umami is not produced by any combination of sweet, sour, bitter and salty. Umami is its own thing, and, some say, addictive because of its ambiguity.

All of these tastes vary in intensity: different sugars register their sugariness in various ways, some bitter foods are a challenge to eat! Consider the difference between honey and molasses, cane sugar and commercial sweetener, or the sweetness of a date versus the sweetness of a plum. Think about the bitterness of an espresso versus the bitterness of raw radicchio, and how bitterness is tempered, or sweetness heightened, when foods are cooked. These five tastes offer an endless playing field for a chef.

Whatever you taste, whether it be wine, cheese, vegetables, fruits, a complicated sauce or stew, a simple egg, or a chocolate bar, try to break it down into taste components. What you are tasting? There are various flavors and aromas at work in your mouth and nose. What are they? Pay attention.

Analyze the food with all of your senses. What does it look like? Does it make a sound when you break it, or bite into it? Smell the food. What aromas do you detect? We've heard oenophiles describe wine in certain terms, such as "I smell cherries, old leather and tobacco." It's ok to appropriate that descriptive language to help you break down flavors and aromas in any food or beverage.

When you hold a square of dark chocolate to your nose, can you smell raisins, mushrooms, or ripe bananas? Does fennel just "smell like fennel," or is there something else you can detect in its odor? Do words like "green" or "piney" come to mind? What about the difference in the smell, taste, appearance and texture between raw fennel and braised fennel?

What cultural associations apply to your food? When you conceptualized or cooked a dish, who did you have in mind? What specific type of person were you thinking of: what ethnicity, gender, socioeconomic level? Food can suggest culture and place as well as a museum, as well as a postcard.

Take all of these things into consideration as you taste, and you will have a deep knowledge of the foods you work with, and what you can do to them, and what other foods you can combine them with.

Use any descriptive language that works for you to help you understand, and to help others understand your concept. Use the language of wine, the language of art, the language of rap music. Can you taste, in a coffee, malt, caramel, blackberries or tar? Can you taste, in a steamed artichoke, a blue sky or the sensation of floating? Does grape soda make you think of midnight movies, root beer floats of walking home form the pool during summer vacations as a teenager? See how this works?

Molecular Gastronomy

Molecular gastronomy is a somewhat new concept—at least when we're speaking of a particular style of culinary inquiry and creativity happening in the late 1990s through 2010, a period which, by virtue of the term being applied by the media,

means that these activities fall under the rubric of "molecular gastronomy." The term is used, most simply, to denote a science used to explain why food tastes the way it tastes.

Gastronomy, or the study of food, has long been a scientific discipline, but it is only now that a "scientific study of deliciousness" is employed to describe the phenomena of using techniques of industrial food production combined with scientific developments. The chemical composition of starches, fats and proteins are studied and manipulated to create new flavors, textures and concepts. All in all, what this means is that experimentation and science are coming to the fore in American professional kitchens.

The term **molecular gastronomy** was originally coined at a 1992 conference of scientists and cooks. Originally it was a field of inquiry that dealt with understanding traditional cooking methods, and how to cook better once one had achieved this understanding. This movement may have happened, unheralded, in kitchens the world over, as many scientific advances do. Yet what helped molecular gastronomy infiltrate the public consciousness was the fact that some of the plates and menu concepts coming out of those kitchens looked like they came from laboratories. They were strange, fascinating, and nearly impossible to recreate at home. Little tubes of food, precious liquid served from pipettes, transparently thin slices of beet, fried mayonnaise, curried cotton candy, foie gras foam—these foods provoked a reaction from diners and critics. At heart molecular gastronomy is not about confusion or amazement; it has to do with understanding the processes of cooking.

Because the term has become charged, chefs who are classified as **molecular gastronomists** have issued a statement about what they do, *The International Agenda for Great Cooking*. Molecular gastronomy is very serious, they say, not facetious or trendy. They explain the principles that guide them. The manifesto of this "new cookery" was written by a pantheon of molecular gastronomists: Ferran Adria of El Bulli, Heston Blumenthal of Fat Duck, Thomas Keller of Per Se and Harold McGee, author of *On Food and Cooking*.

Their principles, the principles of molecular gastronomy, include the following:

- Three basic principles guide our cooking: excellence, openness, and integrity.
- Our cooking values tradition, builds on it, and along with tradition is part of the ongoing evaluation of our craft.
- We embrace innovation—new ingredients, techniques, appliances, information, and ideas—whenever it can make a real contribution to our cooking.
- We believe that cooking can affect people in profound ways, and that a spirit of collaboration and sharing is essential to true progress in developing this potential.

Food, these chefs explain, is an art, an art with "expressive potential." And art is a form of expression. On the plate, these chefs are trying to communicate with diners. They want their customers to see an ingredient that looks familiar, but look at it differently. This open-mindedness opens a realm of possibilities for the diner and for the chef. A restaurant becomes an aesthetic experience on the highest level, like being at a symphony, in an art gallery, at the ballet. The diner is being guided by the chef, but is also a participant in an experience that is meant to make them feel.

Not only do these chefs want food to be considered art, and themselves therefore artists, but they want science to take its proper place in the kitchen. Over time, regarding our food, we embrace science and reject it. These reversals are the typical course in food, as in fashion and art, as trends rise and fall.

For example, in recent history, coinciding with a rising interest in space, television and general technology, processed foods were heralded as the "wave of the future" in the 1960s. Late in that decade and into the 1970s, processed foods were demonzied as everything that went wrong in the way we ate by a food counterculture that embraced organic, natural foods. The once-heroes who created Tang, astronaut ice cream and the TV dinner were dubbed evil technologists. Yet science and experimentation produced every one of our culinary basics, from wheat germ to steaming to cotton candy. Science and experimentation produced heirloom tomatoes and many other plants and fruits that wouldn't grow as they do on farms in the wild.

Even the most diehard "naturalists," like Dan Barber of Blue Hill and Blue Hill at Stone Barns, a restaurant located on and sourcing from a working farm, embrace molecular gastronomy in their craft. They're "respecting the tenets of sustainable agriculture while using the latest technology to create better tasting food" wrote Barber some years ago, in *Food & Wine* magazine. While not creating sauces in a centrifuge or making people wear blindfolds and suntan lotion while they eat, Barber is experimenting with how to cook eggs perfectly in water and using ultrasound on cows to judge the marbling of the meat he serves to his customers.

Innovation is related to things people haven't experienced before. Today's chefs are creating experiences by turning to new tools: industrial gellants, hydrocoloids, protein powders, heating immersion circulators, the Antigriddle with a surface area of 22°F, natural gums like guar and xanthan, thickeners, enzymes, sugar substitutes, liquid nitrogen, food starch sheets, soundscapes, assemblages, extractors,

scientific instrument used to cut biological specimens into thin specimens for microscopic examination, to make vegetable chips and carpaccio.

One of the most widely used techniques associated with molecular gastronomy is **sous vide**. Literally "under vacuum," sous vide, also called vacuum cooking or "Cryovacking" is heating food wrapped in airtight plastic containers at low heat for an extended period of time. The technique seals in flavor, as all juices and aromas of the food are sealed in the little plastic sack rather than dissipating into the air. Other advantages include great heat transfer and thorough, even cooking. Some chefs say this technique makes the foods taste more intensely like themselves, because they're being cooked without being sapped of

If you attempt to cook via sous vide, educate yourself thoroughly, and experiment copiously before serving your product to a customer.

dehydrators, emulsifiers, amalgamators. They're wafting fragrance toward your face with a fan while you sip at a soup and controlling the environment in which food is served by toying with light, sound, aroma and appearance of the food, wait staff, tabletop, restaurant and plate. They're producing crystals, scents, foam, flavored "air," infusing oils with unusual flavors like toasted brioche, pine needle and buttery popcorn. These chefs are using boiling water at the table to release the perfume of dried blossoms, to make them unfurl on demand as a display of nature, arrested and reactivated. They're using a micronome, a

their cooking juices and essential oils, as steaming and boiling do.

Sous vide is still considered somewhat controversial. Customers perceptions are muddled; some don't fully trust or understand it. In 2006, New York City Health Department inspectors cracked down on the practice in several well-publicized raids of high-end kitchens. Under conditions that aren't very carefully controlled, meats and fish cooked at very low temperatures can be a bacterial disaster waiting to happen. Yet it has also been proved that long cooking times followed by proper cooling is just as safe as cooking at higher temperatures. If you attempt to cook via sous vide, educate yourself thoroughly, and experiment copiously before serving your product to a customer.

There are many restaurants at which you can experience molecular gastronomy firsthand. There is one store at which you can get a sense of the movement from the flip side—by examining the tools and ingredients of the trade. At the San Francisco location of Le Sanctuaire, the magical cooking store of Jing Tio (the original location is in Santa Monica), the walls are covered with the gastronomic commitments of those who the media groups together as "molecular gastronomists." On one wall, the words of Fernan Adria; on the opposite wall, the cookbooks and manuals in which the instructions for cooking in this manner are put forth live. In the center of the store, in a giant case that resembles a display in a museum is the equipment. There are plates with fluted edges and a little spout, special tiny forks, covered mugs, and gleaming, tall homogenizing and dehydrating machines.

Two large displays are covered with the purest flavorings from around the world, and Tio's own spice mixtures: curries, rubs, something marked "aphrodisiac" that smells like moussaka baking in an inscense-heavy church: fatty, musky, spicy and sweet, all at once. Peppercorns come to Tio straight from farmers he found in his native Indonesia, pistachio oil comes from the South of France. Mixed in with these gourmet offerings are industrial gellants and packages of agar. This display gives you a sense of what molecular gastronomy is: the finest ingredients, technological tools, a sense of seriousness, a spirit of exploration.

If you experiment with molecular gastronomy, return to the principles, listed above. Focus on highlighting what's unique about certain flavors, how a customer would be used to it tasting it a certain way and how you can accentuate it so it then it tastes different or better. Remember that dining in a restaurant is about a connection to place, not only about the people making the food, but what and how you eat it, and who you share the meal with. Strip away everything, and the simple job of a chef is to make the people leave the restaurant with a positive feeling.

Activity Questions

❶ What does "natural" mean to you?

_____

_____

_____

_____

❷ What do you think of when you hear the word "pure"? How do you apply this to the food you cook?

_____

_____

_____

_____

_____

❸ How do you assess this quote: "A restaurant is not just about getting enough calories to live"? What is a restaurant about, to you? How does your vision gel with or work against what the tenets of molecular gastronomy are?

_____

_____

_____

_____

_____

The Flavor Plate

Far more traditional than molecular gastronomy, the flavor plate is a useful tool to help balance flavors in a dish. On the rim of the plate you can find major flavor groups. Moving from the edge of the plate toward the center, you find a ring of flavor components representing each of the flavors. In the center of the plate you can place the foods you are working with. By conceptualizing foods that are built from various wedges of the plate, the flavor plate can help you balance flavors. The flavor plate does not represent a fixed set of rules, but rather multiple possibilities for flavor. The plate is a way to encourage you to think differently and creatively about the flavors you use in a dish.

THESE ARE COMMON DESCRIPTIONS OF TASTES AND AROMAS IN FOOD:

GREEN	commonly associated with melon, cucumbers or freshly mowed grass.
FRUITY	dried and fresh fruits such as apricots, raisins and plums
EARTHY	a smell like soil, associated with beets and potatoes.
MUSHROOMY	more subtle than earthy, the smell of mushrooms or truffle sometimes found in wine and chocolate.
TERPENE	words that fall into this descriptive category are herby, piney, and citrus, sometimes "leafy," or "fresh." Associated with the aroma of such flavorings as rosemary, roses, mint, caraway.
PHENOLICS	These are woodsy, spicy, warm aromas, such as clove, cinnamon, anise, vanilla, tarragon, and oregano.
PUNGENT	These cause hotness in the mouth, sometimes pain, and are associated with horseradish, garlic, ginger, mustard, chilies, and black pepper. Ginger, for instance, has a taste, a fragrance and causes a prickle: this is the food irritating the cells of the mouth that we "taste."
SULFUR	the smell of cabbage or onions; when it fruit it's often read as musky, as for melons and tomatoes, or more exotic fruit, like guava.
FLOWERY	The fragrance of flowers, which turns up in teas and chocolate.
NUTTY	a smell of toasting or caramelization, in strawberries.
CREAMY	a rich and basic aroma, like the smell of coconut.

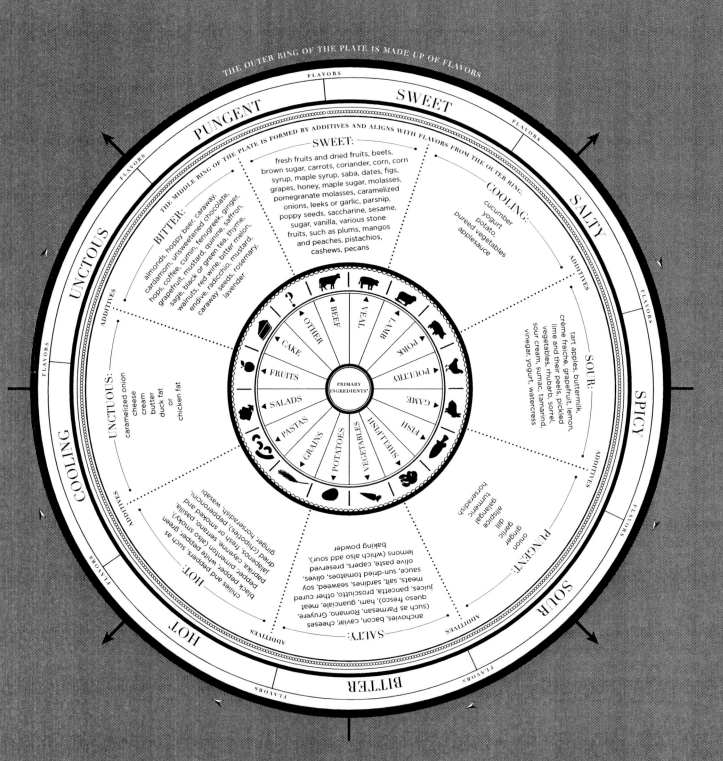

THE OUTER RING OF THE PLATE IS MADE UP OF FLAVORS

FLAVORS

PUNGENT

SWEET

FLAVORS

THE MIDDLE RING OF THE PLATE IS FORMED BY ADDITIVES AND ALIGNS WITH FLAVORS FROM THE OUTER RING

FLAVORS

SALTY

UNCTOUS

SWEET:
fresh fruits and dried fruits, beets, brown sugar, carrots, coriander, corn, corn syrup, maple syrup, saba, dates, figs, grapes, honey, maple sugar, molasses, pomegranate molasses, caramelized onions, leeks or garlic, parsnip, poppy seeds, saccharine, sesame, sugar, vanilla, various stone fruits, such as plums, mangos and peaches, pistachios, cashews, pecans

BITTER:
almonds, hoppy beer, caraway, cardamom, unsweetened chocolate, hops, coffee, cumin, fenugreek, ginger, grapefruit, mustard, quinine, saffron, sage, black or green tea, thyme, walnuts, red wine, bitter melon, endive, radicchio, mustard, caraway seeds, rosemary, lavender

COOLING:
cucumber
yogurt
potato,
pureed vegetables
applesauce

ADDITIVES

ADDITIVES

FLAVORS

BEEF

VEAL

LAMB

PORK

SOUR:
tart apples, buttermilk, crème fraiche, grapefruit, lemon, lime and their peels, pickled vegetables, rhubarb, sorrel, sour cream, sumac, tamarind, vinegar, yogurt, watercress

COOLING

OTHER

CAKE

FRUITS

PRIMARY INGREDIENTS*

POULTRY

GAME

SPICY

FLAVORS

UNCTUOUS:
caramelized onion
cheese
cream
butter
duck fat
or
chicken fat

SALADS

PASTAS

GRAINS

POTATOES

VEGETABLES

FISH

SHELLFISH

ADDITIVES

FLAVORS

HOT:
chiles and peppers, such as green pepper, white pepper, black pepper, cayenne, paprika, pimenton (also smoky), jalapenos, fresh or smoked and dried (chipotles), pepperoncini, ginger, horseradish, wasabi

SALTY:
anchovies, bacon, caviar, cheeses (such as Parmesan, Romano, Gruyère, queso fresco), ham, guanciale, meat juices, pancetta, prosciutto, other cured meats, salt, sardines, seaweed, soy sauce, sun-dried tomatoes, olives, olive paste, capers, preserved lemons (which also add sour), baking powder

PUNGENT:
onion
ginger
garlic
dill
allspice
galangal
turmeric
horseradish

ADDITIVES

COOLING

ADDITIVES

HOT

FLAVORS

BITTER

FLAVORS

SOUR

FLAVORS

*Notice these are all what we would call "plain" foods. They are on the
plate to both contribute to the overall flavor and to "carry" flavor.

Activity Questions:

❶ Can you name additional foods that belong in each of these categories?

_____

_____

_____

_____

❷ Which category would you place aged balsamic vinegar in?

_____

_____

_____

_____

❸ Can you name foods or dishes that represent sweet/sour, salty/sweet or hot/ sweet?

_____

_____

_____

_____

❹ What are you eating for lunch today? Stop. Smell it, taste it, and describe what you smell and taste.

_____

_____

_____

_____

_____

❺ Write down a useful food description that you read somewhere. Why did you choose it? Why did it work for you?

_____

_____

_____

_____

_____

_____

How to transport flavors

Flavors are carried in various mediums, including oil, fat, water, vinegar, wine, pureed starch, and dough. You can layer flavors by combining foods, or you can create flavored oils using herbs and spices. Have you ever popped a few cloves into your mouth, or chewed on a sprig of mint? If not, try it. If you have, you know that herbs and spices are considerably less interesting when eaten plain. When they are diluted, heated, fried, pureed, combined with other foods, or otherwise altered, they become stimulating as their essential oils are released. Essential oils are what are flavorful in herbs and spices, the material found in the cells, glands and interstitial spaces of the leaves, seeds, buds and barks that serve as spices.

**FLAVORED OIL,
VINEGAR PLATFORM**

*Add any of these to a cup
of mild oil, such as olive,
sunflower or grapeseed, or
white vinegar: whole garlic
cloves, citrus peel, herbs,
washed and dried, whole
dried red peppers or other
spices, whole berries. Let
rest, refrigerated, three
days to one week. Strain
and use.*

For a quick infused oil or
vinegar, heat 1 cup mild
oil or vinegar in a small
saucepan. Do not allow to
boil or spit, just warm the
liquid. Add your seasoning
and stir for 30 seconds.
Remove from heat, cool,
then use.

> *...use the world map to change a recipe from a Caribbean flavor to one that reflects the taste of India by simply using different spices.*

You can alter the taste of herbs and spices in many ways, such as exposing them to heat. Whole spices can be toasted, and whole spices, powdered spices and the leaves and stems of herbs can be deep-fried. All herbs and spices can be cooked in liquid, or liquid can be used to extract flavor from the herb or spice, and carry it, as in an infusion.

Remember that oil carries flavor differently than vinegar, water, or wine does; the flavors in oil are more intense. To find the best medium for expressing a flavor in a particular dish, it helps to experiment with different liquids by flavoring them, heating them, letting them rest, and watching how the flavors intensify.

Just as chewing an herb or spice releases the flavor, herbs and spices contribute their flavors to foods differently when they are chopped, crumbled or ground. A larger surface area releases flavor more slowly than smaller particles, which is why whole cloves release their essence more slowly, as in a stew that simmers for four hours, than ground cloves, which releases flavor more quickly, as in cookies that bake for 8 to 10 minutes.

The flavor of herbs and spices can also be released when they are used in the steaming or smoking of foods. And the intensity of the herb or spice flavor can be controlled depending on when the herb or spice is added, at the beginning or end of cooking.

Whole pods are excellent for long stewing, ground spices for long or short cooking periods, and delicate fresh herbs should always be added at the end of cooking.

Flavor Principles

Principles are basics upon which rules are built. A flavor principle is a basic source of flavor, resulting from substances that impart a special quality to food. More simply, the most distinctive flavors of ethnic cuisines are achieved by traditional combinations of seasoning. The foods that result from these combinations reflect flavor principles.

Foods and recipes can be altered and adapted using a number of techniques and/or flavor principles. By substituting and/or adjusting the seasoning components of a recipe, it is easy to alter the premise of the food and manipulate the food into a new or different variation. For example, use the world map to change a recipe from a Caribbean flavor to one that reflects the taste of India by simply using different spices.

The Flavor Map of the World

In her book *Ethnic Cuisine*, food writer Elizabeth Rozin identifies flavor principles as common elements to cuisine in various regions that give the foods of those region distinct flavors. By employing some of these combinations, cooks can begin to reflect the cuisine of a region. By combining them,

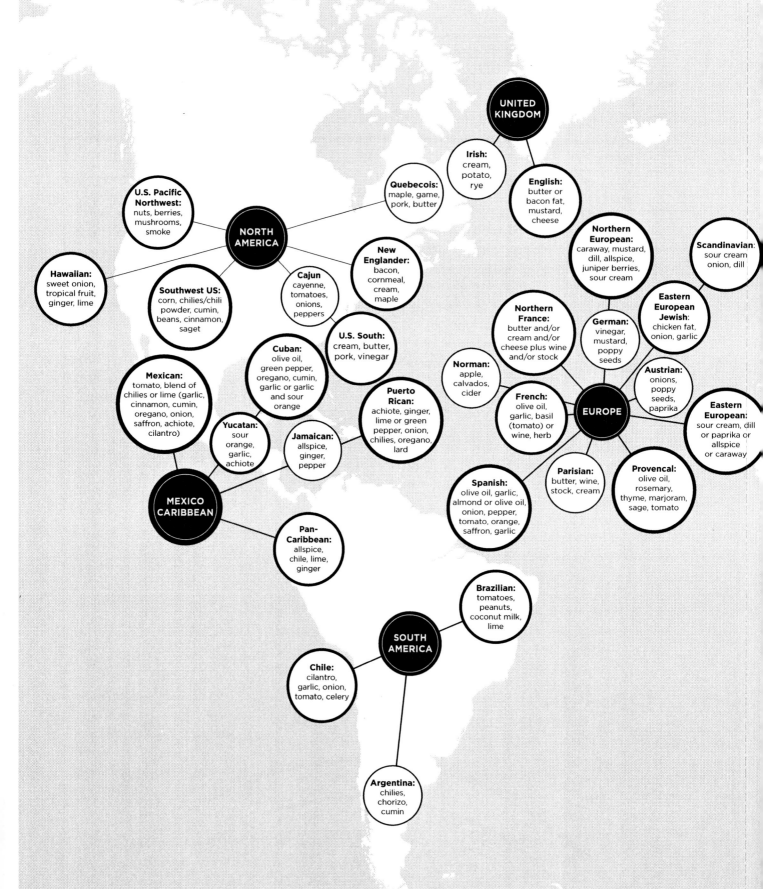

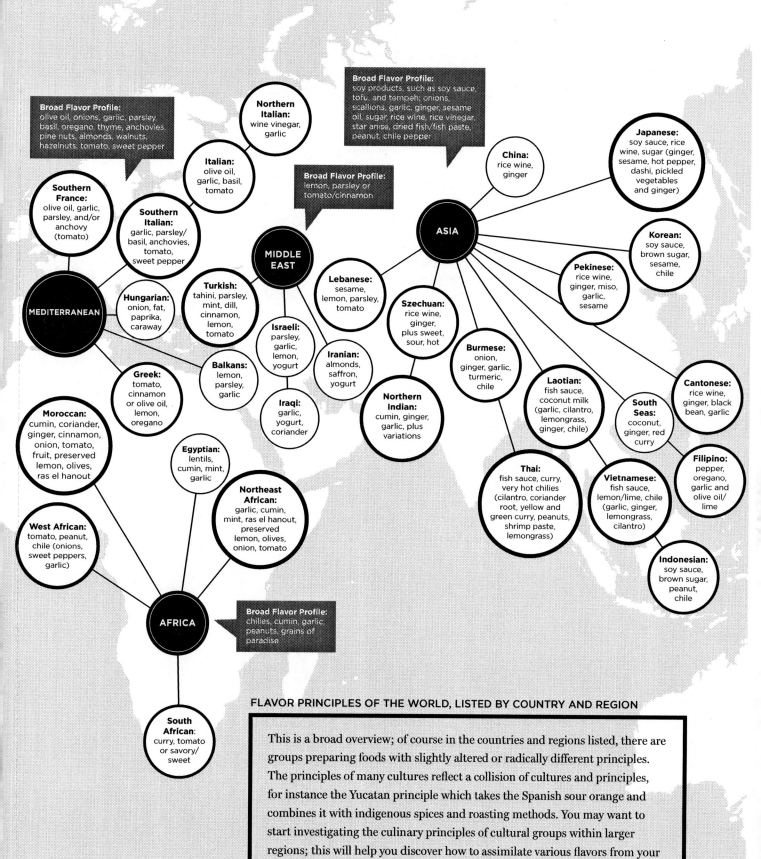

Broad Flavor Profile: olive oil, onions, garlic, parsley, basil, oregano, thyme, anchovies, pine nuts, almonds, walnuts, hazelnuts, tomato, sweet pepper

Broad Flavor Profile: soy products, such as soy sauce, tofu, and tempeh; onions, scallions, garlic, ginger, sesame oil, sugar, rice wine, rice vinegar, star anise, dried fish/fish paste, peanut, chile pepper

Broad Flavor Profile: lemon, parsley or tomato/cinnamon

Northern Italian: wine vinegar, garlic

Italian: olive oil, garlic, basil, tomato

Southern France: olive oil, garlic, parsley, and/or anchovy (tomato)

Southern Italian: garlic, parsley/basil, anchovies, tomato, sweet pepper

MEDITERRANEAN

MIDDLE EAST

Turkish: tahini, parsley, mint, dill, cinnamon, lemon, tomato

Hungarian: onion, fat, paprika, caraway

Israeli: parsley, garlic, lemon, yogurt

Lebanese: sesame, lemon, parsley, tomato

China: rice wine, ginger

ASIA

Japanese: soy sauce, rice wine, sugar (ginger, sesame, hot pepper, dashi, pickled vegetables and ginger)

Korean: soy sauce, brown sugar, sesame, chile

Pekinese: rice wine, ginger, miso, garlic, sesame

Greek: tomato, cinnamon or olive oil, lemon, oregano

Balkans: lemon, parsley, garlic

Iranian: almonds, saffron, yogurt

Iraqi: garlic, yogurt, coriander

Szechuan: rice wine, ginger, plus sweet, sour, hot

Burmese: onion, ginger, garlic, turmeric, chile

Northern Indian: cumin, ginger, garlic, plus variations

Laotian: fish sauce, coconut milk (garlic, cilantro, lemongrass, ginger, chile)

South Seas: coconut, ginger, red curry

Cantonese: rice wine, ginger, black bean, garlic

Moroccan: cumin, coriander, ginger, cinnamon, onion, tomato, fruit, preserved lemon, olives, ras el hanout

Egyptian: lentils, cumin, mint, garlic

Northeast African: garlic, cumin, mint, ras el hanout, preserved lemon, olives, onion, tomato

West African: tomato, peanut, chile (onions, sweet peppers, garlic)

Thai: fish sauce, curry, very hot chilies (cilantro, coriander root, yellow and green curry, peanuts, shrimp paste, lemongrass)

Vietnamese: fish sauce, lemon/lime, chile (garlic, ginger, lemongrass, cilantro)

Filipino: pepper, oregano, garlic and olive oil/ lime

Indonesian: soy sauce, brown sugar, peanut, chile

AFRICA

Broad Flavor Profile: chilies, cumin, garlic, peanuts, grains of paradise

South African: curry, tomato or savory/ sweet

FLAVOR PRINCIPLES OF THE WORLD, LISTED BY COUNTRY AND REGION

This is a broad overview; of course in the countries and regions listed, there are groups preparing foods with slightly altered or radically different principles. The principles of many cultures reflect a collision of cultures and principles, for instance the Yucatan principle which takes the Spanish sour orange and combines it with indigenous spices and roasting methods. You may want to start investigating the culinary principles of cultural groups within larger regions; this will help you discover how to assimilate various flavors from your milieu and create an interesting friction with food on the plate.

using elements of one and merging with another and further experimenting, you can create compelling flavor profiles.

Rozin writes, "Custom, tradition, and familiarity all invest certain flavoring combinations with meaning and with a positive value." We touched on this earlier, when we mentioned how memory and cultural associations can effect your expectations of what particular foods look like, and how they will taste. From the example given earlier, when you hear "noodle," do you think of Italian pasta, Japanese soba, or the broad ribbons of the Pennsylvania Dutch?

When you marry your taste and experience to what you know about flavors and techniques of preparation, you can borrow from different traditions, even combining ethnic backgrounds. "Fusion" cuisines are about reinterpretation. And remember that experimentation is not only about borrowing spices from one ethnic culture, but about using different preparations, too. You can make a terrine using French technique and flavor it with spices that are traditionally Indian, and have been toasted in oil, as Indian cooks do. You can use pistachios, which are common to both cultures, as an ingredient, and decorate the terrine with motifs from Indian textiles.

Roasting a chicken—not a traditional method of preparation in oarts of China, where fuel is scarce and speedy high-heat cooking is common—can nevertheless be done with a soy, ginger and rice wine flavoring. You can make cornbread, a product of the American South, spiced with chermoula and studded with dried apricots, and serve it with a lamb stew, or wrap tortillas around a tofu salad flavored with tomatoes, lime and fresh cilantro.

The possibilities for creative improvisation using flavor principles and techniques are infinite, and that's exciting!

Food with Personality

Food has an emotional power that is not tied only to its associations with culture (Cuban, New York takeout) or nostalgia ("Grandma used to make Red Velvet cake for every birthday!"). Love it or hate it, we've all heard the term "comfort food" and the classic example is mashed potatoes. We've seen the movies in which lovesick teenage girls in fuzzy loungewear mope around eating chocolate ice cream straight from the carton. Why doesn't sushi resonate as a comfort food, or steak with chimichurri? Ask yourself: What distinctions make mashed potatoes so comforting, or comfortable? They're soft, hot, buttery, starchy, and can be eaten with a spoon. Anyone can eat them, from a toddler to an elderly person. Starch carries fat and flavor well, and all these soft, warm, oily things feel good in the mouth.

Comfort food is only one example of the emotive power of food. Just as food can be classified as comforting, it can be masculine or feminine, playful or refined, happy or sad, sophisticated or cute. A food or menu can be created to reflect the personality of your ideal mate: playful, intelligent, sexy, dependable.

Food can also signify events or cultural associations. Fried chicken and cheese grits can be read as "church picnic," whereas Kraft Macaroni and Cheese with cubes of Spam stirred into it might suggest "college dorm food." We associate Shirley Temples with little girls and thick steaks with manly men. In modern American culture we associate the cosmopolitan cocktail with frivolity, and a single-malt scotch with intelligence, brawn and luxury. Flavor, texture and presentation contribute to the categorization, as well as playing on all the principles, tastes and aromas we've listed in this chapter.

Activity Questions:

❶ Can you name a playful food? A sexy food? A sad food?
   What are the distinctive qualities of that food that make it so?

_____

_____

_____

_____

❷ Describe a fusion dish that really worked for you. Why?

_____

_____

_____

_____

❸ Describe a fusion dish that didn't work for you. Why?

_____

_____

_____

_____

❹ What food, scent, color or flavor do you associate with your birthday, or another holiday you celebrate? Why?

_____

_____

_____

_____

_____

❺ What is your cultural heritage? Now name a place you've lived or visited. How could you create a fusion dish by bringing together aspects of both of these? What would it be?

_____

_____

_____

_____

_____

All in the Family

Cooking within families of foods guarantees food affinities. Food in the same plant families may have come from a common ancestor, or have commonalities in chemical makeup, flavor and aroma. Foods can also be grouped by season. You may have heard the saying, "What grows together tastes good together." Plants that come into ripeness at the same time often pair well. We'll talk about that more in the Cooking Seasonally chapter.

Lastly, foods have affinities when they come from the same region or culture. This is a reiteration, in a way, of what grows together tastes good together: the Native American triumvirate of beans, corn, and fish is a fine example. Local fish was buried in the ground, and corn was planted on top of it, with runner beans that climbed the cornstalk. These three foods nourished the soil in different ways and provided support: the fish decayed and fed the plants, the corn stalk held up the bean stalk, and the beans released nitrogen into the soil, nourishing the corn. Combined in a bowl, local fish, corn and beans—whether used fresh or dried—provided complementary nutrition, and a delicious mixture of tastes and textures. When you see, say, grilled salmon served on a bed of corn and cannellini beans (perhaps with sage and shiitake mushrooms), this is a contemporary play on that ancient combination.

Herb and Vegetable Families:

Mints: basil and all its varieties (lemon basil, cinnamon basil, Thai basil, holy basil), bergamot, hyssop, lavender, rosemary, marjoram, oregano, sage, savory, shiso, thyme and its varieties (lemon thyme, nutmeg thyme), and the mints (peppermint, spearmint, pennyroyal, nepitella)

Lettuce: sunchokes, salsify, burdock, lettuces, chicories (Belgian endive, radicchio), dandelions, endives (frisee, escarole), tarragon, curry plant, and thistles: artichoke, cardoon

Carrot: carrots, parsnips, celery, celery root, fennel, angelica, celery, chervil, coriander, cilantro and culantro, dill leaves and seeds, fennel seed and fennel pollen, lovage, parsley, anise, ajwain and caraway, asafoetida, celery seed, coriander, cumin

Cabbage: turnip, radish, cabbages, broccoli, cauliflower, romanesco, kohlrabi, rutabaga, kale, broccolini, cress, mustard, radish, Brussels sprouts, arugula, watercress, broccoli rabe, bok choy, Napa cabbage, mizuna, horseradish, mustard leaves, oil and mustard seeds (black mustard, brown mustard, white or yellow mustard), horseradish, wasabi, capers (distant).

Beans: jicama, mung, soy, alfalfa, green beans, yard beans, peas, pea shoots, lima beans, sugar snap peas, snow peas, favas, licorice root, which is used in syrups, powders and in brewing, fenugreek seeds, tamarind.

Curcubit: squash, cucumber, musk melons, watermelons, gourds, bitter melons, chayote, mirliton, and squashes: acorn, Hubbard, summer, zucchini, pumpkin, butternut, cheese, Kabocha. Borage tastes like cucumber, though it's not a curcubit.

Laurels: bay leaves, California bay leaves, sassafras, avocado, cinnamon (distant)

Nightshades: tomatoes, eggplant, potatoes, tomatillos, bell peppers and all chile peppers: bell peppers, paprika, pimento, jalapeno, ancho, poblano, serrano, cayenne, habanero, scotch bonnet, tabasco, aji

Lilies: yams, lotus root, onions, garlic, leeks, shallots, ramps, chives, asparagus, taro, dasheen, pandan

Goosefoot: epazote, spinach, beets, quinoa, sea beans, amaranth, sorrel, chard

Seaweed: algae, nori, carrageen, dulse, sea parsley, kelp, lombu, wakame

Fungi: truffles, huitlacoche, and mushrooms: white, brown, Portobello, shiitake, maitake, oyster, matsutakes, porcini, wood ear, cloud ear, lobster, morels, chanterelles, fairy ring, puffballs, cepe, cinnamon cap, enokitake, hen of the woods, chicken of the woods, hedgehog, lion's mane

Ginger: ginger, turmeric, galangal, cardamom, grains of paradise

Myrtle: guava, feijoa, allspice, clove

Citrus: orange (sour and sweet), lemon, lime, grapefruit, meyer lemon, sour lime, tangelo, tangor, bergamot, kumquats, yuzu, citron, mandarin, tangerine, pomelo, curry leaf, orange flowers, makrut or kaffir lime, Sichuan pepper

Pepper: black, white, green and rose—not pink, which is a different species—peppercorns, betel leaf, Ahanti pepper and hoja santa

Palm: dates, hearts of palm

Exceptional Produce

Other notable herbs and vegetables that don't fall into any of these families are: Mexican oregano and lemon verbena, from the same South American plant. Some vegetables and spices belong in flower families: sweet potatoes are morning glories, okra is a hibiscus, star anise is a magnolia, pineapple a bromeliad, and saffron a crocus. Tropical roots and tubers include manioc, yucca and cassava. Juniper berries are in the pine family. Wintergreen mint is related to blueberries, lingonberries and cranberries. Figs, mulberries, and breadfruit are in the same family, and mangos, pistachios and cashews are related. Sorrel, rhubarb and buckwheat fall into the same sour herb family. Bamboo shoots and lemongrass are both grasses, and nopales and prickly pears belong in the cactus family.

Think of the interesting combinations that can result from working from this list. We're accustomed to experiencing figs and pistachios together, in a savory context, say, grilled figs wrapped in prosciutto and rolled in crushed pistachios, and in a sweet way, such as a pistachio panna cotta with a fig compote. How can you use other foods related to figs with foods related to pistachios? What about a cashew brittle with a fig sorbet? Mulberries and cashews over plain yogurt? Can you season a buckwheat salad with ingredients that make rhubarb sing, like strawberries?

Food Origins

When grouping foods, it is also useful to know what part of the world they originated in. Why? For all the reasons that were expressed earlier about flavors in sync and cultural touchstones; it's all part of contextualizing your meal and creating an experience for a diner.

From the Middle East and Mediterranean: Vegetables, Fruits, Herbs and Spices: Cabbage, kale, broccoli, cauliflower, Brussels sprouts, mustard, watercress, favas, peas, alfalfa, chickpeas, lentils, hazelnuts, pistachios, wheat

From Asia: Vegetables, Fruits, Herbs and Spices: Turnip, broccoli rabe, bok choy, Napa cabbage, tatsoi, mizuna, radish, horseradish, soybean, mung bean, azuki, pigeon pea, almonds, coconut, walnuts, poppy seeds, barley, rye, oats, rice, buckwheat

From Africa: Vegetables, Fruits, Herbs and Spices: Black-eyed pea, cowpea, groundnut, sesame seeds, millet, sorghum, teff

From the New World (North and South America): Vegetables, Fruits, Herbs and Spices: Beans, haricot vert, lima bean, butter bean, runner bean, peanut, brazil nuts, cashews, pecans, walnuts, sunflowers, corn, wild rice, amaranth, chocolate, vanilla

A World Map of Spices and Seasonings

Here in the United States, we can buy spice mixtures in the grocery store. Pumpkin pie spice, apple pie spice, pizza seasoning—all of these are ready-made mixtures intended to flavor the foods associated with the regional cuisines of the United States. You may have seen these in the spice section of your local grocery store.

Other cultures have their spice-mix standbys as well. The use of these isn't restricted to one particular dish; these mixtures show up throughout that cuisine, in stews, breads and cocktails (I know someone who likes to sprinkle pumpkin pie spice on his popcorn, and I say to each his own!) Classic French spice mixtures were mentioned earlier in the book, and include bouquet garni, herbes de Provence and quatre epices.

Here are some ethnic spice mixtures: From Mexico, in particular the Yucatan, there is *recado rojo*, a spice paste of achiote (or annato seeds—these two are from the same plant), allspice, garlic, cinnamon, cumin and Mexican oregano. The mixture gives depth and a crimson color to stews, soups, rice dishes and a regional specialty of fish wrapped in banana leaves. Spanish *picada* is garlic, parsley, saffron and almonds. It provides a base for cooking, or is spooned onto foods, like tortillas or cooked meats, as a seasoning, like salsa. **Tunisian five-spice powder** is a mixture of cinnamon, cloves, nutmeg, pepper and grains of paradise (and a classic seasoning for lamb), whereas one version of **Chinese five-spice powder** is composed of star anise, Szechuan pepper, clove

anise and cinnamon. Chinese five-spice powder can also be cinnamon, star anise, cloves, and ginger. In either case, Chinese five-spice powder, which is used widely in various cuisines as a seasoning, and in Cantonese cuisine as a classic rub for duck or seasoning in beef stew, reflects the classic Chinese cultural balance of ying and yang in its makeup. A good five-spice mixture keeps salty, sour, sweet, bitter and savory in perfect harmony.

Garam masala, an Indian spice mixture added to many popular dishes, is cumin, cardamom, black pepper, clove, cinnamon, ginger and coriander. **Zaatar**, a classic Middle Eastern spice mixture, is sumac, sesame, thyme, oregano and marjoram. Zaatar adds a zesty touch to salads, roast meats, breads and grains. Chermoula, common to Morocco, Tunisia and Algeria, is a mixture of spices and aromatics, and contains saffron, cumin and black pepper mixed with fresh chilies, cilantro, garlic, and onion. **Chermoula** is used as a marinade or seasoning for fish and seafood, though it is also used on meats and poultry. Made with fresh herbs, chermoula can be used as a salsa with meats, or mixed into grain dishes.

Adobo is a common seasoning blend throughout the Caribbean and Latin Americas. It's a seasoning base for stews and marinades made of pepper, oregano, garlic, salt, olive oil and an acid, such as vinegar or lime juice. **Sofrito**, a cooked mixture similar to picada which is used in Puerto Rican and Cuban cooking, varies by island. Its main ingredients are salt pork or ham, oregano, cilantro, garlic, onion, green peppers and chilies.

The spices contained in curry mixtures are a classic example of how these spice mixtures contain a balance of tastes: the cardamom is the sweet, the mustard is the sour. In sofrito, the pork provides the salty, the

after the fruit that surrounds it has been removed. Green pepper is unripe, greener in flavor as well as color, and often pickled. Pink pepper and pink peppercorns are two different things: **Poivre rose** is made

> *A general statement about balancing flavors:*
> *More doesn't necessarily mean more interesting.*

chiles the heat, and the cilantro the sweet.

A general statement about balancing flavors: More doesn't necessarily mean more interesting. There's a world of spices and a limited number of classic spice mixtures. Not everything works together, for many reasons, including flavor, aroma, color and cultural association. Don't be afraid to experiment; don't try to disgust.

A Review of Common and Not-So-Common Spices

Where do spices come from? What do those colorful powders, flakes or pods look like on the plant they grew on, before they were picked, processed and packaged into little tubes? This is not just a matter of intellectual curiosity; some spices come in many forms and shapes, which an intrepid chef can take great advantage of. Many of these spices have beautiful tales, of how they got their names, how their use spread from culture to culture, the ethnic or religious traditions they've come to be part of.

Peppercorns come in **black, pink, white, green**—all according to how they are processed. Black pepper berries are unripe, and dried to darken. White pepper is the seed at the center of the berry, used

from red pepper berries that have been pickled. **Pink peppercorns** are not from the same pepper plant as white, green and black pepper; they are fruits of a tropical tree, and have a sweeter flavor. **Sichuan peppercorn**s are the dried berries of the prickly ash tree. Sharp and fragrant, they cause a tickling, tingling sensation in the mouth.

Annato/achiote is commonly used in Latin American cooking, and Filipino and Jamaican cuisine as well. These come from the inedible fruit of a small shrub; the seeds are the source of a bright pigment that turns oils and foods bright orange, and infuses oil with a distinctive yet mild, piney flavor when heated. Annato, the whole seeds, or achiote, a paste ground from these seeds, is often added to hot oil then removed so its color and flavor are carried in the oil, but the pebble-like spice isn't directly consumed.

Grains of paradise, a spicy West African plant in the ginger family, is pungent, and sometimes substituted for black pepper. In West Africa, the seeds are used to flavor stews, and they're chewed, to warm the body. When you bite down on them, you initially get hit with the pepper-like tickling heat of them, which turns to a warmer, more cinnamony spiciness, almost a smokiness. In the United States, various chefs have been using grains of paradise lately in conjunction with peppercorns: popping them in a grinder and finishing sauces, salads and soups with grains of paradise, or using it in steak au poive. During the Renaissance, the grains often flavored beer; taking that as a clue, imagine what sorts of infusions you can create with grains of paradise!

Ras el hanout is a savory mixture of many powdered herbs. The name translates roughly from Arabic as "best of shop," and the mixture came about because spice merchants would make specialized mixtures for their customers. Cinnamon, cumin, coriander, ginger, and turmeric are common components. More unusual, ras el hanout can contain grains of paradise, orris root, belladonna and Spanish fly. Ras el hanout is used as a dry rub, or to flavor couscous.

Hoja santa are peppery South American leaves, used to wrap meats and fish. There are all sorts of funny names for this plant, including root beer plant and Mexican pepperleaf. These names get at its elusive flavor, which is similar to the flavor of different root beers, which feature different ingredients such as: sassafras, licorice, spearmint, anise and pepper. Hoja santa leaves are used in mole verde, tamales, cooked into eggs, and used to infuse chocolate drinks with a haunting flavor in Central and South America.

Curry leaves are much milder and totally different from curry powder (a spice mix), and can be simmered in dishes, much like bay leaves. **Makrut (kaffir) lime leaves** are used in the same manner, though often in custards and other desserts as well. Their

sharp, clean flavor is sometimes contributed to a dish when the leaf is julienne very fine, and added at the end of cooking.

Many parts of the **rose**—the dried **petals, extracts, buds, hips** and **petals**— are used the world over, especially in Middle Eastern cuisines, to flavor sweet and savory foods, candies, pastries, stews, sausages, rose hip tea—even a ceviche made of halibut and lime, to which they contribute an interesting, musky, floral note and beautiful hue.

Pandan leaves are used to wrap meats and fish in Southeast Asian cuisines, Indonesian in particular. The leaves can stewed, like bay leaves, for flavor to be extracted in curries and sweet dishes, such as rice pudding or ice cream base. Pandan has a coconutty flavor.

Tamarind is the sour pulp of the pods of an African bean tree, often sold as paste or extract. Sour, sweet and intensely aromatic, it used in drinks, sauces, stews, and desserts, and contributes a tart, perfumey, citrus flavor.

Hops are the dried flowers of a vine related to hemp. The flowers are used to flavor brewed beverages, such as beer, as well as in breads and teas. Hops add a bitter quality and a woody aroma to foods, even notes of pine and citrus. If you have access to a chef garden or a pot with a wall nearby, consider adding hops to your herb plantings; they make a beautiful climber.

Cherry pits and **mahleb**, sour cherry pits, are baked into pastries and breads for flavor, as for cherry claufoutis. They add a subtle nuttiness to the batter. Mahleb is also available ground, and it's mixed into breads, desserts—anything baked—where it adds a subtle bitterness and delicate aroma. Tart, woodsy **sumac** is a crushed berry which is sprinkled on breads and ground for use with other dried spices in Middle Eastern dishes.

Global Techniques

Tandoor

You may have seen the bright orange, sizzling foods at Indian restaurants; these emerged from some version of a traditional tandoor, a cylindrical clay oven. The shape and structure of the oven is unusual to Western eyes, and makes the intense heat and colorful food of Punjabi cuisine possible. Traditionally, tandoor ovens are made from a very fine-textured clay, bound by horsehair and husks and grasses.

The tandoor reaches temperatures at and beyond 500°F. A tandoor is heated with charcoal, which creates and maintains the temperature of a blast furnace within the oven. The fire is built in the bottom of the oven, which creates levels of heat: it's most intense at the middle and cooler at the top.

In India, tandoori ovens are sunk into the ground. Foods are lowered for cooking in them, using special tongs and utensils. Meat lowered into a tandoor is traditionally threaded onto skewers. In restaurants, authentic tandoors (which are not common) are encased in a stainless steel housing.

Use of the oven requires a special technique and turns out distinctive products. Meats, such as chicken, cook rapidly and sizzle. The heat sears their outside, but at their interior they maintain juiciness and flavor. Meats and poultry cooked in a tandoor are often marinated; the marinade or ghee is usually brushed on during cooking, sometimes dropping into the coals and releasing a fragrant smoke. The marinade fuses to the meat when it's lowered into the extreme heat. Breads cooked in the tandoor are flat and textured with bubbles. They have the pleasantly charred taste of a brick oven pizza; naan and roti are examples.

Wok

There are over a billion people cooking in a wok every day the world over. The wok, a rounded-bottomed metal bowl, is multipurpose and efficient. It's shape, and that it is made of highly conductive metal, means that cooking requires very little fuel. Used for stir-frying, stewing, steaming, deep frying, braising or soup-making, the wok comes in many sizes and materials. Carbon steel and cast iron are common wok materials. Cast iron woks are heavy, but their heat retention and distribution are terrific. They're also very durable, though if dropped when very hot, they are prone to shattering.

Carbon steel can be inexpensive; highest quality (read: most expensive) woks are hand-hammered of two sheets of carbon steel, which creates tiny ridges in the sides of the wok. Carbon steel is light, quick to heat and durable. Teflon-coated woks are not recommended, both because they cannot reach the high heat required for wok cookery safely, and because Teflon has been found to emit toxic fumes when heated beyond a certain point.

The bowl shape of the wok is a unique feature. The flattish area at the bottom of the wok gets very hot, and allows for high heat cooking with little oil. Because of the heat conduction, a wok can be operated over a fire that requires very little fuel. The wide are of the wok means that there's less spillage of food; the concave shape herds the food toward the center of the vessel.

Stirfrying

Wok technique is a subject of some debate. In recent years, Chinese cookbook authors have advocated specific techniques. You can perform your own research on wok methods by taking cooking classes or reading Chinese cookery books. Find the details that work best for you, and absorb them into your style. Following, I lay out a basic technique.

Woks have handles because the cooking technique calls for food to be tossed. A very small amount of oil is required for wok cookery. The simple progression of the technique is that pungents, such as ginger or garlic, are often added first, to flavor the oil, them skimmed out. The ingredients that take longest to cook are added next. They're tossed in the oil to coat, then drawn up the sides of the wok to cook. This is when a quality wok comes in handy; the dimpled sides of hand-hammered woks grip the food, suspending it above the oil.

Batch by batch, food is added to the wok, then scooped out for the next thing to be added. When all is cooked, the ingredients are combined in the wok, sauced and reheated.

Before you start heating your wok, you'll want to have all your mise en place prepared; stir-frying happens rapidly, with no time to prep between steps. Have all ingredients chopped, measured and laid out close to where you will be cooking. Ingredients should be cut to a uniform size so the food cooks evenly and into thin shreds or small pieces to cook quickly. Remember the end result of your dish; the appearance will be unified by the similar size and texture of the sliced foods.

Cornstarch, arrowroot or tapioca powder (see discussion of thickeners) is used to thicken the sauce so it coats and clings to the meats and vegetables. Some chefs add thickener to the marinade; others add it to the cooking liquid in the wok; others dredge their meat or chicken in seasoned flour or cornstarch, which helps brown the meat. Adding thickener early also helps thicken the sauce through the gradual process of reduction, which lends a richer flavor then adding thickener at the end of the cooking process does.

To start, heat your wok before you add oil. If you have a carbon steel or cast iron wok, a thin ribbon of smoke will rise from the wok, and you will smell the hot, seasoned metal. Now add your oil. Immediately after, add your pungents and spices: garlic, onion, shallot, chiles, fermented black beans, dried shrimp, scallions, Szechuan peppercorns, and so on. The hot oil will be infused with their flavors.

Add the meat and do not stir. Leave it for one minute or more, until it is seared on one side, and very fragrant. Then toss with the oil and move the meat around. Add a liquid such as soy sauce or cooking wine to deglaze the wok and dislodge all the little brown bits of flavorsome meat and sauce clinging to the bottom and sides of the pan.

Next add vegetables. Add the least succulent vegetables—those that take the longest time to cook, like carrots—first. Add those that cook quickly, like sprouts and shoots, last. The last step is to finish

TANDOOR
a cylindrical clay oven

WOK
a rounded-bottomed
metal bowl

INTENSIFYING FLAVOR

Once you've conceptualized the food you want to make, how do you make it as flavorful, and therefore memorable, as possible? Here are some tips:

❶ *Use products at their peak.* The most intensely flavored strawberry is a ripe, in-season strawberry. This applies to all produce, meat, poultry, seafood, cheeses, other dairy and eggs as well. And remember that spices should be used as quickly as possible. Old, dusty spices have lost their intensity.

❷ *Reducing.* Whether you are working with a stock, wine, or a fruit juice, simmering it until it is thick and syrupy will concentrate its meat/wine/fruity flavor. A reduced sauce is more intense than a starch-thickened sauce.

❸ *Layering.* When you work with the same food, in different forms, you are presenting different flavors and textures of that food, and hitting on different notes, which leads to intensity. Imagine, for instance, preparing a dessert that features dried, fresh, jellied and caramelized apricots together to maximize apricot flavor. The deepest, syrupy sweetness comes from the caramelized fruit, which plays against the tang of the dried, the brightness of the fresh, and the sugariness of the jellied. That's intense apricot flavor!

❹ *Make additions.* A pinch of salt or sugar, a squeeze of lemon juice or dash of vinegar will brighten flavors, or bring them into balance.Now, improvise!

your sauce with broth, hoisin, oyster sauce, and cook until it thickens and coats the meats and vegetables.

Now, garnish! Try highly aromatic toasted sesame oil, chive flowers, carrot flowers, whole or chopped herbs, fried strips of julienned wonton—or anything else that strikes your fancy! Refer to the section in Chapter Three on garnishing for ideas.

Classic Food Pairings

Through experimentation and tasting, you will find that some foods complement each other wonderfully. Chocolate, for instance, does beautifully with cinnamon and hot chiles, nuts, cherries, vanilla, ginger and cognac (not all together at once!). Capers add something magical when paired with mustards, anchovies, raisins and lemons. However, basil and tarragon do not marry well, and a steaming artichoke makes most wines taste like swill.

Two food concepts can help us to understand classic pairings, as "classic," culturally, is often the result of necessity. These things go together because it seems they always have. Core foods are the foods that are consumed daily, the staples of the diet. These can be starches such as rice or potatoes, or proteins, such as beef or fish. Complementary foods are used to elevate these day-in-day-out staples by changing their flavor and texture, and they often add nutritional content. Complementary foods include greens, fruits and vegetables, sauces and bits of protein.

Throughout the games that follow, this chapter including the classic combinations above will prove a valuable resource. Improvisation comes from a knowledge base, and when you're called upon to came up with something off the cuff, think back to these chapters and suggestions. Ethnic techniques, global spices and flavor profiles, classic pairings—these produce "classic" dishes.

Here is a short list of classic pairings, different from the cultural pairings listed earlier in the chapter. When you taste these combinations and the concept of how foods can offset each other really clicks for you, start trying to create your own food matches, or build on these.

APPLES AND PEARS	brown sugar, caramel, Calvados, bleu cheese, cinnamon, custard, ginger, lemon, nutmeg, raisins, rum, vanilla, walnuts.
APRICOTS	almonds, brandy, cream, ginger, lemon, raspberries, vanilla.
ASPARAGUS	butter, egg, hollandaise, garlic, lemon, morels, mustard, Parmesan, vinaigrette.
GREEN BEANS	almonds, bacon, shallots
GREEN PEAS	mushrooms, shallots, chives, cream
BEEF	horseradish, mushrooms, black pepper, béarnaise, red wine.
BEETS	lemon, parsley, sour cream, vinaigrette.
CABBAGE & BRUSSELS SPROUTS	apples, bacon, chestnuts, vinegar, shallots
CARROTS	butter, lemon, orange, parsley
CHERRIES	almonds, chocolate, Kirsch, lemon
CORN	butter, chiles, cream, salt and pepper
DUCK	apples, cherries, currants, figs, garlic, ginger, honey, mint, mushrooms, mustard, orange, port, soy sauce
WHITE-FLESHED FISH	fennel, leeks, lemon, white wine
RED-FLESHED FISH	capers, olives, mustard, tomatoes
MELON	ginger, lemon, lime, port, prosciutto, raspberries, vanilla
SPINACH AND OTHER GREENS (CHARD, KALE)	ricotta, nutmeg, garlic, bacon, oinions, pine nuts, raisins
STRAWBERRIES	almonds, bananas, Champagne, cream, chocolate, lemon, rhubarb, sugar, balsamic vinegar, black pepper
RASPBERRIES	chocolate, hazelnuts, cream
BLUEBERRIES	lemon, mint, yogurt
ORANGES	chocolate, rose, cinnamon, almonds, cranberries
FIGS	red wine, salty ham, basalmic vinegar, creamy cheeses like chevre and ricotta, hard, salty cheeses such as Parmigiano Reggiano, Manchego or Pecorino Romano, and blue cheeses such as Saga blue and gorgonzola

To Summarize...

A final word: Keep in mind that although there are principles and classic combinations in this chapter, these are simply guidelines, not laws. Take what you've learned and build on it. Question it. Take classic combinations and subvert expectations. Remember: some rules are meant to be broken. Others deserve their status as "classic" pillars of cuisine. Play with the flavors, spices, marinades, vegetables, meats, etc. to find combinations that work for your needs and tastes—some will work deliciously and others will leave room for growth and further experimentation.

Chapter 4 Assessment Questions

❶ Name the senses, and describe how each of them contributes to the appreciation of flavor.

_____

_____

_____

_____

❷ Define "improvise" in your own words

_____

_____

_____

_____

❸ Can the leaves of nightshades be eaten?

_____

_____

_____

_____

❹ How many types of peppercorns are there?

_____

_____

_____

_____

_____

❺ Does the flavor plate assist you in thinking of taste components? How, or not?

_____

_____

_____

_____

_____

❻ Create a menu item drawing from the flavor ideas presented in this chapter.

_____

_____

_____

_____

_____

5/

The Food System and Cooking Seasonally

Foods at the peak of ripeness taste best. Period. However masterful and creative, your dish is only as good as the raw ingredients you put into it.

In this modern consumerist era, we are accustomed to having what we want when we want it: fresh strawberries all year, a Caprese salad of tomatoes, basil and mozzarella in February, honeydew on demand. The globalization of markets and advanced systems of transportation have made it possible to import those strawberries from Chile in March, overnight the tomatoes to a Manhattan restaurant from a hothouse in New Mexico, and have honeydew turn up in countless pale fruit salads in restaurants across the nation.

What is the effect of our food system on the way food tastes? Fruits and vegetables that remain unblemished and edible after being picked by a machine, packed, shipped, unloaded, put on display in a grocery—enduring days of handling and varying temperatures—have been bred specifically for the purpose of surviving transport, rather than to embody the unique flavor of a particular fruit or vegetable. Technology and transportation is almost always performed—at the expense of Flavor.

We may want to taste a strawberry in December, but what is the flavor of that strawberry compared to the tiny, deeply red strawberries that make up the first crop of the season in May? The flavor of a strawberry in season is pure, intensely sweet and utterly unique. This pure flavor is heightened by the unique aroma of the berry, absent in the December fruit, yet irresistible when the fruit is in season and the scent of one pint fills your apartment with warm sweetness. The texture of the May strawberry, picked at the height of ripeness, is succulent and soft, even juicy, with tiny seedy flecks, and it slips easily from its stem. The strawberry in season epitomizes all the qualities we associate with the word "strawberry," and captures the essence of the fruit: the juiciness, flavor, and fragrance that scream "strawberry."

CHAPTER OBJECTIVES

① To understand the importance of seasonality

② To recognize when foods are at peak ripeness

③ To understand when foods come into season at the same time

④ To associate particular foods with a season

⑤ To explain the U.S. food system

In contrast, mid-winter berries do not ripen on the stem, because ripe berries cannot be shipped. Instead these berries are hard, even starchy, with a faint sweet flavor that barely registers through their wan wateriness. Sure, these berries can be doctored with some sugar and liquor, and even be made to taste good. But the out-of-season berry, no matter how it is prepared, will win no contests against the berry in season; it cannot match the intensity of the flavor, aroma, or texture of the ripe berry. Even a strawberry frozen at its prime or preserved as a jam or fruit spread tastes better than an out-of-season fruit.

Cooking with Foods at their Peak Season

Cooking with foods at their peak season, allows you to capitalize on all of their finest qualities. This is why, in recent decades, a simple, straightforward style of cooking that relies on top-notch ingredients has been very successful, in all restaurant price brackets. These restaurants, with menus and publicity that utilize catch phrases like "locally-grown" and "seasonal"—even the names of heirloom fruits and vegetables, or the farms they are grown on—appeal to consumers for many political and personal reasons.

One major reason for success is that foods taste their best when they are in season. As with anything, there are those who embrace it and those who despise it.

Yet eating locally— or what has lately been come to be called "place-based eating"— has become a mantra for many chefs and consumers. Concerns such as food miles and pressure on water and fuel resources used in transporting fruits and vegetables from around the world bring this issue to the forefront. Some scientists say that as consumers in the United States, the largest percentage of our individual carbon footprint comes not from the cars we drive, but from the food we eat. The global food system consumes a massive amount of energy, as we eat fruits that are flown or trucked from point to point, refrigerated all the while, a system that consumes vast amounts of fossil fuel energy.

Farms and Food Production— Your Choice

Crops produced on an industrial scale take a tremendous amount of energy in the form of machines and chemical inputs such as fertilizers and pesticides to plant, grow, pick and package. Animals, too, consume an unusually large amount of energy to feed and raise on a feed lot instead of a pasture. Not only do they eat corn or other feed that has been grown and shipped many miles, but the animals are trucked from point to point at different times in their lives, for finishing, to the stockyard, to slaughter. Animals—cows especially—produce gases in their bodies which are released into the atmosphere. But cows pass a large amount of gas, specifically methane, a major greenhouse gas. Many foods—fruits, vegetables and meats—are imported from faraway countries, and those are flown in or transported by boat.

The way to opt out of this production system, to the extent you can, is to find national or regional companies that utilize a different, more energy-efficient method of production. Major food companies such as Niman Ranch and Stonyfield yogurt are prime examples of companies striving for what's known as "carbon neutrality." What this means is that the companies have either reduced or offset (by investing in carbon reduction programs globally) their emissions to the extent that they are not just adding carbon emissions to the universe.

Another way of opting out of the industrial food system to some degree is to join a smaller producer network. Many moderate to fine-dining restaurants are now relying on a network of cooperatives, farmers and purveyors based in their region. Often this network is close at hand, in the community or region of your restaurants; sometimes it is a bit more removed, if you are in a concentrated urban area. A network of regional producers allows you to forge reciprocal relationships with community growers and purveyors to bring the ripest, freshest and most trustworthy food to the table.

An advantage of regional eating is that it provides a way to differentiate yourself from the broader marketplace of restaurants, by serving the specialties of your region. A regional food is one that tells you you're in a particular place. The ingredients and preparation are particular to a specific geographical and cultural area of cuisine: how the regional cuisine of New Orleans is very different from that of Western Texas, how the food in Providence, Rhode Island differs from that in Burlington, Vermont, though both are Northeastern areas.

Seasonality

Regional produce reflects the growing season as well as the tastes of the people that live in that community. Another word for this is provenance. **Provenance** is simply another word for source. Provenance is a sense of place. In the food world, a related term is **terroir**. Like Provenance, terroir, a term commonly used in French winemaking, translates roughly to "sense of place." Terroir is a geographic term, while provenance is more cultural. In the case of terroir, it is said that certain geographic regions impart certain qualities to a product through everything from air to soil, and the product comes to embody the place. Think of a Cote du Rhone wine, or certain cheese of particular regions.

We have heard the refrain that if chefs or restaurateurs choose to restrict themselves to buying regionally, they will lose variety on their menus, and customers will not be satisfied. The regional diet is monotonous, right? Ask yourself: How monotonous is a diet composed only of commodity produce such as sugar, soybeans, rice, corn and wheat? It may sound strange, but buying regionally ensures genetic diversity in crops, which gives you more to feed your customer, who doesn't come into a restaurant to eat the same thing over and over.

You don't have to rely only on what is grown in your region during certain seasons. Just be logical about buying. Are Chilean raspberries, at $6 a pint in February, a smart choice? Or are winter-season kumquats from California just as lovely as a garnish, compote or sorbet? What about canning seasonal fruits and vegetables, and relying less on processed foods and long-distance fruits and vegetables? This allows you to capture the bounty of particular seasons, and really offer your customer something unique. In Chapter

Four, there is a section about preserves and jams to get you thinking about this, and started on your way.

Network with Suppliers

A great advantage of cultivating a network of suppliers is that it puts you in contact with interesting people, every single day. Every person has a story; some growers and artisanal producers have amazing, beautiful stories. In other words, putting a face to the food you serve by buying direct from people means that you're collecting stories, stories you can relate to your customers. Because dining out is, to a large degree, entertainment, think of how this contributes to the customer's entertainment, to hear these stories. Think of how these stories make your restaurant unique. When diners come in to your restaurant for an experience, a story helps to make that experience happen.

Food Safety and the Food system

Finally, food safety has become a hot-button issue. E. coli scares, related to beef and spinach here in the United States, have forced an examination of our food system. Evidence of neurological damage and antibiotic immunities in people who consume lots of fish raised in large aquaculture operations make us skeptical of what we buy, and in turn we look for restaurants with transparent sourcing. Different regulatory measures in countries like China, from which we now import a substantial portion of our food supply, may make us lean toward foods grown close to home.

Keeping all these issues in mind, buying direct from the grower ensures food quality, freshness and safety. And there are benefits to your community, as well. Every dollar into a farmer's pocket recirculates in the community, helping local economies stay vibrant. Vibrant local economies mean there are more people who can afford to eat in your restaurant.

Buying directly from the farmer or artisanal producer preserves family farms. Agricultural land is beautiful. Also, small farms often grow heirloom varieties of fruits and vegetables because they are best suited to the climate where they grow, or heritage breeds of animal that produce distinctive meat and eggs. Or, small farmers will experiment on different varieties of plant, instead of owning one giant farm and raising only one crop. The larger issue is that these farming commitments and experiments encourage biodiversity.

Here is a mantra for you: food in season tastes good, and choosing to buy it from local purveyors and farmers works hard to bring better products and producers to market.

Why Cook Seasonally?

Cooking with a sense of season is acknowledging the world we live in. In a way, it's showing a respect for the products of the earth, by using them when they have achieved a natural state of ripeness. Cooking seasonally celebrates freshness, and offers foods at the height of their character. As in the example above, a fruit in season has all the attributes that make a strawberry a strawberry, a peach a peach, an artichoke and artichoke. When produce is at its seasonal peak, it is at the height of its flavor, aroma and texture. This is when you want to use it.

Cooking seasonally also offers opportunities to learn food affinities. Foods that grow together—or grow at the same time of year—taste good together. An example is the classic pairing of tomatoes and basil. Tomatoes ripen in August, at the same time the basil—often recommended for companion planting with tomatoes, to ward off certain pests that afflict the plant— planted at the plant's base, gets bushy, dark green and fragrant. The two come to peak together, and taste delicious together, demonstrating the principle that using foods in season in tandem leads to wonderful combinations.

Choices

When you buy what's in season and go from there, you realize that seasonality lends structure in a world of stimulating choices. Learning to cook seasonally also allows you to exercise your creativity, by opening the door for originality and expression. How? Instead of relying on the ingredients a recipe calls for, you go to the market and see what's available. From that point, you know what you have to work with. How can you use it creatively? How can you prepare something different with it for every service, or change it on the menu for every new week? How you use what you can get when it is at its best is particular to you, and a way of distinguishing yourself in the kitchen.

Appearance and Texture

Cooking seasonally, you'll realize there's a tremendous variety to the appearance and texture of foods. There's not only one kind of tomato, but thousands; their flavors are slightly different, some sweeter, some tangier, but they are always "tomato." Carrots are orange, purple, magenta, yellow, and pale white; they're as long as your forearm or as tiny as your pinkie finger. Broccoli and cauliflower appear in shades from milky white to deep purple, with a speckled yellow-green Romanesco in the middle of the spectrum. Beans can be a foot long or the size of a toothpick. There are so many ways to present these foods that surprise and please a customer, and make cooking, for you, a constant challenge and surprise.

Variety

Using all this variety in your kitchen, it's possible to achieve visual complexity and interesting combinations of tastes and textures, simply by using foods in their prime. Imagine a lusciously juicy peach, warm as flesh. You can serve that, solo, as dessert, because it's a perfect food. Imagine spinach so fresh it's never been refrigerated; the green of it is so brilliant, the crunch so enticing, the whorls and ridges on the leaves perfect for cradling mustard vinaigrette. In addition, when you shop directly from farmers, either to supply your kitchen directly or at a farmers market, you benefit from their experimentation with different varieties, and knowledge of the product. If they're selling it, they're also eating it. They know what it grows with, and how to make it taste slightly different every day. Ask them what they're doing with it—how they would cook it at home— to develop your own knowledge base of the product, then riff on their suggestions to make them your own.

Control Expenses

Cooking seasonally is also a way of controlling expense. What's in season is abundant, meaning it is also less expensive. Long-distance shipping, storage and brokerage add dollars to your ingredients. Buying locally and in season is getting a whole lot of bang for your buck.

Seasonal Associations

We associate certain fruits and vegetables—though they are available throughout the year—with certain seasons. That is because, not so long ago, most fruits and vegetables were only available at that time of year, during their growing season. Wow—with global transport and technologies that extend or imitate the growing season, we can often have what we want when we want it. Some fruits and vegetables marked a particular time of year, in the common imagination, or at festivals celebrating the fruit, vegetable, animal or bird. People associated eating these foods with time or experiences.

Seasonal cooking also involves playing upon these associations, which are culturally specific. When you offer a customer a salad of just-picked tomatoes in season, that dish says "summer." You are tapping into their experience, if they have had it, or even if they cherish a romantic ideal about farming, of walking among the rows of plants growing, of smelling the sharp fragrance of tomatoes growing in the sun.

We also associate seasons with color. We crave green things in the spring: tender shoots of asparagus, pale leaves of mint, a pile of peas. Green is associated with newness and growth. In summer, colors are riotous: red-red tomatoes, bright golden corn, peppers in every hue of yellow, orange, purple, red. Bright colors capture the hotness and exhilaration of summer vacation. The shades of autumn are the rich tones of russet apples, coppery squashes and garnet pomegranate seeds; noble and fitting for the harvest, and the last days of heat and light. Winter brings a more subdued palate of brown tubers and emerald kale, comforting in a time of hibernation. Cooking seasonally involves playing upon these associations as well as using produce at its peak.

The weather also prompts cravings, and taking this into account is seasonal cooking. In most parts of the United States, spring can be alternately warm and very cold, and your menu or meal for each particular day should reflect the world beyond the kitchen. We don't often crave cold soups during winter, or stews on a hot summer night. A wide variety of culinary traditions, from Mexico to Sri Lanka, can be called into play, since customers associate place with climate. Many people associate English shepherd's pie with cold weather, and cold Japanese soba noodles with hot days. People crave tropical foods on steamy summer nights, and blood-warming Korean when the temperature drops.

Techniques reflect the seasons as well. We don't braise or slow-cook when it's 85 degrees outside, and nor do we bake cakes—but grilled tuna steaks sound appealing. Canning captures the bounty of late summer, but is less of an option in winter, when the type of produce that's in season stores well in its natural form, like parsnips and carrots. These can be "wintered" in a basement, if you have access to one.

Cooking seasonally involves a combination of ingredients, techniques and associations. Your ingredients are the raw materials for your meal, and they should be of the highest possible quality. Produce in season, at its prime, is the finest it can be, and will lift your preparations to a new level.

Questions:

❶ Use the list on page 130 to pick a fruit from each season. Think of three different ways you can use that fruit in a preparation with at least one other fruit from the same season.

_____

_____

_____

_____

_____

❷ Repeat question one, using the list of vegetables, page 130.

_____

_____

_____

_____

_____

❸ Think of foods, sensations, feelings, textures and colors you associate with a particular season. Make a list. Now, could you build a menu that incorporates these characteristics?

_____

_____

_____

_____

_____

_____

_____

❹ Can you think of a food with terroir? What qualities does the geography of the food impart to the food?

_____

_____

_____

_____

_____

_____

_____

❺ If you had free rein to build a network of farmers and artisanal producers to supply your restaurant, where would you start? How would you find them? What do you think the benefits of your association would be, and how would you reveal those relationships to a customer?

_____

_____

_____

_____

_____

_____

_____

❻ Describe a food you associate with a season, and why.

_____

_____

_____

_____

_____

_____

_____

_____

_____

Seasonal Food Associations

Different regions have different growing seasons. The growing season is a time at which crops can be grown in different regions, and it is reliant upon several key factors. Growing season is determined by climate, daylight hours, the amount of rainfall, and the crop being grown (all crops have different light and temperature requirements). For many regions, the end of the growing season for most crops is marked by the first frost.

There are also foods we associate with particular times of the year. This is usually because these foods are at their peak at these times, and have historically been eaten at this time. Food associations are cultural.

Seasonality of Dairy Products

This may be a surprise: some of our most perishable supermarket staples are also seasonal. We think of milk as one of the most constant, consistent substances we consume, but in fact the quality, flavor and composition of milk changes with the seasons and fluctuations in temperature as the cows (or goats, sheep, buffalo, etc.) that provide it react to changes in their environment. Of course, the animals reacting to an environment are those that have one beyond concrete enclosures and milking stalls: pasture-grazed and grass-fed animals that, thankfully, provide the milk for most artisanal cheeses and butters produced in the United States and Europe.

Seasonal fluctuations in milk greatly influence the flavor, texture and aroma of cheeses. The information on cheese production in Chapter Three taught us that cheesemaking is reliant on the salts, sugars, enzymes, fats, acids and proteins in milk, all of which vary at different times of the year, or due to natural bodily cycles of birth, lactation and age. Milk-bearing animals also cope with changes in weather, feed, and forage, external factors that result in changes in the amount of milk produced, its fat content, and flavor.

Milkfat content rises and falls with the lactation cycle, and according to how hot it is (cows give less milk when they're overheated and stressed). Milk that is higher in fat and protein is produced during autumn and winter; a low-fiber pasture diet of tender grasses in the spring and the heat and humidity of summer result in milk that is more watery. Higher milkfat often results in creamier cheeses, and changes in nutrition affect the presence of bacteria that spur fermentation during the cheesemaking process.

Seasonal variations in milk affect the saltiness, sourness, and bitterness of cheese, as well as the flavor and quality of the whey. What the animal ate influences the flavor of the cheese, and this often varies by season as well. For instance, cheeses made from the spring milking of pasture-fed cows that ate garlic shoots and dandelions will exhibit hints of greenness and garlic, as well as a golden color. Goat cheese made from autumn milk of goats that ate high, dry grasses and nuts that fell from a tree can have a toasty flavor, contributed by the nuts and the golden grasses.

Some highly perishable cheeses are only available at particular times of the year, when they are at their peak, before they age too much; others are made in correspondence with festivals or animal events—or

HERE ARE SOME LISTS OF FOODS COMMONLY ASSOCIATED WITH A PARTICULAR SEASON.

SPRING	SUMMER	AUTUMN	WINTER
artichokes	wild Pacific salmon	cranberries	quinces
asparagus	shad	apples	grapefruit
Fava beans	basil	pears	Brussels sprouts
blood oranges	blackberries	runner beans	black truffles
lemons	blueberries	lima beans	cardoons
soft-shell crabs	raspberries	broccoli rabe	cabbage
cucumbers	melons	celery root	chocories and endives
fiddlehead ferns	cantaloupe	chestnuts	kumquats
green garlic	cherries	chanterelles	greens
ramps	sweet corn	figs	kale
lamb	frozen desserts	grapes	parsnips
shoots and sprouts (pea, sunflower, amaranth)	peaches	garlic	potatoes
	nectarines	duck	rosemary
lettuces	peppers	dates	winter squash
mint	plums	leeks	sweet potatoes
morels	zucchini	mushrooms	turnips
nettles	squash blossoms	persimmons	lamb and veal shanks
peas	yellow squash	pomegranates	short ribs
new potatoes	tomatoes	pumpkins	warm spices (cinnamon, allspice)
sardines	maple syrup	squashes	chocolate
sorrel	pineapples	rabbits	stewing
strawberries	mangoes	radishes	braising
apricots	coconut	turkey	celeriac
fresh herbs	watercress	venison	fennel
pistachios	saffron	sunchokes	sunchokes
wild mushrooms	grilling	currants	salsify
roasting	searing	gooseberries	dried beans
avocados	arugula	halibut	lentils and dried fruits
carrots	celery	stewing	
cucumbers	halibut	cauliflower	
dandelion greens	eggplant	white truffles	
haricot verts	porcinis		
rhubarb	butter beans		
fresh butter	chard		
eggs are more abundant.	lychees		
	watermelon		
	lemon verbena		

they are reliant on certain temperatures, which only happen at certain times of the year.

Some cheeses keep well; these tend to be harder, or have longer aging processes.

Foods That Have no Season

Farm-raised animals, fish and birds are available year-round, as "harvest" of these is timed in waves, so there is a fresh supply of meat regardless of season. These include: beef, veal, lamb, pork, buffalo, ostrich, elk, venison, chicken, guinea hen, quail, duck, abalone, arctic char, barramundi, catfish, crayfish, scallops, mussels, oysters, striped bass, tilapia, shrimp, sturgeon and paddlefish caviar, trout, and clams. In addition, many fish are fished year-round, and these include: black sea bass, bluefish, striped bass, Pacific cod, croaker, Petrale sole, grouper, Haddock, marlin, opah, rockfish, snapper, swordfish, and wahoo.

Fruits and vegetables produced in greenhouses or other artificially-conditioned systems are also immune to seasonality. Tomatoes sold in the United States are commonly raised in greenhouses.

CHEESES THAT ARE GOOD ALL YEAR LONG:

Bel Paese, Brillat-Savarin, Caciocavallo, Camembert, Cantal, Chabichou, Cheddar, Cheshire, Comte, Crème de Gruyere, Derby, Edam, Emmenthal, Excelsior, Feta, Fontainbleau, Gjetost, Gloucester, Gorgonzola, Gouda, Gruyere, Lancashire, Limburger, Liptauer, Manchego, Mimolette, Mozzarella, Munster, Neufchatel, Parmesan, pecorino, Port-Salut, Provolone, Reblochon, Ricotta, Saint-Nectaire, Sardo, Scamorze, Stracchino, Tilsitt, Tomme.

THESE CHEESES ARE BEST WHEN CONSUMED IN SUMMER TO LATE-FALL (MAY TO NOVEMBER):	THESE CHEESES ARE BEST WHEN CONSUMED IN LATE FALL TO MID-SPRING (NOVEMBER TO APRIL):
Blue farmhouse cheeses, Bleu d'Auvergne, Cabecou, Cachat, Caerphilly, Chabichou, Chevrotin, crottin de chavignol, Dauphin, Epoisses, Fontina, Livarot, Laguiole, Pave d'Auge, veined cheeses, Ribbesdale, Roquefort, Saint-Marcellin, Saint-Nectaire, Sancerre, English soft cheeses, Sharpham, Vacherin.	Appenzell, Asiago, Beaufort, Blue des Causses, Brie, Cheshire, Farmhouse Cheddar, Gapron, Pont l'Eveque, Stilton, Vacherin, Vendome, Reblochon, chevre, Stilton, Single Gloucester, Cabrales

Fruit	JAN	FEB	MAR	APR	MAY	JUN
APPLE/ BRAEBURN, CAMEO, GALA, GOLDEN DELICIOUS, GRANNY SMITH, RED DELICIOUS	●	●	●	●	●	●
APPLE/ CORTLAND	●	●	●	●		
APPLE/ CRABAPPLES	●	●	●	●	●	●
APPLE/ CRISPIN, MCINTOSH	●	●	●	●	●	●
APPLE/ EMPIRE	●	●	●	●	●	●
APPLE/ IDA RED APPLE	●	●	●	●	●	●
APPLE/ JONAGOLD	●	●	●	●		
APPLE/ JONATHAN	●					
APPLE/ LADY	●					
APPLE/ NORTHERN SPY	●	●	●			
APPLE/ PINK LADY	●	●	●			
APPLE/ ROME, STAYMAN WINESAP, YORK	●					
APPLE/ WINESAP	●					
APRICOTS					●	●
APRIUM					●	●
BANANA (IMPORT YEAR ROUND)	●	●	●	●	●	●
BERRY/ BLACKBERRY						●
BERRY/ BLUEBERRY				●	●	●
KUMQUAT	●	●	●			
BERRY/ RED, BLACK, WHITE CURRANTS			●	●	●	●
BERRY/ GOOSEBERRY			●	●	●	●
BERRY/ LOGANBERRY						●
BERRY/ ELDERBERRY BERRY						●
BERRY GOLDEN RASPBERRY						●
RED RASPBERRY PEAK						●
BERRY/ RED RASPBERRY	●	●	●	●	●	●
BERRY/ STRAWBERRIES (IMPORTED)	●	●				
BERRY/ STRAWBERRIES		●	●	●	●	●
BERRY/ WILD STRAWBERRIES				●	●	●
CACTUS OR PRICKLY PEAR				●	●	●
CHERIMOYA (CUSTARD APPLE)				●	●	●
CHERRIES/ BING, RAINIER, MONTMORENC						●

	JAN	FEB	MAR	APR	MAY	JUN

Fruit	JAN	FEB	MAR	APR	MAY	JUN
CITRON	●					
CLEMENTINE	●	●				
COCONUT	●	●	●	●		
DATES (DEGLET NOOR, MEDJOOL, THOORY, ZAHIDI)	●	●	●	●	●	●
FEIJOA (PINEAPPLE GUAVA)	●	●				
FEIJOA (PINEAPPLE GUAVA)				●	●	●
FIGS/ MISSION					●	●
FIGS/BROWN TURKEY					●	●
FIGS/KADOTA					●	●
GRAPEFRUIT/ PINK, RUBY OR RED	●	●				
GRAPES/ CHAMPAGNE						●
GRAPES/ BLACK	●	●				
GRAPES/ GREEN, RED					●	●
GRAPES/ GLOBE	●	●				
GRAPES/ MUSCAT (IMPORTED)			●	●	●	●
GRAPES/ MUSCATO						●
GUAVA			●	●		
GUAVA						●
HORNED MELON	●	●			●	●
JACKFRUIT					●	●
KUMQUAT		●	●	●		
LAVENDER						●
LEMONS/ EUREKA AND LISBON	●	●	●			
LEMONS/ MEYER	●	●				
LIMES/ PERSIAN	●	●	●			
LIMES/ KEY						●
LONGAN	●	●	●	●	●	●
LOQUAT (JAPANESE MEDLAR)			●	●	●	●
LYCHEE					●	●

PEAK SEASON OF FRUITS
IN THE UNITED STATES (unless noted)
Alphabetically from A–L

APPLE/ CORTLAND

APPLE/ CRABAPPLES

APPLE/ CRISPIN, MCINTOSH

APPLE/ EMPIRE

APPLE / GINGER GOLD

APPLE/ GRAVENSTEIN, HONEYCRISP APPLE

APPLE/ IDA RED

APPLE/ JONAGOLD

APPLE/ JONATHAN

APPLE/ LADY APPLE

APPLE/ MACOUN

APPLE/ NORTHERN SPY

APPLE/ PINK LADY

APPLE/ ROME, STAYMAN WINESAP, YORK

APPLE/ WINESAP

PEAK

BERRY/ BOYSENBERRY

BERRY/ MARIONBERRY, MULBERRY

BERRY/ CAPE GOOSEBERRY

BLACK RASPBERRY

JUL	AUG	SEP	OCT	NOV	DEC

CITRON

CLEMENTINE

COCONUT

CRANBERRIES

PEAK

DRAGONFRUIT (PITAYA)

FEIJOA (PINEAPPLE GUAVA)

FIGS/CALIMYRNA

CELESTE FIGS (DEPENDS ON REGIONS)

GRAPES/ BLACK

GRAPES/ CONCORD

GRAPES/ GLOBE

GUAVA

HORNED MELON

JUJUBE (CHINESE DATE)

KIWI

LEMONS/ MEYER

LIMES/ PERSIAN

LIMEQUAT

LONGAN

MANDARIN

MANGOES/ TOMMY ATKINS

MANGOES/ HADEN MANGO

MANGOES/ KENT

MELON/ CANARY, CASABA, CRENSHAW, GALIA AND PERSIAN MELON
MELON/ CANTALOUPE, HONEYDEW
MELON/ CHARENTAIS, SHARLYN, HAMI AND SPRITE
NECTARINES/ WHITE AND YELLOW

ORANGE/ BLOOD
ORANGE/ CARA CARA

ORANGE/ JAFFA
ORANGE/ NAVEL ORANGE
ORANGE/ SEVILLE OR SOUR ORANGE (IMPORT YEAR ROUND)
ORANGE/ VALENCIA
ORANGE/ VOLCANO

ORO BLANCO
PAPAYA: IMPORT YEAR-ROUND IMPORT
PASSIONFRUIT: YEAR-ROUND FROM FLORIDA, JULY TO MARCH FROM CALIFORNIA

PEACHES/ WHITE AND YELLOW
PEACHES/ SATURN PEACHES
PEARS/ BARTLETT, RED BARTLETT, BOSC

PEARS/ BARTLETT, RED BARTLETT, BOSC
PEARS/ COMICE
PEARS/ D'ANJOU
PEARS/ FORELLE

PEARS/ SECKEL

PEARS/ASIAN/ KOREAN PEARS (IMPORT)

JAN	FEB	MAR	APR	MAY	JUN

PINEAPPLE: DOMESTIC AND IMPORTED
PLANTAINS: IMPORT

PLUOTS
PLUMCOTS

POMMELO

RAMBUTAN

STARFRUIT (CARAMBOLA)

TAMARINDO: IMPORT
TANGERINE
TANGERINE/ FAIRCHILD
TANGEL / ORLANDO
TANGELO/ HONEYBELL
TANGELO/ MINNEOLA: (CALIF.) / FEB TO APRIL (FLORIDA)
TANGOR/ HONEY MANDARIN
TANGOR/ HONEY MURCOTT
TANGOR/ TEMPLE

TOMATILLO (TREE TOMATO): IMPORT
UGLIFRUIT (CALIF.)   UGLIFRUIT: IMPORT

WATERMELON

PEAK SEASON OF FRUITS
IN THE UNITED STATES (unless noted)
Alphabetically from M–Z

MAMEY SAPOTE

MANDARIN/ SATSUMA

MANDARIN

MANGOES/ KETIT

ORANGE/ BLOOD
ORANGE/ CARA CARA
ORANGE/ HAMLIN ORANGE
ORANGE/ JAFFA ORANGE
ORANGE/ NAVEL ORANGE
ORANGE/ SEVILLE OR SOUR

ORO BLANCO

PAWPAWS
PEACHES/ INDIAN

PEARS/ COMICE
PEARS/ D'ANJOU
PEARS/ FORELLE
PEARS/ KIEFFER
PEARS/ SECKEL
PEARS/ASIAN/ YALI (IMPORTED)
PEARS/ ASIAN: IN UNITED STATES
PEARS/ASIAN/ KOREAN (IMPORT)
PERSIMMONS/ FUYU AND HACHIYA

JUL	AUG	SEP	OCT	NOV	DEC

DINOSAUR EGG PLUOT

POMMELO

PLUM/ ELEPHANT HEART
PLUM/ ITALIAN PRUNE PLUM (LATE SUMMER)
PLUM/ SANTA ROSA
POMEGRANATE
QUINCE
RAMBUTAN

TANGERINE
TANGERINE/ FAIRCHILD
TANGEL / ORLANDO
TANGELO/ MINNEOLA: (CALIF.)

UGLIFRUIT: IMPORT   UGLIFRUIT: (CALIF.)

YUZU

	JAN	FEB	MAR	APR	MAY	JUN
AMARANTH						
ARTICHOKES						
ARUGULA						
ASPARAGUS/ WHITE: IMPORT FROM EUROPE						
ASPARAGUS/ PURPLE: IMPORTED FROM EUROPE YEAR-ROUND		U.S. PEAK				
ASPARAGUS/ GREEN				PEAK		
AVOCADO/ HASS AND FUERTE				PEAK		
AVOCADO/ FLORIDA					AVOCADO/ FLORIDA (60 VARIETIES)	
CARDOONS						
CARROTS						
BAMBOO SHOOTS: IMPORTED FROM ASIA						
BEANS/ CRANBERRY BEANS						
BEANS/ FAVA						
BEANS/ LIMA (BUTTER)						
BEANS/ FRESH GARBANZO						
BEANS/COMMON SHELL (BLACK TURTLE,						
BEANS/ SNAP BEANS (GREEN BEANS, STRING BEANS, HARICOT VERTS): IMPORT YEAR-ROUND					BEANS/ SNAP (U.S.A.)	
BELL PEPPERS						
BEET						
BITTER MELON						
BOK CHOY, CHOY SUM, GAI CHOY						
BROCCOLINI						
BURDOCK						
CABBAGE/ NAPA, RED AND SAVOY						
CELERY						
CELERIAC (CELERY ROOT)						
CHARD/ GREEN, RED AND RAINBOW						
CHILES						
CHILES						
CHINESE BROCCOLI (GAI LAN)						
CORN						
CUCUMBER						
CUCUMBER/ LEMON						
CUCUMBER/ PICKLING						

	JAN	FEB	MAR	APR	MAY	JUN
DANDELION (PEAK)						
EGGPLANT						
EGGPLANT/ CHINESE, JAPANESE, THAI						
EGGPLANT/ WHITE						
ENDIVES AND CHICORIES (BELGIAN, CURLY ENDIVE, CATALONIA, PUNTARELLE, FRISEE, ESCAROLE, RED BELGIAN)						
RADICCHIOS (ROSSO DI CHIOGGIA, TREVISO, DI VERONA, TARDIVO, CASTELFRANCO)						
FENNEL						
FIDDLEHEAD FERNS						
GALANGAL						
GALANGAL						
GARLIC/ COMMON AND ELEPHANT: YEAR-ROUND, HARVESTED IN EARLY SUMMER AND AGAIN IN LATE FALL						
GARLIC/ GREEN						
GARLIC SCAPES: SPRING						
GARLIC/ ROCAMBOLE						
GREENS/ BEET, COLLARD, SPINACH , PEAKS DECEMBER TO APRIL						
GREENS/ TURNIP						
GREENS/ MUSTARD						
HEARTS OF PALM						
HORSERADISH						
JICAMA: IMPORT						
KOHLRABI						
LEEK				LEEK		
LEMONGRASS						
LOTUS ROOT: IMPORT						
MALANGA: IMPORT						
MICROGREENS (MIZUNA, TAT SOI)					PEAK	
MUSHROOMS/ BEECH, CREMINI, ENOKI, WHITE, MAIITAKE, MATSUTAKES. OYSTER, PORTOBELLO, SHIITAKE, WOOD EAR						
MUSHROOMS/ HEDGEHOG						
MUSHROOMS/ CHANTERELLE						
MUSHROOMS/ MOREL						
MUSHROOMS/ PORCINI						

PEAK SEASON OF VEGETABLES
IN THE UNITED STATES (unless noted)
Alphabetically from A–M

ARTICHOKES

PEAK

CARDOONS

BEANS/ CRANBERRY BEANS

ROMANO, BORLOTTI, HARICOT VERTS, PURPLE & YELLOW WAX, DRAGON TONGUE)

BEANS/ SNAP: IMPORT

PEAK

BRUSSELS SPROUTS

CELERIAC (CELERY ROOT)

.... (ANAHEIM, BANANA, CHERRY BELL, CHILACA, CUBANELLE, HUNGARIAN, FRESNO, HABANERO, JALAPENO)
.... (MANZANA, PASILLA, POBLANO, SCOTCH BONNET, SERRANO, THAI, BIRD'S EYE, YELLOW)

JUL	AUG	SEP	OCT	NOV	DEC

EDAMAME (FALL)

PEAK
PEAK
PEAK

GARLIC/ GREEN

GARLIC/ ROCAMBOLE

GREENS/ TURNIP
GREENS/ MUSTARD

3EHOG

MUSHROOMS/ CHANTERELLE
MUSHROOMS/ LOBSTER

MUSHROOMS/ PORCINI

NETTLES
NOPALES
OKRA

ONIONS/ APAZ

ONIONS/ MAUI SWEET

ONIONS/ OSO SWEETS
ONIONS/ PEARL

ONIONS/ RED

ONIONS/ TEXAS 1015s

ONIONS/ TEXAS SWEET

ONIONS/ VIDALIA

ONIONS/ WALLA-WALLA

PARSNIP
PEAS/ BLACK-EYED (SOUTHERNPEA, COWPEA) PEAS

PEAS/ ENGLISH

PEAS/ PEA SHOOTS

PEAS/ PEA GREENS: LATE WINTER, EARLY SPRING

PEAS/ SNOW
PEAS/ SUGAR SNAP

RAMPS

POTATOES/ FINGERLING

POTATOES/ NEW

POTATOES/ RUSSET AND CREAMER

RADICCHIO

RADICCHIO

RADISHES/ BREAKFAST, FRENCH AND SMA

RADISHES/ BLACK AND WATERMELON, DAIKON (FALL AND WINTER)
RAPINI (BROCCOLI RABE)

RHUBARB

RUTABAGA
SALSIFY: IMPORT
SEA BEANS: IMPORT

SEA VEGETABLES

SHALLOT

JAN	FEB	MAR	APR	MAY	JUN

SQUASH BLOSSOMS

SUNCHOKES

TURNIPS

WINTER MELON

SQUASH/ ACORN

SQUASH/ BABY CROOKNECK, BABY GOLD BAR, PATTYPAN, BABY ZUCCHINI

SQUASH/ BANANA

SQUASH/ BUTTERNUT

SQUASH/ CHAYOTE, MIRILTON
SQUASH/ CROOKNECK

SQUASH/ GOLDBAR

SQUASH/ KABOCHA

SQUASH/ SPAGHETTI

SQUASH/ SUMMER GREEN, SUMMER YELLOW

SQUASH/ ZUCCA (LATE FALL AND WINTER)

SQUASH/ ZUCCHINI

SUNCHOKE (JERUSALEM ARTICHOKE):
SWEET POTATOES...
JAPANESE SWEET POTATOES
TARO (DASHEEN)
TURMERIC
WASABI
WATER CHESTNUTS, IMPORT YEAR-ROUND, DOMESTIC PEAK IN SUMMER AND FALL   DOMESTIC PEAK IN SUMMER AND FALL
WATER SPINACH

PEAK SEASON OF VEGETABLES
IN THE UNITED STATES (unless noted)
Alphabetically from N–Z

FRESH OLIVES

OLIVE OIL HARVEST

OLIVE OIL HARVEST

ONIONS/ PEARL   PEAK

PEAK

POTATOES/ FINGERLING

PUMPKINS

RADISHES/ BLACK AND WATERMELON, DAIKON (FALL AND WINTER)

RAPINI (BROCCOLI RABE)

RUTABAGA

PEAK

JUL	AUG	SEP	OCT	NOV	DEC

SUNCHOKES

SUNFLOWERS

TURNIPS

SQUASH/ ACORN

SQUASH/ BANANA

SQUASH/ BUTTERCUP

SQUASH/ BUTTERNUT

SQUASH/ CARNIVAL

SQUASH/ CUSHAW, DELICATA

SQUASH/ GOLD NUGGET, HUBBARD

SQUASH/ KABOCHA

SQUASH/ KURI

SQUASH/ SPAGHETTI

SQUASH/ SWEET DUMPLING, TURBAN

SQUASH/ ZUCCA (LATE FALL AND WINTER)

SUNCHOKE (JERUSALEM ARTICHOKE):

SWEET POTATOES (JEWEL, GARNET AND JERSEY)

JAPANESE SWEET POTATOES

COD
FLOUNDER

HALIBUT

JOHN DORY

MAHI-MAHI

WILD SALMON/KING

WILD SALMON/PACIFIC

WILD SALMON/STEELHEAD
SARDINES (WINTER)
SEA BASS

SEA TROUT

YELLOWFIN TUNA

CRABS/ BLUE: THE SEASON MIGRATES UP THE EASTERN COAST OF THE U.S.

CRABS/ DUNGENESS

AMERICAN LOBSTER

SPINY LOBSTER
OYSTERS   OYSTERS
SCALLOPS/ NANTUCKET BAY
SCALLOPS/ DIVER

SHRIMP...

SQUID
SOFT SHELL CRABS

STONE CRAB

JAN	FEB	MAR	APR	MAY	JUN

YOUNG LAMB (3-4 MOS): CALIFORNIA   YOUNG LAMB (THREE TO FOUR MONTHS)
LAMB (OLDER THAN FOUR MONTHS): YEAR-ROUND
PARTRIDGE
PHEASANT
RABBIT

NUTS/ GREEN ALMONDS

NUTS/ PECANS

PEAK SEASON FOR NUTS, MEATS, POULTRY,
SHELLFISH, & FISH IN THE UNITED STATES
(unless noted)

ANCHOVIES

BLUEFISH

DOVER SOLE

FISH/ HERRING

MULLET

WILD SALMON/COHO

WILD SALMON/SOCKEYES

WILD SALMON/STEELHEAD

SEA BASS

TURBOT

CRABS/ DUNGENESS

CRABS/ KING

OYSTERS

SCALLOPS/ NANTUCKET BAY

SCALLOPS/ DIVER

VARIES BY REGION. GEORGIA, FLORIDA SUMMER

STONE CRAB

JUL	AUG	SEP	OCT	NOV	DEC

WILD DUCK

BLACK BEANS

WILD RICE

NUTS/ ALMONDS

NUTS/ CHESTNUTS

NUTS/ HAZELNUTS

NUTS/ PECANS

NUTS/ WALNUTS

To Summarize...

Understanding how the food system and seasonality can improve the flavor, color and complexity of the food you prepare will help you create a unique dining experience for your guests in any venue. This knowledge will enhance food pairings, allow you to keep the bottom line low by purchasing what's plentiful in season, ground your restaurant in a sense of place, or to meet the expectations of guests who grow ever more sophisticated in their tastes. Seek this information by talking to farmers, distributors and other chefs and digging in to the wealth of titles and articles on the subject; reading and talking build great ideas!

Chapter 5 Assessment Questions

❶ During which months of the year are strawberries at their peak in California? In New Jersey? In Minnesota? How did you find this information?

_____

_____

_____

_____

_____

❷ What are some causes of energy consumption relating to industrial agriculture?

_____

_____

_____

_____

_____

❸ Name three benefits of seasonal cooking.

_____

_____

_____

_____

_____

❹ Does seasonal cooking or local sourcing ensure food safety?

_____

_____

_____

_____

❺ Create a menu item featuring local foods for the time of year you are answering this question.

_____

_____

_____

_____

_____

UNIT 2/

THE GAMES

All of the games in this book are focused on allowing you to practice and improve under different competency areas. Some will be very realistic exercises closely resembling real-world applications. For example, many guests have dietary restrictions so a game challenging you to eliminate certain food items from a menu is highly realistic and practical. Other games will challenge you to improve your skills in general but may not be related to a real-world situation. For example, preparing a menu without speaking to your classmates or coworkers allows you to realize the importance of communication and improve non-verbal forms of communication. But, of course, it is a rare kitchen where speaking is banned. Nevertheless, like the actor who plays an unlikely character or a jazz musician who plays some dissonant chords to experiment, such skills building can give you portable skills to apply when needed. So have fun, good luck, and improvise!

6/
Problem Solving Games

Foodservice operation owners and managers look for problem solving skills in their employees. Chefs and managers are busy women and men and rely on a staff that can take the initiative to solve problems on the ground level.

CHAPTER OBJECTIVES

By the end of these games you should be able to:

① Demonstrate problem solving skills in the kitchen.

② Adapt a basic recipe (platform) to one or more situations such as cuisine style and/or dining scenario.

③ Improvise using available ingredients and equipment.

④ Use your understanding of platforms to create appropriate concepts.

⑤ List and explain some potential problems in a foodservice environment and how they could be solved.

⑥ Design and implement a dish or menu within a set of constraining parameters.

While:

❼ Demonstrating effective communication with team members.

❽ Demonstrating appropriate knife skills.

❾ Demonstrating appropriate cooking techniques.

❿ Demonstrating appropriate kitchen sanitation and safety procedures.

⓫ Demonstrating appropriate seasoning and flavor balance.

⓬ Cultivating advanced culinary technique.

Does the owner need to know that a restroom is soiled, that a diner was unhappy with the doneness of her steak or that a credit card was rejected at the cash register? These are problems that can be quickly solved by employees who take initiative and ownership of the problems. Foodservice operators are happy to have team members who can think on their feet and get the problems solved. When the problems are bigger—a food order doesn't arrive before dinner service, a guest claims he suffered a case of food-borne illness at the establishment, or the truck breaks down on the way to catering an off-premise event—effective problem solving can make or break an operation.

An example: In class there was a power failure, causing the kitchen to go dark, with only a few emergency lights remaining. There was palpable relief among the class—it was a tough night in an introductory hot foods class with an ambitious menu and a demanding chef-instructor. The chef let out a sigh of frustration and the students imagined themselves chatting casually on the quad until the power was restored. A few students began to put products away and remove their aprons. The chef responded, "Where do you think you're going? We have people to feed! Do you think your guests won't be hungry because it's dark? Get to work!" They cooked by the dim emergency lights and were held to the same standard of excellence as we would have been under ideal conditions. The lesson is clear: problems happen but must be quickly dealt with. A problem is not an excuse to falter on service excellence. If anything, it is even more important to provide excellent hospitality when problems occur.

Problems are unfortunately a common and unavoidable feature of business so it might be helpful to establish a working definition of the word **problem**. A definition that we like is that **a problem is a negative difference between what is expected and what is provided.** If you think about problems in your life, most of them will fall into this situation.

FOOD for THOUGHT   Think about a problem you had in your life. Describe it. Does it fit into the definition given above? What was the difference between what you expected and what was provided?

_____

_____

_____

_____

_____

_____

_____

_____

_____

_____

_____

For example, it is a problem in a restaurant when a food order does not arrive on time from the purveyor. The problem is this negative difference between what is expected and what is provided. The expectation of the restaurant is to have the food delivered by, perhaps, noon. But what is provided is a five PM delivery, not allowing ample prep time before service. To take another example, a bride and groom who pay $50 per guest for Beef Wellington at their wedding expect a hot, beautifully presented, perfectly-cooked tenderloin of beef inside a pastry crust.

If there is chicken, raw steak, or the cook's wedding ring inside the crust, there is a problem—a negative difference between the couple's expectations for the dish and what was provided.

Conversely, when there is a positive difference between expectations and what is provided, you can create a great experience that truly wows your guests. When an unremarkable hole-in-the-wall restaurant provides the best barbecue you have ever tasted; when you expect a long wait at a restaurant but are immediately ushered to a table with a great view; when the sommelier's unusual recommendation pairs perfectly with your dessert; or you have perfectly cooked and seasoned, beautifully presented food on your hospital tray, there is a positive difference between what you expect and what is provided. There is always room in what you do to create a positive difference in the experience you provide your customer.

Being a good chef or food service manager is really about managing problems in two ways: preventing them from happening in the first place and dealing deftly with those that inevitably arise. By hiring the right people, providing first-rate employee training, having a facility that is well-designed with ample space, maintaining a clean and sanitary facility, buying excellent ingredients and structuring an appealing menu that provides good value, you can avoid having many problems in the first place. For example, an experienced and dedicated employee trained in sanitation might prevent a problem for a restaurant by preventing food-borne illness. But even chefs from the best operations tell us about problems that they cannot avoid or those that arise unexpectedly. Such problems are of course unexpected and can consist of nearly any scenario—a guest with strict dietary restrictions, equipment failures or limitations, problems with product quality or availability, a breakdown in communication, or even a personality problem can be challenges.

A good team member can transform this negative difference between expectation and what is provided into a positive one. Let us present a final example of how this transition may occur. When Jon, one of this book's authors, was new to industry, he cooked in a cramped 70-seat restaurant with only a six-burner stove and single oven, making the dinner rush tough to manage. The problem then was that the expectation of the cook is to have an ample cooking service to prepare multiple meals simultaneously and efficiently. The negative difference between the reality and this expectation resulted in a problem. Similarly guests at that restaurant had an expectation that they could arrive at any point in the evening and receive a wonderfully prepared meal within a reasonable timeframe, perhaps twenty minutes. The solution to the problem was to move some of the burden from the kitchen to the server and garde manger stations by focusing on a quick appetizer menu that featured freshly prepared soups, salads and cold appetizers. That way guests could get good food fast and the burden at the stove and oven was more evenly distributed. Ultimately these changes turned the negative discrepancy between expectation and reality into a positive one.

FOOD for THOUGHT

Imagine you are a restaurant chef facing a particular problem. Describe the problem and how you might change this negative difference in expectation and reality into a positive one for you and the guest.

_____

_____

_____

_____

_____

_____

_____

_____

_____

_____

_____

_____

_____

_____

From the Line: Case Study

PASTRY CHEF LEI SHISHAK, STONEHILL TAVERN, DANA POINT, CALIFORNIA

Before becoming a pastry chef, Lei Shishak studied the sciences for her pre-med college major and worked in the marketing department of a large financial institution. Chef Lei has been able to cross-pollinate the skills she gathered from her education and work experiences. What she has used most are problem-solving skills.

Critical thinking within the world of medicine revolves around the use of a decision tree. Essentially, the philosophy of solving medical problems uses a series of deductions to lead to the most fitting diagnosis. This thought process can also be applied to the kitchen. When faced with a predicament or situation in the kitchen, there are a certain number of possible solutions one can implement to resolve it. Chef Lei explains, "When baking, if I'm missing an ingredient, I ask myself, 'What are the recipe's components and what is the missing ingredient's role?' I can either find something to mimic the role of the missing food or make it from other ingredients."

Like her pre-med studies, baking revolves around science. In both fields, Chef Lei applies formulas, science, and math skills to the process

of critical thinking. Problem solving skills are similar and applicable in the kitchen.

"There is no such thing in our kitchen as '86'ing a menu item. You have to make more... and quickly!" Often times this rule has put Chef Lei in a situation where she has to solve a problem rapidly. "A customer has ordered an item and they are waiting for it. You have to think quick and sometimes that means solving the problem of not having that dish made. The only solution at that point is to make it quickly!" For example, Chef Lei was plating a dessert that used crème anglais. She discovered that the crème anglais had soured and couldn't take the time to make more in the middle of the dinner rush. She asked herself, "What is crème anglais made of?" She quickly recognized that it has the same components as vanilla ice cream. Chef Lei slightly melted ice cream and added a touch of cream to adjust the texture. Without fail, the solution served well throughout the evening's dinner service.

On another occasion, Chef Lei realized mid-recipe that she had run out of buttermilk. She asked herself, "What does the buttermilk add, so what component needs to be replaced?" Sour. She solved her problem by simply adding vinegar to milk, to impart acidity, saving the recipe.

On a cold winter morning Chef Lei came into work at 6 a.m. to make bread and discovered that the proofers were not functioning. The kitchen was too cold for the dough to rise. Chef Lei used her ingenuity and her problem solving skills to identify and create the warmest environment possible within the restaurant. With dough in hand, Chef Lei grabbed a couple of trash bags and towels she soaked in hot water. She placed the wet warm towels inside the trash bags, along with the dough and sealed the bags tightly. In no time at all, Chef Lei was pleased to see that the dough had risen and could be used that day.

Temperature was the source of yet another problem Chef Lei had to solve. When first learning to make biscuits, Chef Lei learned the hard way that the butter had to be particularly soft in order to cut it into the dough. While Chef Lei was in the process of making the dough, she realized that the butter was too cold and was going to cause a problem in the final result of the biscuit. Chef Lei determined that she needed to cut the butter into a fine texture in order to save the consistency of the recipe. She used a cheese grater to shred the butter and then added it to the dough—which worked perfectly!

Chef Lei believes that an important part of developing problem-solving skills involves experimentation, the opportunity to make mistakes and to learn in a safe environment, the goals of this book. In culinary school, Chef Lei learned her pastry skills by reading a recipe at night, reviewing the recipe in the morning, and then preparing the recipe in class. She recalls having particular difficulty when learning to prepare buttercream. When making buttercream, it is important for the butter to be soft in order for it to blend with ease. Chef Lei had no way of knowing this fact until she was in the process of making it for class and it was too late. She was embarrassed when the buttercream didn't blend well. Her instructor took one look at her buttercream, made her throw it away, and asked her to start over. Since she was working with a partner, the partner's grade was also affected. Chef Lei felt terrible. She stayed in the kitchen and made the buttercream over and over again until she was able to find the proper consistency.

Chef Lei compares problem solving to walking in the dark with a flashlight; "You point the flashlight in front of you. You see what's ahead and then you move on." To apply this analogy to problem solving in the kitchen, first see the challenge in front of you, then use your analytical skills to decide how to move forward. Today, Chef Lei solves problems daily by using the lessons she learned in culinary school, in addition to trial and error. She was thrilled to participate in this interview and contribute to this book because she truly wishes that there would have been a book teaching her these problem solving skills and an open-minded classroom kitchen when she was in culinary school!

Today, the problem solving for Chef Lei continues. Lei wanted to create a flaming flan. When she tried to make the flan the first couple times, she struggled with the alcohol. First there was too little alcohol to make the flame stay lit. Then when she got the flame the right size, she realized that she used too much alcohol to make the dessert cost effective in production. As of this writing, Chef Lei was still struggling with solving this problem—but we're confident she'll solve it!

CASE STUDY Questions

❶ Were you impressed with any of the solutions that Chef Lei used to solve problems in her kitchen? Why or why not?

_____

_____

_____

_____

_____

❷ Give an example from your own life of when a problem turned into an unexpected opportunity.

_____

_____

_____

_____

_____

❸ As Chef Lei relies on her science background, what skills or early learning from your life has informed your decision-making in the kitchen?

_____

_____

_____

_____

❹ Point to a potentially negative situation that Chef Lei converted to a positive experience, and explain how.

_____

_____

_____

_____

❺ Give an example of a kitchen trick or substitution that you've used to solve a problem as Chef Lei did. How did you think of it?

_____

_____

_____

_____

Game: Hands-On Eating

The Scenario

Reservations for the college foundation's annual fundraising dinner are going swimmingly. As the caterers for the event, you've designed a fabulous menu that includes elaborate platters, soup, salad, entrée and dessert. The menu will impress the guests and showcase your culinary talents:

> *Cheese and Crudités Platters with Vegetable and Ice Carvings*
>
> *Seafood Bisque*
>
> *Salad with Spring Roll and Soy Miso Vinaigrette*
>
> *Navarin of Lamb with Baby Vegetables*
>
> *Molten Chocolate Cakes*

But there's a problem: The room only seats about 200 donors for a sit-down dinner but already reservations are topping 300. The fundraising director comes to you and humbly explains the situation. It would be a bad thing to turn down so many potential donors. With 300 guests instead of 200 you can increase your revenue by 50 percent. But no alternate space is available.

The client has a creative solution to the problem. What if the entire menu were able to be served butler-style as passed hors d'oeuvres? This would eliminate the need for large tables and could pack the donors in for a creative and swanky event. Are you up to the task?

In this game, Hands-on Eating, your team is required to adapt two food items from the menu that can be eaten neatly out of hand. To make things more interesting, no plates or bowls allowed! You can depart from the menu significantly but some aspect of the original menu item needs to be clearly recognizable.

Activity:

Design an alternate menu that you think would be appropriate for an event like this one.

_____

_____

_____

_____

_____

Game Details

This game is for a student with medium to advanced skills. You should be comfortable in a kitchen and be familiar with basic preparations and applications, at minimum. There is no maximum skill level. Even professional chefs have fun with and are challenged by this game.

In this game you are challenged to think creatively to solve a problem—how to adapt a traditional menu to be eaten out of hand. How far you deviate from the original menu depends on your creativity. The main rules are:

- Your menu item must reflect the original menu in some way.
- No plates or bowls and the food item should be capable of being eaten entirely hand-held.
- Don't be so obsessed with the engineering of the hand-held item that you forget to make it taste wonderful!

Game Specifications

ANTICIPATED TIME:	3–4 HOUR LAB
Concept Presentation	20 minutes
Student Planning and Station Set-up	30 minutes
Cooking	80–140 minutes
Tasting, Discussion and Debriefing	30 minutes
Clean-up	20 minutes

Ingredients Needed

Note: students should form teams of 2-3. Depending on class size all or part of the menu may be used. Quantities are recommended for a class of 18 and should be adjusted depending on class size, time allowed and how much of the menu is being used. Finally, keep in mind that the original menu from the game description need not be made – an alternate from the instructor or the student activity could be substituted—and additional items are included to encourage creativity in adapting these items to be hand-held.

In addition to a variety of pantry items and staples always on hand (see p. 67):

CHEESE AND CRUDITÉS PLATTERS WITH VEGETABLE AND ICE CARVINGS	SEAFOOD BISQUE	SALAD WITH SPRING ROLL AND SOY MISO VINAIGRETTE	NAVARIN OF LAMB WITH BABY VEGETABLES
About 2 pounds of assorted cheeses About 3 pounds of assorted vegetables	About 1.5 pounds assorted seafood 1 pt. heavy cream 2 qt. fish stock	About 1 lb. assorted salad greens About 1 lb. of other vegetables—carrot, red pepper, daikon, cucumber, bean sprouts Small amounts of soy sauce, miso, rice wine vinegar, mirin, peanut oil, sesame oil, vegetable oil, chili oil garlic, ginger and scallions Spring roll wrappers About ½ lb. of ground pork or shrimp, if desired	About 2 lb. lamb shoulder About 1 qt. brown stock About 1 lb. turnips About 1 lb. assorted baby vegetables

MOLTEN CHOCOLATE CAKES	OTHER POSSIBLE INGREDIENTS	SPECIAL EQUIPMENT NEEDS
About 8 ounces semi-sweet chocolate About 1 cup heavy cream About ½ lb. flour About ½ lb. sugar 1 dozen eggs Small amounts of baking powder	Puff pastry Phyllo dough Belgian endive, red leaf Romaine lettuce or spinach Nori Lasagne pasta	Skewers Toothpicks Assorted Flatware

Student Guidelines

- **Safety First.** Put knife safety and safe food handling at the fore. Wash hands frequently, keep station clean and organized and observe time and temperature requirements for safe food handling.
- Use the tools in the flavor chapter to help you brainstorm initial ideas and guide you through the game. Discuss merits of all suggestions and reach consensus on leading concepts. Develop concept fully, including the engineering of how the item could be hand-held before beginning cooking. Remember that the item must also be served from a passing tray.
- Write a plan for recipe execution. Do not be afraid to alter the design as you go.
- Taste as you go. For unsafe or raw ingredients, cook a small sample to determine seasoning balance and flavor.
- Divide the prep work among the team.
- Maintain constant communication.
- Present finished product in a way that is visually appealing and is served at the appropriate temperature. Use the plating template in the activity tear-out as a guide.
- Keep an eye on the clock—start long-cooking items immediately and quickly assemble your mise-en-place.

Supporting Activities

Which menu item or items will you work on for this activity?

_____

_____

_____

_____

_____

_____

What is the essence of the item that you think must be preserved during the variation?

_____

_____

_____

_____

_____

_____

Sketch some ideas regarding how to turn a menu item into a handheld one.

Refine your ideas.

What engineering considerations come into play in making your item a handheld one?

_____

_____

_____

_____

_____

_____

_____

Create a prep list and plan of attack for this game.

_____

_____

_____

_____

_____

_____

_____

_____

_____

_____

_____

Reflection Questions

❶ If you had to grade yourself on your performance on this game, what grade would you give yourself and why?

_____

_____

_____

_____

_____

❷ What did you do that you feel was particularly innovative and worked well?

_____

_____

_____

_____

_____

❸ If you could do it all over again what would you do differently?

_____

_____

_____

_____

_____

❹ What's the most important thing you learned in playing this game?

_____

_____

_____

_____

_____

_____

_____

❺ Describe a real-world application different from the scenario where you might apply something you did in this game.

_____

_____

_____

_____

_____

Variations to Game

This game can be adapted for any number of recipe items and flavor profiles. A different menu could easily be substituted for the one given. To keep the game challenging, the foods in the menu should be those that do not easily lend themselves to being hand-held. Students can work individually or in teams. If time is limited, advance steps can be taken, including cleaning and par-cooking some ingredients or selecting recipes like green salads, more dependent on assembly than cooking. The essential element of the game that should be maintained is the experience of solving this specific problem.

Game: Guess Who's Coming to Dinner

"You are quite a cook. I was here at your restaurant last week. I had the braised pork shank—to die for! No really, you're good. Your food is delicious. And not only that. You have a way with menu design and flavor combinations that make the whole sequence exquisite.

"There are just a few things you need to know before we order. The kids only eat buttered noodles. My husband has allergies to wheat, black pepper and eggs. My daughter's a vegetarian but eats fish and doesn't really like vegetables. I eat everything. But nothing too crunchy—I have a toothache."

For a chef this is an exaggeration of an all too familiar and frustrating but ultimately important conversation. Who are cooks here for if not for guests? But sometimes adapting to their needs can be challenging and frustrating. It is easy to substitute egg whites for whole eggs in making an omelet to accommodate a heart healthy diner. It is much more challenging to ensure that every item on the plate — including stocks, sauces and component ingredients—is entirely free of garlic and black pepper to accommodate a food intolerance.

Customizing recipes to the specific needs of guests is a challenging problem in many cases and is also an important thing we can do as cooks. It is the obligation of the hospitality professional to meet the needs of the guest. A mistake of, for example, forgetting that a vinaigrette is made with peanut oil or that the codfish broth is made with shrimp shells to add flavor and color can be a lethal error, not the best way to get a mention in the local newspaper!

Of course the flip side to this challenge is that chefs spend a lot of time and effort to design menu items and prepare great food. It frustrates us when someone asks for the chicken without the salsa verde, which, we all know, is the best part; asks for mashed potatoes without butter, since they are prepared in advance and taste so much better this way; or messes up our rhythm on the line by asking for a side from one dish to be paired with a center-of-plate item from another. Many cooks find guests who have these special requests to be annoying. Such an attitude reminds me of what our culinary school colleagues jokingly say around registration and advisement time, "This school would be great if it weren't for the pesky students." Just as we know there could be no school without students, there can be no hospitality industry without guests, so accommodating special needs is both the pain and the pleasure.

This game challenges you to take problem solving in accommodating guests to extremes. After this, an allergic, picky or dieting customer in the real world will seem easy! Have fun and good luck!

FOOD for THOUGHT Imagine a guest is allergic to onions. What typical components in an a la carte restaurant would have to be avoided in cooking for this guest if she ordered a roast chicken with pan gravy, roasted potatoes and creamed spinach?

_____

_____

_____

_____

_____

_____

_____

_____

_____

_____

_____

> *Arugula Salad with Red Onion and Parmesan Crostini*
>
> *Sautéed Fish of the Day with Shaved Fennel and Confetti Orzo*
>
> *Crème Brulee*

Here is a standard menu you may use as a starting point:

- Next, cut out the table from the page and randomly draw one card from each column:
- Next, sketch out how you might adapt your menu items to the parameters listed on your cards—one health concern, one quirk and the age of the diner. Age may or may not be a relevant concern.

Game Specifications

ANTICIPATED TIME:	3–4 HOUR LAB
Concept Presentation	20 minutes
Student Planning and Station Set-up	30 minutes
Cooking	80 - 140 minutes
Tasting, Discussion and Debriefing	30 minutes
Clean-up	20 minutes

Ingredients Needed

Note: students should form teams of 2–3. Depending on class size all or part of the menu may be used. Quantities are recommended for a class of 18 and should be adjusted depending on class size, time allowed and how much of the menu is being used. Finally, keep in mind that the original menu from the game description need not be made—one of the instructor's or students' design could be substituted. In addition to a variety of pantry items and staples always on hand:

Game Details

This game is for a student with medium to advanced skills. You should be comfortable in a kitchen and be familiar with basic preparations and applications, at minimum. There is no maximum skill level. Even professional chefs have fun with and are challenged by this game.

In this game you are challenged to think creatively to solve a problem—how to adapt a menu for various constraints ranging from common, everyday challenges, to unlikely scenarios. The main rules are:

- Your adaptation should be as creative as you like but should reference the original menu.
- You most honor every limitation provided in your adaptation.

ARUGULA SALAD WITH RED ONION AND PARMESAN CROSTINI	SAUTÉED FISH OF THE DAY WITH SHAVED FENNEL AND CONFETTI ORZO	CRÈME BRULEE	OTHER POSSIBLE INGREDIENTS, ESPECIALLY FOR VARIATIONS:
3 bunches arugula	One small whole fish per team (good opportunity to practice filleting)	1 qt. Milk	Lactaid
1 red onion		1 pt. Heavy Cream	Soy Milk
1 baguette	2 bulbs fennel	1 dozen Eggs	Rice
¼ pound parmesan cheese	1 lb. orzo	Sugar	Potatoes
Variety of oils and vinegars for vinaigrette	A variety of vegetables for "confetti" (good opportunity to practice brunoise)		Matzoh
			Tapioca
			Chocolate

HEALTH ISSUE	QUIRK	AGE
HEALTH ISSUE: Low Sodium (hypertension)	QUIRK: Hates vegetables	AGE: Young Adult
HEALTH ISSUE: Lactose-free (lactose intolerance)	QUIRK: Loves rich food	AGE: Child
HEALTH ISSUE: Fat free	QUIRK: Likes food spicy	AGE: Senior
HEALTH ISSUE: Difficulty swallowing (dysphasic)	QUIRK: Likes food with high-impact flavors	AGE: Teen
HEALTH ISSUE: Gluten-free (celiac)	QUIRK: Likes beautifully-presented food	AGE: Baby Boomer
HEALTH ISSUE: Seafood Allergy (food allergy)	QUIRK: Likes exotic flavors	AGE: Toddler

✂

Page intentionally
left blank, back side
of cutout cards

Student Guidelines

- **Safety First.** Put knife safety and safe food handling at the fore.
- Use the tools in the flavor chapter to help you brainstorm initial ideas and guide you through the game. Discuss merits of all suggestions and reach consensus on leading concepts. Develop concept fully, including how the concept meets each parameter before beginning cooking.
- Write a plan for recipe execution. Do not be afraid to alter the design as you go.
- Taste as you go. For unsafe or raw ingredients, cook a small sample to determine seasoning balance and flavor.
- Divide the prep work among the team.
- Maintain constant communication.
- Present finished product in a way that is visually appealing and is served at the appropriate temperature. Use the plating template in the resource section as a guide.
- Keep an eye on the clock—start long-cooking items immediately and quickly assemble your mise-en-place.

Supporting Activities

Which cards did you draw for this activity? How do you anticipate that these factors may influence the approach you take to the game?

_____

_____

_____

_____

_____

_____

What is the essence of the item that you think must be preserved during the variation?

_____

_____

_____

_____

_____

_____

_____

Sketch some ideas regarding how to modify these items to meet the parameters.

Refine your ideas.

How might you evaluate the success of your approach?

_____

_____

_____

_____

_____

Create a prep list and plan of attack for this game.

_____

_____

_____

_____

_____

Reflection Questions

❶ How easy or difficult was it to accomplish this task? What did you do that you feel was particularly innovative and worked well?

_____

_____

_____

_____

❷ If you could do it all over again what would you do differently?

❸ What's the most important thing you learned in playing this game?

❹ Have you had an experience like this in industry? If so, how did you deal with it? If not, how would you anticipate dealing with it?

❺ Do you feel it is appropriate for diners to make special requests in restaurants? Or should they eat somewhere else? Support your answer with examples. How might your opinion change if the question were applied to a managed care dining setting like a nursing home?

_____

_____

_____

_____

_____

_____

_____

Variations to Game

This game can be adapted for any number of recipe items and flavor profiles. A different menu could easily be substituted for the one given. To make the game easier, teams could draw only one or two cards. Students can work individually or in teams. If time is limited, advance steps can be taken, including cleaning and par-cooking some ingredients or selecting recipes like green salads, more dependent on assembly than cooking. The essential element of the game that should be maintained is the experience of solving the problem of adapting a menu for various needs, preferences and restrictions.

Game: Technique Trio

Sometimes in improvising, cooks rely on tried and true platforms and techniques. Dredge a tender piece of meat, poultry or fish in flour, sauté in clarified butter and make a small sauce with shallots, butter, wine and herbs is a pretty reliable classic French formula for success. But this game may challenge you to stray from your comfort zone as a cook. You may be comfortable working the range but how about using the same ingredients in a savory pastry application?

This game, Technique Trio, challenges you to cook from a mystery basket using specific techniques. It is also a good opportunity to test yourself on:

- Whether you have mastered various techniques
- Whether you can use these techniques in an improvisational way.

Unlike the last game, *Guess Who's Coming to Dinner*, that had you performing a task you will do often in industry—adapting a menu or recipe for a specific dietary need—this problem-solving game is a bit more "out there."

That also means it can be more fun! Being able to creatively and incorporate a specific culinary technique into a dish is an important skill. Being able to do so "on the fly," in an improvisational way is a great skills-building exercise. We learned, from the passage on Molecular Gastronomy in Chapter Four, that combining seemingly incongruous ingredients or techniques can lead to exciting new culinary experiences. So give this a whirl and see if you create something totally unexpected – and amazing!

Game Details

This game is for a student with medium to advanced skills. You should be comfortable in a kitchen and be familiar with basic culinary techniques outlined below. There is no maximum skill level. Even professional chefs have fun with and are challenged by this game.

In this game you must use three specific culinary techniques in preparing a dish from a mystery basket of ingredients. These techniques will range from moist and dry heat cooking methods, sauces, standard baking preparations and knife skills. The platforms presented in Section I of this book and your basic culinary text will give you helpful reminders of some of these techniques.

The instructor will provide you with a mystery basket of ingredients. This may be one recommended in the text or an entirely different basket.

Next, your team should randomly draw THREE culinary techniques from the table below, cut into cards:

Specifications for Game

ANTICIPATED TIME:	3–4 HOUR LAB
Concept Presentation	20 minutes
Student Planning and Station Set-up	30 minutes
Cooking	80–140 minutes
Tasting, Discussion and Debriefing	30 minutes
Clean-up	20 minutes

Ingredients Needed

Note: students should form teams of 2-3. Quantities are recommended for each team and should be multiplied by the number of teams. Nearly any type of mystery basket could be used but it is recommended to give the same basket ingredients to each team so that teams can see very different results depending on the techniques employed.

In addition to a variety of pantry items and staples always on hand:

SUGGESTED MYSTERY BASKET

1 lb. meat, poultry, fish, seafood or tofu
One bunch green vegetable (about ½ pound)
One bunch red, yellow, or white vegetable (about 1 pound)
Starch or grain (about ½ pound)

Braise	Starch-Thickened Sauce	Puree
Sauté	Baked En Croute	Tourner
Pan-Fry	Fine Brunoise	Steam
Deep Fry	Chiffonade	Stuff
Roast	Reduction Sauce	Stew
Stir-Fry	Compound Butter	Julienne
Warm Emulsified Sauce	Grill/Broil	Cold Emulsified Sauce

✂

Page intentionally
left blank, back side
of cutout cards

Student Guidelines

- Safety First. Put knife safety and safe food handling at the fore.
- Take time if needed to review the techniques being used. Base your creations on other recipes if needed.
- Use the tools in the flavor chapter to help you brainstorm initial ideas and guide you through the game. Discuss merits of all suggestions and reach consensus on leading concepts.
- Write a plan for recipe execution. Do not be afraid to alter the design as you go.
- Taste as you go. For unsafe or raw ingredients, cook a small sample to determine seasoning balance and flavor.
- Divide the prep work among the team.
- Maintain constant communication.
- Present finished product in a way that is visually appealing and is served at the appropriate temperature. Use the plating template in the resource section as a guide.
- Keep an eye on the clock—start long-cooking items immediately and quickly assemble your mise-en-place.
- Be sure to highlight all of the techniques drawn. If making julienne cuts, for example, make it a prominent feature of the dish and not an afterthought.
- Compose a dish with a variety of flavors, textures and shapes for appeal.

Supporting Activities

Which cards did you draw for this activity?

How do you anticipate that these factors may influence the approach you take to the game?

_____

_____

_____

_____

_____

_____

Looking at the ingredients and techniques can you begin to see ingredient and technique pairings that may work well together? Describe.

_____

_____

_____

_____

_____

Sketch some ideas regarding how you might combine these ingredients and techniques.

Refine your ideas.

How might you evaluate the success of your approach?

_____

_____

_____

_____

_____

Create a prep list and plan of attack for this game.

_____

_____

_____

_____

Reflection Questions

❶ If you had to grade yourself on your performance on this game, what grade would you give yourself and why?

_____

_____

_____

_____

_____

❷ How easy or difficult was it to accomplish this task? What did you do that you feel was particularly innovative and worked well?

_____

_____

_____

_____

_____

❸ If you could do it all over again what would you do differently?

_____

_____

_____

_____

❹ What's the most important thing you learned in playing this game?

_____

_____

_____

❺ Did you identify any skills or techniques where you need a refresher? Describe.

_____

_____

_____

_____

Variations to Game
Nearly any mystery basket and techniques could be used. Different baskets could be used and additional techniques could be added. The essential element of the game that should be maintained is the experience of creating a dish incorporating and highlighting specific culinary techniques.

Game: Today's Special

Look in the refrigerator at a food service establishment where you work or at your culinary school. Chances are there is some food product that was purchased in excess, is nearing the end of its life, and needs to be used soon or will go to waste. One of the challenges of managing a food establishment is that all of the inventory is decaying at varying rates. Some products like fish need to be used almost immediately and others, like oil, will last for many weeks but eventually everything in inventory will need to be used—hopefully by being prepared for sale—or discarded.

The chef's challenge, then, is to profitably use every ingredient in inventory while it can be safely, deliciously and profitably consumed—before the end of its shelf life. This is a common problem in industry and an important contributing factor to daily specials and creative family meals (meals for staff). Many specials employ great culinary creativity to both maximally utilize products and provide appealing meals to guests that showcase the chef's talents; many beloved family meals have become hits on a restaurant menu.

This game, Today's Special, will be very familiar to viewers of the television show Iron Chef. The problem solving exercise is to incorporate a featured ingredient in a variety of menu items: soup, salad, appetizer, entrée or dessert in a way that will appeal to guests and be profitable in a foodservice setting.

Game Details

This game is for a student with beginning to advanced skills. You should be comfortable in a kitchen and be familiar with basic preparations and applications, at minimum. There is no maximum skill level. Even professional chefs have fun with and are challenged by this game.

In this game you are challenged to think creatively to solve a problem—how to feature a food item in one or more dishes.

First, select a featured item randomly or per your instructor's directions. Some possibilities include:

Specifications for Game

ANTICIPATED TIME:	3–4 HOUR LAB
Concept Presentation	20 minutes
Student Planning and Station Set-up	30 minutes
Cooking	80–140 minutes
Tasting, Discussion and Debriefing	30 minutes
Clean-up	20 minutes

Ingredients Needed

Note: students should form teams of 2-3. Because this game has one primary featured ingredient, there should be a variety of other ingredients on hand.

In addition to a variety of pantry items and staples always on hand:

- Featured ingredient: about one pound per team

OTHER INGREDIENTS TO HAVE ON HAND FOR VARIATIONS MIGHT INCLUDE:

Stock	Butter
Onions	Phyllo Dough
Garlic	Puff Pastry
Carrots	Pasta
Celery	Rice
Flour	Quinoa
Eggs	Potatoes
Milk	Shallots
Wonton Wrappers	Oils
Chocolate	Vinegars
Sugar	Spices

Student Guidelines

- **Safety First.** Put knife safety and safe food handling at the fore.
- Use the tools in the flavor chapter to help you brainstorm initial ideas and guide you through the game. Discuss merits of all suggestions and reach consensus on leading concepts.
- Write a plan for recipe execution. Do not be afraid to alter the design as you go.
- Taste as you go. For unsafe or raw ingredients, cook a small sample to determine seasoning balance and flavor.
- Divide the prep work among the team.
- Maintain constant communication.
- Present finished product in a way that is visually appealing and is served at the appropriate temperature. Use the plating template in the resource section as a guide.
- Keep an eye on the clock—start long-cooking items immediately and quickly assemble your mise-en-place.

Supporting Activities

Which ingredient were you given or did you select for this game? What immediately comes to mind as associated with that ingredient?

_____

_____

_____

_____

_____

_____

What other flavors might pair well with the featured ingredient? What cooking techniques could be used to highlight the flavors?

_____

_____

_____

_____

_____

_____

Potatoes	Mushrooms	Chicken
Fresh Pasta Dough	Pork Shoulder	Apples
Salmon	Chocolate	Grapes
Cheddar Cheese	Parmesan Cheese	Spinach
Bacon	Garlic	Onions
Eggs	Peaches	Fennel
Asparagus	Corn	Peanuts

✂
Page intentionally
left blank, back side
of cutout cards

Sketch some ideas regarding how you might feature this item.

Refine your ideas.

How would the item be presented?

_____

_____

_____

_____

_____

How might you evaluate the success of your approach?

_____

_____

_____

_____

_____

Create a prep list and plan of attack for this game.

_____

_____

_____

_____

_____

_____

Reflection Questions

❶ If you had to grade yourself on your performance on this game, what grade would you give yourself and why?

_____

_____

_____

_____

❷ How easy or difficult was it to accomplish this task? What did you do that you feel was particularly innovative and worked well?

_____

_____

_____

_____

❸ If you could do it all over again what would you do differently?

_____

_____

_____

_____

_____

❹ What's the most important thing you learned in playing this game?

_____

_____

_____

_____

_____

_____

❺ Have you had an experience like this in industry? If so, how did you deal with it? If not, how would you anticipate dealing with it?

_____

_____

_____

_____

_____

Variations to Game

Depending on time, skill levels, and ingredients available teams could make anywhere from one to four dishes featuring their ingredient. Again it is instructive for each team to have the same item to feature so that comparisons can be drawn. Further restrictions could be introduced such as desserts only or a soup and entrée both required.

Game: Alternative School Lunch

It is a popular pastime to complain about the quality or palatability of public school lunches. One reason, of course, is that there are a host of parameters that shape offerings.

Brainstorm a list of parameters that influence school lunch menu choices:

_____

_____

_____

_____

_____

_____

In this game you are challenged to develop a school lunch that balances the need to run an efficient operation with the need to provide wholesome and delicious food, all with a variety of constraints.

Student Guidelines

- Safety First. Put knife safety and safe food handling at the fore.
- Taste as you go. For unusual combination experiments, try a small amount before proceeding with the whole batch wherever possible.
- Divide the prep work among the team.
- Maintain constant communication.
- Present finished product in a way that is visually appealing and is served at the appropriate temperature. Use the plating template in the resource section as a guide.
- Guide classmates through tasting process.

Some parameters:

- The dish cannot have an estimated cost more than one dollar per portion.
- The dish cannot use any specialty equipment such as mandolines, slicers, grills, etc. Only: knives, pots, pans, oven and range.
- The dish must contain foods from all food groups.
- The food must be culturally relevant to a specific group of students but appeal to a general population as well.
- It must take less than one hour to prepare.
- It must include at least one whole grain and one reduced fat item.
- You must be able to articulate how you've fulfilled the parameters above.

Game Details

This game is for a student with basic to advanced skills. You should be comfortable in a kitchen and be familiar with basic preparations and applications, at minimum. There is no maximum skill level. Even professional chefs have fun with and are challenged by this game.

For fun presentation and authenticity, school-style lunch trays should be used for plating.

A variety of pantry items and low-cost foods such as inexpensive cuts of meat, fish and poultry, root vegetables, leafy vegetables, fruits, starches and grains should be made available.

Specifications for Game

ANTICIPATED TIME:	2.5 HOURS
PART I	
Concept Presentation	10 minutes
Menu Concept Planning and Formulation	15 minutes
Game Plan	5 minutes
PART II	
Station Set-up and Mise en Place	10 Minutes
Cooking	60 Minutes
Tasting and Comments	20 Minutes

Supporting Activities

How do you think you can design a menu that meets all these parameters?

_____

_____

_____

_____

Sketch some preliminary ideas.

Refine your ideas.

Create a work plan for creating the menu. Double check this plan against the parameters.

_____

_____

_____

_____

Create a prep list.

_____

_____

_____

_____

_____

_____

Reflection Questions

❶ Describe the process you followed during today's game. What worked well? What could have been better?

_____

_____

_____

_____

_____

❷ What's something you learned about cooking from this activity? What's something you learned about yourself from this activity?

_____

_____

_____

_____

_____

_____

_____

_____

❸ Which dishes would you want to see at school lunch? Why? Would they work within the parameters?

_____

_____

_____

_____

_____

_____

Variations to Game

Depending on the level of the students and the instructional goals, the parameters of this game could be made much more specific to include specific nutritional targets, more specific costing targets, specific surplus commodities or explicit cultural relevancy references.

Chapter Summary

The ability to use improvisation to solve problems is a mark of a good chef. Good chefs prevent problems before they happen and are skilled at handling those that inevitably arise. Some of the games in this chapter represent very realistic scenarios and others are fun but definitely not everyday situations! Regardless, having an opportunity to practice thinking and cooking creatively to solve problems will serve you well in your career.

The games in this chapter also taught us about customizing to meet specific guest needs, highlighting a featured ingredient, and showcasing unexpected combinations. The games developed a basic understanding of problem solving and emphasized the skills required to transform a potentially negative experience into a positive one.

Chapter 6 Assessment Questions

❶ Define and give an example of a problem, as the term is used in this chapter.

_____

_____

_____

_____

_____

❷ Describe the process of solving a problem in one of the games. What challenges or obstacles did you face? Where did your team excel?

_____

_____

_____

_____

_____

_____

❸ Describe the cooking process you used for each game. What worked well? What would you have done differently?

_____

_____

_____

_____

_____

❹ Describe your group's decision making process. Where did you easily agree? Where was more debate involved? How did you ultimately reach decision points?

_____

_____

_____

_____

_____

❺ Assess your final outcome. What worked in your concept? What didn't? What would you do differently in the future?

_____

_____

_____

_____

_____

Assessment Rubric for Problem-solving Games

CRITERIA	PROFESSIONAL	DEVELOPING	NOVICE
Cooking Advanced Culinary Techniques	Student demonstrated professional-level knife skills and cooking techniques, needing little support. Student worked neatly, observing all safety and sanitation guidelines.	Student demonstrated some professional-level knife skills and cooking techniques, needing support or correction. Student did not neatly maintain station or did not observe some important safety and sanitation guidelines.	Student demonstrated developing skills and cooking techniques, needing help. Student did not maintain station or failed to observe critical safety and sanitation guidelines.**
Problem Solving Skills	Student clearly identified problem posed in the game and designed a creative solution following game guidelines.	Student identified problem posed in the game and designed a workable solution following game guidelines.	Student failed to clearly identify problem posed in the game or designed an inappropriate solution.
Adaptive skills Working in groups	Student was an active and engaged participant in the team and team members could clearly point to student's contribution. Student fully understood scenario and quickly adapted to situation, helping other students along.	Student worked with team but was not a key contributor to the final result. Student understood scenario and took direction from classmates in order to adapt to the situation.	Student did not show evidence of engagement with team and did not significantly contribute to the result. Student misunderstood scenario or did not adapt to situation.
Written Communication Informal writing and reflection	Student work exhibited thoughtful reflection on process and included concrete and significant conclusions.	Student work exhibited reflection on process and awareness of issues.	Student work lacked reflection on process or awareness of issues.
Style and Creativity Professional presentation	Student brought innovative and creative ideas: dish was attractive and restaurant quality.	Student did some innovative or creative things: dish was acceptable but unremarkable.	Student did not show evidence of creativity or innovation: dish was only attention-getting due to inadequacies.

*Note: Criteria could be given equal or various weights at instructor's discretion and tied to letter or number grades as desired.

**Note: Critical Safety and Sanitation Violations include: Cross-Contamination, Time/Temperature Violations, and knife handling hazardous to self or others.

7/

Flavor & Palate Development Games

Cooking is a business of taste. Cooking is much more than the mechanics of grilling a steak or rolling a pie crust. Cooks are constantly using all of their senses in concert, and, especially, smell and taste, to prepare great food.

Think of the decision process when you taste a chicken soup that lacks something.

What does it need?

- Salt, sweet, acid, or meaty flavor?
- Something spicy?
- An herb for aroma and color?
- Some potato for body?

Such assessments and adjustments may seem intuitive to a talented and experienced cook but they can be learned through practice, studying recipes, tasting to train the palate and trial and error – the cornerstone of this book. As young cooks we often threw the proverbial everything but the kitchen sink at a bland or insipid dish in an effort to spice it up. Now with a more sophisticated palate, we understand that what is required may be a bit of sear and a sprinkle of sea salt; a dash of hot pepper sauce and a whisk of cold butter; or a drizzle of curry powder-infused oil.

Since foods are agricultural products that can vary widely with the seasons, weather, location of origin and age of the product, it is not sufficient to cook something to a recipe.

Even the best recipes may work great one time and not the second because of variations in weather, altitude, product freshness, product flavor, equipment, or the culinary techniques of the cook. For example, when amateur cooks cook in our commercial teaching kitchen for the first time they are often frustrated by how differently it feels to cook on a powerful range or with a convection oven and surprised at how different flavors may be when ingredients come from premium suppliers. The best way to adjust to these variations and to make consistently great food is to have a good palate and know how to combine flavors for optimum result.

To follow an executive chef around a busy kitchen, you see a nose and mouth that never stop:

"Something smells like it's burning. Check the toasting sesame seeds."

CHAPTER OBJECTIVES

By the end of these games you should be able to:

① Demonstrate techniques for flavor and palate development in the kitchen.

② Create dishes with contrasting and complementary flavors using culinary improvisation.

③ Improvise using available ingredients and equipment.

④ List and explain some challenges in flavor combinations and how they might be overcome.

While:

❺ Demonstrating effective communication with team members.

❻ Demonstrating appropriate knife skills.

❼ Demonstrating appropriate cooking techniques.

❽ Demonstrating appropriate kitchen sanitation and safety procedures.

❾ Cultivating advanced culinary technique.

KEY TERMS

Platform

Concept

"Let me taste that sauce."
"This stock smells old—what's the date on it?"
"Mmm, those caramelized onions smell great."

Like most chefs, when I walk into a busy kitchen that I'm running or in which I'm involved, I can tell what is going on before anyone says anything. I know if we're on time or in the weeds. I know which cook is making the soup. I know if our vendor was able to supply that special fish we asked for. I know if the sink faucet is acting up again. The sounds, feels, smells, sights and tastes of the kitchen provide immediate feedback.

One day when you're not busy, stand out in an out of the way place in a working kitchen. Most chefs won't mind your asking to do this unless you're on the clock. Try to tune out your thoughts and just focus on your senses. What are you feeling? Smelling? Touching? Seeing? Hearing? Can you smell and hear distinct foods cooking? Can you tell what they are without looking? Can you tell from people's movements how things are going? If you shut your eyes and listen do you sense the tone of the kitchen? Can you smell something wonderful and appetizing? Can you smell something less than wonderful?

Even tasting a bite of something employs all five senses. It is misleading to think of tasting as employing simply the sense of taste. Of course, you taste the food. Before you've even tasted, though, you've formed an opinion on what it will taste like, first by sight and then by smell as it makes its way to your mouth and continuing from the back of your palate once inside your mouth. Once in your mouth, the flavors you detect are still provided mainly by the food's aromas. You also feel the texture and

temperature of the food with your tongue, mouth and inner cheek, feeling how it yields or pulls between your teeth, and even continuing as the food makes its way down your throat. You hear it crunch or slurp around your mouth through your jaw bones directly up to your inner ear.

Understanding, respecting and preparing for this full sensory experience of eating and drinking is an important skill set for a cook. Something needs to not only taste good but also provide appealing colors, arrangement, textures, aromas, mouthfeels and even sounds. In a multi-course meal or one complemented by a particular beverage or accompaniment, varying and balancing these elements not only across a dish but across the time span of multiple courses becomes complex, challenging and of critical importance. Chefs tell us that that distinction between knowing how to cook, and having a great palate and understanding of how tastes, colors, shapes, textures and aromas work together forms another dividing line between cooks and chefs. Cooks can execute a recipe, unquestionably an important skill in itself. Chefs can execute a recipe, improve it, or create a new one altogether based on their sensory impressions of the dish as it evolves.

In this chapter we provide you with some games to play that can expand your practice and understanding of flavor combinations and palate development. These exercises, together with the chapter on flavors, provide the knowledge and skills practice you need to develop creative dishes with a good balance of flavors, textures and colors, while expanding your own understanding of how flavors can work together to reinforce or contrast with one another.

From the Line: Case Study

TONY LIU, EXECUTIVE CHEF, AUGUST, NEW YORK CITY

In the following case study, consider the ways in which the important skill of culinary improvisation emphasizes the use of flavor and palate development in the restaurant kitchen.

Flavor and palate development through culinary improvisation was a necessity for Chef Tony Liu as he designed the menu for August, a 60-seat full-service restaurant in New York City's Greenwich Village that focuses on regional European cuisine.

Chef Tony was challenged with creating a menu for a very unique restaurant space. Previously, the venue was a pizzeria with a large brick oven as the predominant feature of the space. There is not much kitchen space besides the oven that sits in the center of the restaurant; eight burners comprise the line with a small prep kitchen in the basement. In addition, like many small restaurants in New York City, August does not have a large storage space for fresh or dry ingredients. Rather than letting the cramped space and pizza equipment confine Chef Tony's style, he used his creativity to develop a working set of recipes that took advantage of this problem-laden cooking environment. He creatively adapted the traditional flavors created from a brick-oven and created a menu of regional European dishes that complemented the use of equipment and palate of the target customers.

Chef Tony displayed ingenuity in his menu development. Take a minute to review the following lunch, brunch, and dinner menus. Can you see how Tony used his given equipment and space to his advantage? Describe.

_____

_____

_____

_____

APPETIZERS

Daily Selection Of Oysters and Raw Bar	MP
Minestra di Arzilla	11
Lenten skate salad with Roman broccoli and grapefruit	
Charcuterie Plate	15
Cured european meats with mustard and traditional garnish	
Roasted Stuffed Artichoke	15
Minted breadcrumbs and lemon anchovy mayonnaise	
Beef Borscht	9
Hearty soup of beets, barley, and cabbage	
Fava Bean Crostino	9
Sheep ricotta and truffled pecorino	
Bibb Lettuces and Radishes with Lemon Dressing	9
Brandade de Morue with Sage	9
Whipped salt cod and potato casserole	
White Salad	11
Raw salad of white asparagus, salsify, celery root, and hearts of palm	
Skagen med Knackebrod	15
Swedish shrimp salad on housemade rye crispbread	
Tarte Flambe	12
Alsatian onion and bacon tart with creme fraiche	

APPETIZERS

Daily Selection Of Oysters and Raw Bar	MP
Minestra di Arzilla	11
Lenten skate salad with Roman broccoli and grapefruit	
Charcuterie Plate	15
Cured European meats with mustard and traditional garnish	
Roasted Stuffed Artichoke	15
Minted breadcrumbs and lemon anchovy mayonnaise	
Beef Borscht	9
Hearty soup of beets, barley, and cabbage	
Fava Bean Crostino	9
Sheep ricotta and truffled pecorino	
Bibb Lettuces and Radishes with Lemon Dressing	9
Brandade de Morue with Sage	9
Whipped salt cod and potato casserole	
White Salad	11
Raw salad of white asparagus, salsify, celery root, and hearts of palm	
Skagen med Knackebrod	15
Swedish shrimp salad on housemade rye crispbread	
Tarte Flambe	12
Alsatian onion and bacon tart with creme fraiche	

AUGUST
Regional European Food
LUNCH

Beef Borscht	9
Hearty soup of beets, barley, and cabbage	
Brandade de Morue with Sage	9
Whipped salt cod and potato casserole	
White Salad	11
Raw salad of white asparagus, salsify, celery root, and hearts of palm	
Fava Bean Crostino	9
Sheep ricotta and truffled pecorino	
Bibb Lettuces and Radishes with Lemon Dressing	9
Tarte Flambe	12
Alsatian onion and bacon tart with creme fraiche	
Skagen med Knackebrod	15
Swedish shrimp salad on housemade rye crispbread	
AUGUST Burger	13
with Pommes frites & house made mayonnaise	
Crispy Cod Sandwich	14
Dill brioche bread, tartar sauce, and lemon	
Pressed Ham and Chorizo Sandwich	13
Dare mustard, gruyere, and salad	
Half Sandwich and Cup of Soup	13
Choice of Cod or Chorizo Sandwich	
Eggs en Cocotte	10
Your choice of Roman, Bordelaise, or Florentine	
Grilled Beef and Wild Spring Salad	14
Sunchokes and watercress, parsley sauce	

ENTREES

Spaghettini with Ramps	18
Spicy almond pesto, currants, and ricotta salata	
Slow Roasted Halibut with Lardo	24
Mixed beets, fennel, and citrus	
Oven Roasted Whole Orata	24
Sicilian salmoriglio	
Cod and Cockles Estofado	24
Roasted cauliflower, chorizo, saffron, yellow raisins	
Braised Rabbit	22
Confit carrots, peas, ramp polenta, and tarragon	
Grilled Leg of Lamb Salad	24
Green garlic, pea shoots, and fava beans	
Lapi's Chicken Matzoh Ball Soup	20
Early spring vegetables and poached breast	
Grilled Bavette of Beef	23
Sunchokes and watercress, parsley sauce	

Pommes Frites with Mayonnaise	7	Sunchokes and Wild Greens	8
Braised Whole Fava Pods	8	Roasted Asparagus	8

Gratuity of 20% added to parties of 6 or more

ENTREES

Spaghettini with Ramps	18
Spicy almond pesto, currants, and ricotta salata	
Slow Roasted Halibut with Lardo	24
Mixed beets, fennel, and citrus	
Oven Roasted Whole Orata	24
Sicilian salmoriglio	
Cod and Cockles Estofado	24
Roasted cauliflower, chorizo, saffron, yellow raisins	
Braised Rabbit	22
Confit carrots, peas, ramp polenta, and tarragon	
Grilled Leg of Lamb Salad	24
Green garlic, pea shoots, and fava beans	
Lapi's Chicken Matzoh Ball Soup	20
Early spring vegetables and poached breast	
Grilled Bavette of Beef	23
Sunchokes and watercress, parsley sauce	

Pommes Frites with Mayonnaise	7	Sunchokes and Wild Greens	8
Braised Whole Fava Pods	8	Roasted Asparagus	8

Gratuity of 20% added to parties of 6 or more

AUGUST BRUNCH

Greek Yogurt and Fruit Parfait	6
Beaujolais poached cherries	
Matzoh Brie with Lingonberry Compote	6
Pain Perdu	12
Wild blueberry compote and whipped cream	
Cast Iron German Pancake	12
Oven roasted with seasonal garnish	
Wood Oven Baked Eggs en Cocotte	11
choose your regional style	
Alsatian, bacon and onion with creme fraiche	
Florentine, spinach and garlic cream	
Bordelaise, mushrooms and red wine	
Roman, tomato and mozzarella	
Frittata of the Day	10
Ham and Egg Galette	11
Crepe with ham eggs and cheese	
AUGUST Burger	13
with pommes frites and mayonnaise	
Fire Grilled Steak with Eggs	14
Housemade Gravlax with Scrambled Eggs	14
Pumpernickel, herb creme fraiche, and red onions	
Lentil, Pork, and Chicken Crepinette	13
Endive salad and mustard vinaigrette	
White Salad	11
Raw salad of white asparagus, salsify, celery root, and hearts of palm	
Bibb Lettuces and Radishes with Lemon Dressing	9

SIDES

Smoked Bacon	6	Swiss Potato	6
Pain au Chocolat	4	Grilled Chorizo	7
Fresh Fruit	5	Croissant with Jam	4

Can you identify places where he highlights flavors within the menu that come from using this pizza oven?

_____

_____

_____

_____

_____

_____

_____

As you can see, Chef Tony embraced the pizzeria's equipment and positioned August as regional European bistro that emphasizes the use of the large brick oven. Instead of being frustrated with the boundaries the kitchen defined for the menu, Chef Tony welcomed the situation by offering foods flavored by the brick oven and that are easily prepared in such equipment; for example "eggs en cocotte" are offered instead of omelets on the brunch menu; there are a number of casseroles, tarts, braised and roasted dishes as opposed to sautéed or grilled options. The bread served has been heated directly on the floor of the oven—and in turn flavored as such. Even the bacon reflects the flavors of the brick oven. Ham and potato _raclette_, caramelized onion tart, and the baked eggs all evolved into signature dishes that make reviewers swoon.

Chef Tony uses these cooking techniques and simple flavors that are enhanced by the oven to another advantage: Because many of these dishes can be prepared in advance, he can limit the number of cooks in the kitchen during meal times, cutting back on labor costs.

Chef Tony also uses culinary improvisation and adapts flavors to assist in ingredient availability at August. A classically trained chef at The Culinary Institute of America, Hawaiian-born Chef Tony studied in Hawaii and Spain, and worked at renowned high-end French and Italian restaurants in New York City including Daniel and Babbo. He often pulls flavor and palate techniques, ingredients and recipes from his background and past culinary experiences to create his own versions of classic dishes for the menu at August. One dish that Chef Tony is particularly fond of making is a recreation of a classic dish from Spain. Typically, a pepper from Padron is sautéed in olive oil and served with sea salt. Chef Tony had a difficult time trying to find the right type of pepper—at the required quality specifications—to replicate the recipe and create the same flavors using ingredients available in the United States. After testing a number of ingredients, he was able to achieve a similar taste using a Hawaiian shishito pepper, which imparted a taste as close as one could find to the Spanish pepper.

Chef Tony implements culinary improvisation techniques on a regular basis in his restaurant operations, design of the menu, and daily operations. His flexibility and improvisational skills allow him to creatively adapt flavors and dishes using the restrictions of the restaurant space, while pleasing his customers with delicious cuisine.

Case Study Questions

❶ Give an example of a classic dish you would modify to adapt the flavor using the brick oven. What would you do to modify it?

_____

_____

_____

_____

❷ Give an example from your own life of how you adjusted the flavors of a dish to improve the finished product.

_____

_____

_____

_____

_____

❸ Looking at Chef Tony Liu's menus, write another menu item that you think would complement the types of flavors currently offered. Explain what you think your menu item could offer. Sketch a design of its presentation.

_____

_____

_____

_____

_____

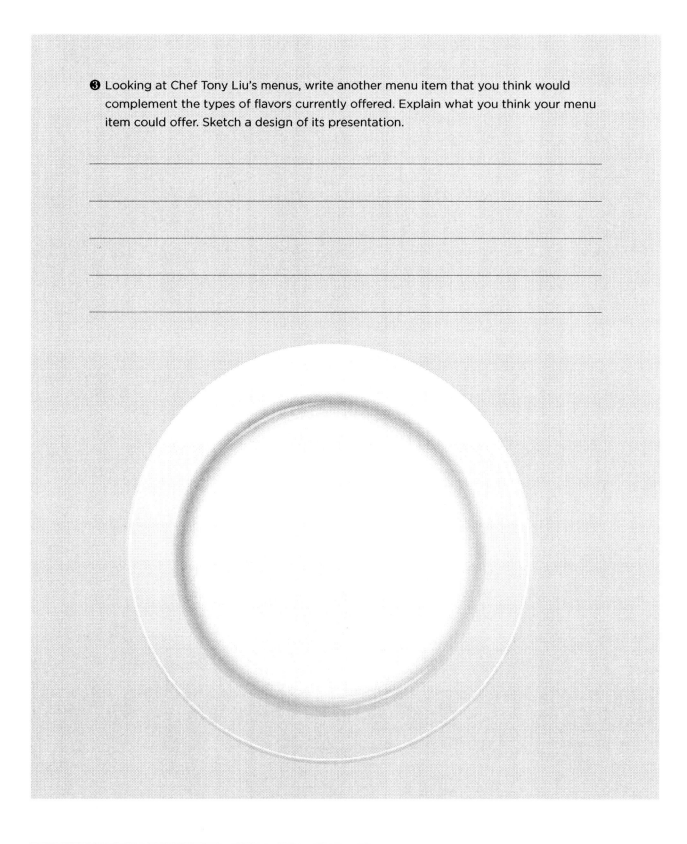

Game: Same Recipe—Different Style

Did you ever wonder how a classic American diner menu could possibly be so large? How can one establishment offer so many hundreds of items? The answer, of course, is that they have a core *mise en place* of basic ingredients that are altered for various recipes. Consider a breaded pan-fried chicken cutlet. The cook can bread, fry and safely chill a large batch of these in the morning. These cutlets may then be reheated topped with tomato sauce and cheese for chicken Parmesan, chopped on top of a salad with bleu cheese for a composed salad, or warmed and ladled with hot sauce for a Buffalo chicken sandwich. From one basic idea—**breaded pan-fried chicken cutlet**—a cook can build a variety of menu concepts.

What are some other concept ideas that you can generate using this simple item?

_____

_____

_____

In this game each team will be given the same recipe as a recipe **platform**. A platform is a simple basic recipe upon which a **concept** can stand. For example, a broiled beefsteak is a platform—it involves ingredients (beefsteak, salt, pepper; garlic if you know what I like) and technique (broiling). By itself, it is not a dish or menu concept. But a broiled chili and lime-rubbed steak served with fried onion rings and a salsa verde may be an appealing concept based on that simple platform. A broiled steak sliced thinly on the bias and served over a salad of radicchio, arugula, marinated red onions and bleu cheese crumbles is another concept based on the same platform.

Specifications for Game

ANTICIPATED TIME:	THREE HOUR LAB
Concept Presentation	20 minutes
Student Planning and Station Set-up	20 minutes
Cooking	90 minutes
Tasting, Discussion and Debriefing	30 minutes
Clean-up	20 minutes

A **concept** in this case is an integrated menu idea based on a platform combining ingredients, techniques and flavor elements.

Two platforms suggested for this game are mashed potatoes as an introductory exercise, and dumplings as an advanced exercise. Your instructor may introduce her or his own platform. Chicken soup, composed salads and hearty sandwiches are other fun options. Next you will be assigned or will randomly draw a certain style of cuisine in which to build from your basic platform. Depending on the goals of your instructor, it may be a certain regional cuisine or flavor profile and/or a certain dining situation. It could have you adapt to an equipment scenario as in the case of Chef Liu in this chapter, or even have you cook toward a feeling as a way of communicating with food. You will adapt your basic platform to suit the style you draw.

Game Details

This game is for a student with basic to advanced skills. You should be comfortable in a kitchen and be familiar with basic preparations and applications, at minimum. There is no maximum skill level. Even professional chefs have fun with and are challenged by this game.

In this game you are challenged to draw on your knowledge and skills in the culinary arts, in cultural foods, in geography and in flavor principles in order to take a basic recipe and adapt it to various styles and situations. Think of each team having the same basic canvas and color schemes, but having the ability to paint very different pictures.

PLATFORM 1: MASHED POTATOES: BEGINNER SKILL LEVEL

Ingredients

Potatoes	1 lb.	Peeled and Diced
Butter (or fat)	3 T.	Warmed
Milk (or liquid)	1 c.	Warmed
Salt and Pepper (seasonings)		To Taste

PROCEDURE

Cook potatoes. Drain and dry.

Mash and mix potatoes with butter and milk.

Season and serve.

SAMPLE INGREDIENTS FOR VARIATIONS	SPECIAL EQUIPMENT NEEDS
Additional root vegetables	Ricers
Cheeses	Food Mills
Spices	Mashers
Condiments	Mixers
Oils	
Vinegars	
Aromatics	
Creams	
Dairy Alternatives	

PLATFORM 2: DUMPLINGS: ADVANCED SKILL LEVEL

Dough Ingredients

Flour, All Purpose	1 ¼ c.	
Water	2 oz.	Cold
Water	6 oz.	Boiling
Salt	½ tsp.	
Flour	Additional for Dusting	

PROCEDURE

Divide flour and salt into two bowls. Add cold water to one bowl and boiling water to other. Mix both separately until balls form. Dust work surface with flour. Combine doughs and knead together until supple, approximately ten minutes.

Cover and allow to rest (approximately thirty minutes) while preparing filling.

Roll, shape and fill as desired.

SAMPLE INGREDIENTS FOR VARIATIONS	SPECIAL EQUIPMENT NEEDS
Ground meats	Rolling pins
Vegetables	Pasta machines (optional)
Herbs	Steamers
Spices	Meat grinders (optional)
Vinegars	
Condiments	
Alternate flours such as whole wheat, buckwheat, chickpea, rice	
Coloring agents such as beet juice, pureed spinach, squid ink	
Cornstarch for binding	
Cottage or Farmers Cheese	

Student Guidelines

- **Safety First.** Put knife safety and safe food handling at the fore.
- Use the tools in the flavor chapter to help you brainstorm initial ideas and guide you through the game. Discuss merits of all suggestions and reach consensus on leading concepts. Develop concept fully, including the regional style, dining situation and other factors.
- Write a plan for recipe execution.
  Do not be afraid to alter the design as you go.
- Taste as you go. For unsafe or raw ingredients like raw meat dumpling filling, poach or sauté a small sample to determine seasoning balance and flavor.
- Divide the prep work among the team.
- Maintain constant communication.
- Present finished product in a way that is visually appealing and is served at the appropriate temperature. Use the plating template in the resource section as a guide.

Supporting Activities

List some other ingredients that you think would be interesting variations for either game.

_____

_____

_____

_____

Which menu item will you work on for this activity?

_____

_____

_____

What variation will you need to incorporate? What is the essence of the item that you think must be preserved during the variation? What do you think the variation can add?

_____

_____

_____

_____

How will you approach this scenario?

_____

_____

_____

_____

Sketch some ideas regarding how you might present this item to enhance the theme.

Refine your ideas.

Create a prep list and plan of attack for this game.

_____

_____

_____

_____

_____

_____

Reflection Questions

❶ If you had to grade yourself on your performance on this game, what grade would you give yourself and why?

_____

_____

_____

_____

_____

❶ What did you do that you feel was particularly innovative and worked well?

_____

_____

_____

_____

_____

_____

❷ If you could do it all over again what would you do differently?

_____

_____

_____

_____

_____

❸ What's the most important thing you learned in playing this game?

Variations to Game

This game can be adapted for any number of recipes—pasta dishes, chicken dishes, and soups and stews work well. Students can work individually or in teams. If time is limited, advance steps can be taken, including purchasing wrappers or making dough in advance of class, par-cooking potatoes, or selecting recipes like green salads, more dependant on assembly than cooking. The essential element of the game that should be maintained is the experience of adapting a foundation recipe to a specific setting.

_____

_____

_____

_____

❹ Describe a real-world application different from the scenario where you might apply something you did in this game.

_____

_____

_____

_____

Sample Ingredients for Variations (card cutouts)

Ground meats	Vegetables	Herbs	Spices
Vinegars	Condiments	Alternate flours such as whole wheat, buckwheat, chickpea, rice	Coloring agents such as beet juice, pureed spinach, squid ink

Sample Feelings for Either Platform (card cutouts)

Happy	Sad	Bored	Excited
Angry	Frustrated	Mellow	Confused

✄

Page intentionally
left blank, back side
of cutout cards

Sample Regional Styles for Either Platform (card cutouts)

Argentine	Brazilian	Cajun
Cantonese	Cuban	Eastern European
Egyptian	Greek	Israeli
Jamaican	Japanese	Lebanese
Mexican	Moroccan	New England
New Latin	Northern Indian	Pan Caribbean
Persian	Puerto Rican	Scandinavian
Sichuan	South African	Southeast Asian
Southern Indian	Southern Italian	Tibetan
Tuscan	US Pacific Northwest	US South
US Southwest		

✂

Page intentionally
left blank, back side
of cutout cards

Sample Dining Situations for Either Platform (card cutouts)

A la minute	Airplane	Bar mitzvah
Batch cooking	Breakfast	Brunch
Cruise	Festival	Formal
Formal reception	Funeral	Graduation
High volume	Hospital	Kids
Limited equipment	Low budget	Nursing Home
Pub	Romantic	School cafeteria
Small kitchen	Snack	Take out
Wedding	Dairy Allergy	Nut Allergy
Sustainable (Green)	Loss of Electricity	Loss of Gas
Loss of Running Water		

✂

Page intentionally
left blank, back side
of cutout cards

Game: Unlikely Marriage

Chef Lara Brumnach, a pastry chef featured in the next chapter, made a name for herself by stretching the boundaries of flavors that are considered appropriate for dessert. Her trained palate and innovative approaches to flavor combinations result in desserts with ingredients that initially seem at odds but at first bite, and then second, work together in a way not possible using only classic dessert flavors like vanilla, almonds, cinnamon or mint.

For example, a dish of quenelles of strawberry ice cream is garnished with fresh pea shoots, a vegetable normally used only in savory preparations. But the linear shoots in contrast to the rounded quenelles, the crunchiness of the vegetable in contrast to the smoothness of the ice cream and the fresh vegetal flavor in contrast to the rich and smooth fruit and cream flavor all work together to provide a compelling contrast. How did Chef Lara envision such a dish? She tasted the pea shoots, newly arrived in the kitchen for the spring season, tasted another early spring product—strawberries—and let her creativity, palate and knowledge of flavors guide her to this winning combination.

This game, Unlikely Marriage, challenges you to practice trying to make similarly unlikely flavor combinations work. In the previous game, you had latitude to develop your own flavor combinations, perhaps a more realistic but not as challenging exercise. In this game you will draw or be given a set of ingredients that you may not be able to envision working together from a culinary perspective. The challenge is to use your palate and practice combining flavors in a way that will work into a soup, salad, appetizer, main course or dessert that you think could be a viable restaurant item. Some will be highly appealing and some will be a real stretch of our notions of palatability but either way, you will have practice challenging yourself to think creatively about flavor combinations and have an opportunity to practice.

....

Specifications for Game

ANTICIPATED TIME:	THREE HOUR LAB
Concept Presentation	20 minutes
Student Planning and Station Set-up	20 minutes
Cooking	90 minutes
Tasting, Discussion and Debriefing	30 minutes
Clean-up	20 minutes

SPECIAL RULES:

The flavors should be used together. Including just a small amount of a flavor to hide it in the dish is foul play.

This is a challenging and not-everyday game. Don't be afraid to mess up flavor-wise but follow the student guidelines to keep focused professionally.

Game Details

This game is for a student with medium to advanced skills. You should be comfortable in a kitchen and be familiar with basic preparations and applications, at minimum. There is no maximum skill level. Even professional chefs have fun with and are challenged by this game.

The unlikely ingredient combinations are divided into medium and advanced levels of difficulty.

....

Student Guidelines

- **Safety First.** Put knife safety and safe food handling at the fore.
- Use the tools in the flavor chapter to help you brainstorm initial ideas and guide you through the game. Discuss merits of all suggestions and reach consensus on leading concepts.
- Write a plan for recipe execution. Do not be afraid to alter the design as you go.
- Taste as you go. For unusual combination experiments, try a small amount before proceeding with the whole batch wherever possible.
- Divide the prep work among the team.
- Maintain constant communication.
- Present finished product in a way that is visually appealing and is served at the appropriate temperature.

Ingredients Needed (per team of 2-3)

Obviously, the flavor pairings selected will need to be purchased in small quantities. Quantities are added:

MEDIUM	ADVANCED
1 lb. Sirloin Steak	1 small bottle Cold Pressed Peanut Oil
4 ea. Peaches	4 Peaches
1 lb. Shrimp	1 small bottle Chili Oil
4 oz. Bleu Cheese	4 oz. Bleu Cheese
½ ea. Chicken or 2 Breasts or Whole Legs	1 small bottle Soy Sauce
4 oz. Chocolate	4 oz. Chocolate
¾ lb. Salmon	4 each Onions
2 Vanilla Beans	2 Vanilla Beans
1 ½ lb. Lamb Shoulder	1 ½ lb. Potatoes
1 bunch Rhubarb	1 bunch Rhubarb
1 whole small Flounder	2 heads Garlic
¾ lb. Cherries	¾ lb. Cherries
In addition, if using the medium-level pairings, students should have access to a well-stocked pantry of spices, vinegars, oils, sauces and grains; staples like flour, sugar, eggs, butter, vegetable oil, olive oil, and stock and a small variety of fresh vegetables.	In addition, if using the Advanced pairings, a wide variety of small amounts of protein items, fresh fruits and vegetables and grains should be offered in addition to seasonings and staples listed along with the medium table.

Supporting Activities

Which cards did you draw for this activity? How do you anticipate that these flavors may influence the approach you take to the game?

_____

_____

_____

_____

_____

_____

MEDIUM:

Sirloin Steak

MEDIUM:

Peaches

MEDIUM:

Shrimp

MEDIUM:

Bleu Cheese

MEDIUM:

Chicken

MEDIUM:

Chocolate

MEDIUM:

Salmon

MEDIUM:

Vanilla

MEDIUM:

Lamb Shoulder

MEDIUM:

Rhubarb

MEDIUM:

Flounder

MEDIUM:

Cherries

MEDIUM:

Other...

MEDIUM:

Other...

MEDIUM:

Other...

MEDIUM:

Other...

✂
Page intentionally
left blank, back side
of cutout cards

ADVANCED:

Peanut Oil

ADVANCED:

Peaches

ADVANCED:

Chili Oil

ADVANCED:

Bleu Cheese

ADVANCED:

Soy Sauce

ADVANCED:

Chocolate

ADVANCED:

Onions

ADVANCED:

Vanilla

ADVANCED:

Potatoes

ADVANCED:

Rhubarb

ADVANCED:

Garlic

ADVANCED:

Cherries

ADVANCED:

Other...

ADVANCED:

Other...

ADVANCED:

Other...

ADVANCED:

Other...

✁
Page intentionally
left blank, back side
of cutout cards

What is the essence of the flavors that you think you can combine? Will you try to have flavors complement? Contrast? Parallel?

_____

_____

_____

_____

Sketch some ideas on a dish you might create.

How might you evaluate the success of your approach?

_____

_____

_____

_____

Create a prep list and plan of attack for this game.

_____

_____

_____

_____

Reflection Questions

❶ If you had to grade yourself on your performance on this game, what grade would you give yourself and why?

_____

_____

_____

❷ How easy or difficult was it to accomplish this task? What did you do that you feel was particularly innovative and worked well?

_____

_____

_____

_____

❸ If you could do it all over again what would you do differently?

_____

_____

_____

_____

❹ What's the most important thing you learned in playing this game?

_____

_____

_____

❺ What did you learn from this game that you could directly or indirectly apply in the professional kitchen?

_____

_____

_____

Variations to Game

This game can be adapted for any number of flavor combinations. Students can create their own unlikely flavor combinations, can draw cards at random, or can challenge other teams to use pairings of their devising. Nearly any type of dish can be created and the instructor can limit the exercise to a certain type of dish such as a salad or main course. Students can work individually or in teams. The essential element of the game that should be maintained is the experience of experimenting with unlikely flavor combinations.

Game: Crab Libs

In the previous game, Unlikely Marriage, the challenge was to improvise an interesting and palatable dish with two unlikely ingredients. This game, Crab Libs, is a variation of Unlikely Marriage that is a bit more complicated.

This game challenges you to create a composed dish that "works" in terms of innovative flavor combinations, using complementary or contrasting flavors, textures and colors; an appealing plate presentation; and a feasible concept of professional quality.

Here's how it works. You will select cards from two different categories:

- Technique (Select 2 Cards)
- Ingredient (Select 3 Cards)

Arrange the cards how you think they will work best to complete the following phrase:

| Technique | Ingredient | with | Technique | Ingredient | over | Ingredient |

Then, cook a dish to these specifications in a way that maintains innovative but appropriate flavor balance. Use the tools in the flavors chapter to help you with this.

Special Rules:

- The flavors should be used together. Including just a small amount of a flavor to hide it in the dish is foul play.
- This is a challenging and not-everyday game. Don't be afraid to mess up flavor-wise but follow the student guidelines to keep focused professionally.

Game Details

This game is for a student with medium to advanced skills. You should be comfortable in a kitchen and be familiar with basic preparations and applications, at minimum. There is no maximum skill level. Even professional chefs have fun with and are challenged by this game.

Cards are arranged by technique and ingredient categories. Each team should draw two technique cards and three ingredient cards.

Specifications for Game

ANTICIPATED TIME:	THREE HOUR LAB
Concept Presentation	20 minutes
Student Planning and Station Set-up	20 minutes
Cooking	90 minutes
Tasting, Discussion and Debriefing	30 minutes
Clean-up	20 minutes

Ingredients Needed
(per team of 2–3)

Obviously, the flavor pairings selected will need to be purchased in small quantities. Instructor should choose cards to be used in advance, with none left over, and order accordingly. In addition, the instructor could issue one center-of-plate, protein item to each group to ensure an even distribution of these items.

Pantry staples such as flour, butter, sugar, eggs, grains, stock and sauces should be available as always.

Quantities are added to ingredient sheets.

TECHNIQUE: Braised	TECHNIQUE: Spiced	TECHNIQUE: Pureed
TECHNIQUE: Sautéed	TECHNIQUE: En Croute	TECHNIQUE: Turned (Tourne)
TECHNIQUE: Pan-Fried	TECHNIQUE: Emulsion of	TECHNIQUE: Steamed
TECHNIQUE: Deep Fried	TECHNIQUE: En Papillote	TECHNIQUE: Stuffed
TECHNIQUE: Roasted	TECHNIQUE: Macedoine of	TECHNIQUE: Stewed
TECHNIQUE: Caramelized	TECHNIQUE: Pie of	TECHNIQUE: Julienned
TECHNIQUE: Reduction of	TECHNIQUE: Grilled/Broiled	TECHNIQUE: Salad of
TECHNIQUE: Other	TECHNIQUE: Other	TECHNIQUE: Other

✂
Page intentionally
left blank, back side
of cutout cards

1 lb. Potatoes	½ lb. Mushrooms	4 Chicken Thighs
Fresh Pasta (Dough or Flour, Eggs and Oil)	1 ½ lb. section Pork Shoulder	4 ea. Apples
1 Whole Fish per market availability	5 oz. Chocolate	1 lb. Grapes
6 oz. Cheddar Cheese	4 oz. Parmesan Cheese	4 bunches Spinach
½ lb. Slab Bacon	4 heads Garlic	2 lb. Onions
6 ea. Eggs (plus staples)	4 ea. Peaches	2 heads Fennel
1 bu. Asparagus	6 ears Fresh Corn or 12 oz. Frozen Corn	6 oz. Unsalted, Shelled Peanuts or 1 lb. Shell-On Peanuts
1 c. Uncooked Rice	1 ea. Eggplant	2 bu. Arugula
2 lb. Carrots	1 bunch Leeks	1 ½ lb. Turkey Wings
1 head Escarole	3 ea. Red Pepper	1 pt. Berries
¾ lb. Ground Turkey	¾ lb. Italian Sausage	1 ea. Butternut Squash
1 ea. Red Onion	1 lb. Tofu	½ ea. Cantaloupe
2 ea. Grapefruit	4 ea. Tomatoes	2 Heads Belgian Endive

Page intentionally
left blank, back side
of cutout cards

Student Guidelines

- **Safety First.** Put knife safety and safe food handling at the fore.
- Use the tools in the flavor chapter to help you brainstorm initial ideas and guide you through the game. Discuss merits of all suggestions and reach consensus on leading concepts.
- Write a plan for recipe execution. Do not be afraid to alter the design as you go.
- Taste as you go. For unusual combination experiments, try a small amount before proceeding with the whole batch wherever possible.
- Divide the prep work among the team.
- Maintain constant communication.
- Present finished product in a way that is visually appealing and is served at the appropriate temperature. Use the plating template in the resource section as a guide.

Supporting Activities

Which cards did you draw for this activity? How do you anticipate that these factors may influence the approach you take to the game?

_____

_____

_____

_____

_____

_____

Looking at the ingredients and techniques can you begin to see ingredient and technique pairings that may work well together? Describe.

_____

_____

_____

_____

_____

_____

_____

Sketch some ideas regarding how you might combine these ingredients and techniques.

Refine your ideas.

How might you evaluate the success of your approach?

_____

_____

_____

_____

_____

Create a prep list and plan of attack for this game.

_____

_____

_____

_____

_____

_____

Reflection Questions

❶ If you had to grade yourself on your performance on this game, what grade would you give yourself and why?

_____

_____

_____

_____

_____

_____

❷ How easy or difficult was it to accomplish this task? What did you do that you feel was particularly innovative and worked well?

_____

_____

_____

_____

❸ If you could do it all over again what would you do differently?

_____

_____

_____

❹ What's the most important thing you learned in playing this game?

_____

_____

_____

❺ Did you identify any skills or techniques where you need a refresher? Describe.

_____

_____

Variations to Game

This game is an especially good opportunity for you or your instructor to adjust the focus to specific techniques or seasonal ingredients, whether those listed or those from the "other" category. Students can also create their own technique and ingredient cards (though ingredient cards need to be written and vetted well in advance to allow for purchasing). The instructor can assign certain techniques to individual teams who need development in a given area. Students can work individually or in teams. The essential element of the game that should be maintained is the experience of experimenting with flavor combinations and problem solving to create a unique and compelling dish.

Game: Reverse Food and Beverage Pairing

Chefs, servers and sommeliers are asked every day what beverage would best complement a dish. Knowledge and mastery of flavors and flavor combinations needs to go beyond food to include food and beverage pairing, whether alcoholic in the case of wine, beer and spirits or even nonalcoholic beverage pairings.

Less typical is developing a menu item to match a beverage. But it does happen. For example, dinners designed to market a particular wine, beer or spirit are not unusual events held by vintners or beverage companies.

This game, played in two parts, has you tasting a beverage, alcoholic or non-alcoholic, depending on your age, school policy, and preference, and developing a dish of complementary flavors.

In part one, taste the beer, wine, spirit, non-alcoholic beer, non-alcoholic wine, soft drink or sparkling juice supplied by your instructor. Really taste it. Using tasting techniques from the flavor chapter, diagram the predominant tastes and flavors of the beverage.

Next, using the techniques described in the Culinary Improvisation chapter, develop a menu concept, soup, salad, appetizer, entrée, or dessert that would complement the beverage, superimposing complementary, contrasting or bridging flavors upon your initial diagram above. Describe those factors in both the beverage and the food that you think would work together to form a strong combination:

1.

2.

3.

4.

5.

Finally for Part I, prepare an ingredient list and shopping list (if not using exclusively available pantry items) for the menu item you have developed and submit to your instructor for approval.

In Part II, cook the dish and organize a tasting for your classmates to evaluate the strength of the pairing.

Specifications for Game

ANTICIPATED TIME: FOUR HOUR LAB IN TWO PARTS
one hour initial tasting and planning separated by time for purchasing. three-hour lab to follow.

PART I

Concept Presentation	10 minutes
Student Tasting and Notes	10 minutes
Menu Concept Planning and Formulation	25 minutes
Ingredient and Shopping Lists and Game Plan	15 minutes

PART II

Review of Concept and Game Plan	10 Minutes
Station Set-up and Mise en Place	15 Minutes
Cooking	95 Minutes
Structured Tasting and Comments	30 Minutes
Clean-Up and Debriefing	30 Minutes

Ingredients Needed (per team of 2-3)

There should be sufficient amounts of beverages to allow for multiple tastes, before, during and after cooking and in both Part I and Part II. Instructors should require spitting for alcoholic beverages.

Students will prepare shopping lists for this exercise or can be told to limit their designs to those incorporating the larder of available ingredients.

Pantry staples such as flour, butter, sugar, eggs, grains, stock and sauces should be available as always.

Game Details

This game is for a student with medium to advanced skills. You should be comfortable in a kitchen and be familiar with basic preparations/applications, at minimum. There is no maximum skill level. Even professional chefs have fun with and are challenged by this game.

The instructor should choose the beverage and have enough on hand for both parts of the game.

Some beverage suggestions are:

Beer: complex styles from the US, Canada, Belgium and Germany prove interesting.

Wine: a limitless range of quality and reasonable options from light (Vinho Verde, Prosecco) to medium (Sauvignon Blanc, Chardonnay, Light Reds) to heavier (Cote du Rhone, Zinfandel, and Shiraz). Try for wines with pronounced food flavors.

Cordials (especially for Baking and Pastry applications)

Sparkling Juice—effervescence adds complexity

Juice Blends

Quality Non-alcoholic Beer

Quality Non-alcoholic Wine

Student Guidelines

- **Safety First.** Put knife safety and safe food handling at the fore.
- Use the tools in the flavor chapter to help you brainstorm initial ideas and guide you through the game. Discuss merits of all suggestions and reach consensus on leading concepts.
- Write a plan for recipe execution. Do not be afraid to alter the design as you go.
- Taste as you go. For unusual combination experiments, try a small amount before proceeding with the whole batch wherever possible.
- Divide the prep work among the team.
- Maintain constant communication.
- Present finished product in a way that is visually appealing and is served at the appropriate temperature. Use the plating template in the resource section as a guide.
- Guide classmates through tasting process.
- Compare the flavors of the food and beverage periodically during the cooking process to see flavors evolve.

Supporting Activities

Which beverage were you given or did you select for this game? What flavors immediately come to mind as associated with that ingredient?

_____

_____

_____

_____

What other flavors might pair well with the featured beverage? What cooking techniques could be used to highlight the flavors? Will you contrast, complement or bridge?

_____

_____

_____

_____

Sketch some ideas regarding the dish you might prepare.

Refine your ideas.

How would the item be presented?

How might you evaluate the success of your approach?

_____

_____

_____

_____

_____

Create a prep list and plan of attack for this game.

_____

_____

_____

_____

_____

Reflection Questions

❶ If you had to grade yourself on your performance on this game, what grade would you give yourself and why?

_____

_____

_____

_____

_____

❷ How easy or difficult was it to accomplish this task? What flavor combinations do you feel were particularly innovative and worked well?

_____

_____

_____

_____

_____

❸ If you could do it all over again what would you do differently?

_____

_____

_____

_____

❹ What's the most important thing you learned in playing this game?

_____

_____

_____

_____

❺ Have you had an experience like this in industry? If so, how did you deal with it? If not, how would you anticipate dealing with it?

_____

_____

_____

_____

_____

Variations to Game
If sufficient variety and quantity of ingredients are on hand, this game could be completed in one session.

Game: Quick Fix

In many ways bold flavors can speak for themselves. While few tastes or textures can rival slowly cooked barbecue or a braised cut of meat, there are many foods with flavors that pop with high impact immediately out of the package, off the vine, or off the shelf. Red wine, fresh orange zest, chocolate, anchovies, soy sauce, curry paste, vanilla bean, chili paste, and cinnamon are all intense flavors that need little in the way of preparation to enhance their impact.

What are some other flavors of high impact?

_____

_____

_____

_____

_____

_____

_____

In this game you are challenged to use one or more of these intense flavors to create a dish of high impact. Easy so far? But in under twenty minutes. Because flavors like these are so intense, they don't need much manipulation to provide high impact delicious dishes, provided other quick-cooking ingredients like pasta, fish, chicken, rice and vegetables are available.

Specifications for Game

ANTICIPATED TIME:	2 HOURS
PART I	
Concept Presentation	10 minutes
Student Tasting and Notes	10 minutes
Menu Concept Planning and Formulation	25 minutes
Ingredient and Shopping Lists	
and Game Plan	15 minutes
PART II	
Review of Concept and Game Plan	10 Minutes
Station Set-up and Mise en Place	15 Minutes
Cooking	95 Minutes
Structured Tasting and Comments	30 Minutes
Clean-Up and Debriefing	30 Minutes

Game Details

This game is for a student with basic to advanced skills. You should be comfortable in a kitchen and be familiar with basic preparations and applications, at minimum.

Student Guidelines

- **Safety First.** Put knife safety and safe food handling at the fore.
- Since you only have twenty minutes to prepare your dish, spend plenty of time in the preparation, design and planning phase so that you can make every second count in the kitchen.
- Divide the prep work among the team.
- Maintain constant communication.
- Present finished product in a way that is visually appealing and is served at the appropriate temperature.
- Guide classmates through tasting process.

Ingredients Needed

A variety of high-impact high-flavor items. These can be distributed one or more per team.

In addition, a variety of quick-cooking items such as rice, pasta, couscous, seafood, meat or poultry and a variety of fruits and vegetables, in addition to the usual pantry items, should be made available.

Anchovies	Parmesan Cheese	Bleu Cheese
Chili Oil	Chili Paste	Harissa
Dried Shrimp	Fish Sauce	Curry Paste
Pesto	Lavender	Dill
Canned Sardines	Curry Powder	Cinnamon
Sherry Vinegar	Wine or Non-Alcoholic Wine	Cardamom
Sambal Oelek or Sriracha	Olives	Lemon
Rosemary	Black Peppercorns	Grapefruit
Other...	Other...	Other...

✂

Page intentionally
left blank, back side
of cutout cards

Supporting Activities

How can you design a menu that features one or more of these high-impact flavors and can be cooked entirely in under twenty minutes? What elements might you have to modify in order to meet the timing goals?

_____

_____

_____

_____

_____

Sketch some preliminary ideas.

Refine your ideas.

Create a work plan for creating the menu. Double check this plan against the time requirement.

_____

_____

_____

_____

Create a prep list.

_____

_____

_____

_____

_____

_____

Reflection Questions

❷ Describe the process you followed during today's game. What worked well?
What could have been better?

_____

_____

_____

_____

_____

❷ What's something you learned about cooking from this activity? What's something you learned about
yourself from this activity?

_____

_____

_____

_____

_____

❸ What's the practical application of this game to the commercial kitchen?

_____

_____

_____

_____

_____

_____

> **Variations to Game**
> Depending on the level of the students and the
> instructional goals, students could select or be as-
> signed flavors to work with. A popular variation with
> students is to have each student bring a particular
> item with them to class and then exchange.

Chapter Summary

In this chapter you experienced a variety of ways to expand your ideas about flavors and flavor combinations in some very challenging settings, some realistic everyday-type situations and some less-realistic. Either way, you were challenged to think creatively and improvise while cooking dishes that employ unique but effective flavor combinations.

Many of us in the culinary world worship at the altar of the senses. We want to see, taste, touch, do, work with our hands—a need to channel our sensory intoxication drove us into the kitchen. A good chef can execute a recipe, improve it, or create a new one altogether based on their sensory impressions of the dish as it evolves. Developing the palate through an exploration of flavors using all of the senses—smell, taste, touch, even sound—will improve your craft and differentiate you from the pack.

Chapter 7 Assessment Questions

❶ Describe a flavor combination you tried that worked especially well. Why did it work?

_____

_____

_____

_____

_____

❷ Describe a flavor combination you tried that didn't work. Why not?

_____

_____

_____

_____

_____

_____

❸ Describe the process of solving a problem in one of the games.
What challenges or obstacles did you face? Where did your team excel?

_____

_____

_____

_____

_____

❹ Describe the cooking process you used for each game. What worked well?
What would you have done differently?

_____

_____

_____

_____

_____

❺ Assess your final outcome. What worked in your concept? What didn't?
What would you do differently in the future?

_____

_____

_____

_____

_____

8/
Teamwork Games

Commercial kitchens, whether in hotels, restaurants, institutions or other settings are operations that must generate revenue and control costs. Chefs and managers seek employees who can cook well, of course. But whether that cook can work as part of a cohesive team so that management can achieve its larger goals is also important. The cook who makes the most delicious hollandaise sauce is worth little to the organization if she or he has bad work habits, angers coworkers, wastes food, steals, or is otherwise a bad team member.

CHAPTER OBJECTIVES

By the end of these games you should be able to:

① Demonstrate a leadership role in the kitchen.

② Overcome leadership challenges in the kitchen.

③ Work as a team member in the kitchen.

④ Overcome challenges as a team.

⑤ List and explain some challenges in leadership and team building and how they might be overcome.

While:

❻ Demonstrating appropriate knife skills.

❼ Demonstrating appropriate cooking techniques.

❽ Demonstrating appropriate kitchen sanitation and safety procedures.

❾ Cultivating advanced culinary technique.

Conversely, with experience and practice, a new cook can always improve on culinary technique. But to be a valued employee, that cook first has to work well as part of the team. As a young cook my knife skills left a lot to be desired, both in terms of speed and accuracy. But I was a good team member—I showed up on time or early and eager to work, communicated with coworkers and persevered. Over time, and after cutting through countless cases of produce, my knife skills gradually improved.

Kitchens are workplaces that are highly dependent on a group of people—a **team**—performing a variety of tasks in harmony. No one can do it all alone. Here's an example of work in the kitchen:

Our team was really excited to have Jared, a culinary school extern, come on board for a summer externship. On his first day, Jared learned the importance of treating everyone on the team, from the dishwasher, Felix, to the executive chef, Lisa, with respect. After being given the usual tour around the kitchen and meeting the entire staff, Lisa asked Jared to prep a few things. Lisa told Jared that part of the culture of that kitchen is that everyone works together on prep in the morning and does his or her own dishes until Felix switches from prep to the dish machine for lunch service.

Jared made good headway on his prep list—chopping three bunches of parsley, roasting a pint of garlic cloves, rendering some lardons, and chopping onions. But as he completed each task, rather than cleaning his station and pots and beginning the next step, he let things pile up on Felix's station.

Felix said nothing and cleaned up Jared's mess.

At dinner service, Jared worked the salad station. As the night got busier, Jared noticed that Felix was visiting each station stocking warm clean plates at the hot food stations and putting clean plates in the lowboy refrigerators at the cold food stations. But he didn't visit Jared. As Jared got to his last plate he asked Felix for some clean ones. But they were already distributed throughout the kitchen. He asked the pastry cook for some cold plates from the pastry station but was told there were none to spare. He asked at the garde manger station where the cook, Su, claimed to have none, but then eventually handed over a few.

By that point, Jared had been away from his station for ten minutes at the height of the dinner rush. He was in the weeds and struggled through the rest of service to catch up on salads. No one helped him.

The next morning, Jared apologized to Felix and cleaned up after himself during prep. During dinner service, Jared had all of the clean cool plates he needed at his station and even had time to visit the other stations during service to get to know the menu and the plating of each item.

A kitchen is dependent on each link the chain fulfilling its function. If the food is not received in a timely manner and to quality specifications, storage, butchery, prep and cooking not done correctly, clean equipment not available or not fully functional, or food not delivered to the guest efficiently, the chain breaks, and the guest could have a bad experience.

When we speak with chefs about the characteristics that they seek in their employees, the idea of teamwork is peppered throughout: "a team player," "someone who works well on a team," "someone who can feel like part of the family," "someone who can get along with everyone."

This chapter will challenge you and your teammates through some games where you will need to come together as a team and overcome obstacles to succeed. Some of these situations may be harder than those you will face in the industry, so if you can play these games well you should do well at work! As importantly, some of the games may put you in the position of leading the team, an important role not to be taken lightly, and one that is good to practice in school before you need to do it for real.

From the Line: Case Study

CHEF DE CUISINE FORTUNATO NICOTRA AND
EXECUTIVE PASTRY CHEF LARA BRUMNACH, FELIDIA, NEW YORK CITY

A leader is a key element in any team. But a leader would not be able to lead without a team that works together to support the leader and the team as a whole. This concept is true in many aspects of life including sports, politics, communities, and of course, kitchens.

A restaurant begins with a team that includes all of the restaurant staff—from the owners to the cooks to the dishwashers. This larger team is broken down into multiple groups, or teams, including front of the house and back of the house staff. Those two teams are divided further into smaller groups—and each group has a leader to facilitate responsibilities. As demonstrated in the example of Jared, every member of the team must keep up their part for the whole to succeed; even a dishwasher with a grudge can put a line chef in the weeds. A leader's primary responsibility is to make sure that every person is working in sync with the system. Often a lack of leadership and teamwork creates the most negative dynamic in a restaurant. An environment that is negative overall - or positive - can affect the morale of the establishment as a whole, in turn affecting staff, food, and sometimes even the clientele.

In this case, Chef de Cuisine Fortunato Nicotra and Executive Pastry Chef Lara Brumnach of Felidia in New York City share their thoughts on how effective communication plays out in the kitchen at Lydia Bastianich's New York upscale Italian restaurant.

Chef Fortunato and Chef Lara both agree that one of the most important characteristics when hiring a team member is the individual's consideration for the team as a whole. They look for a demonstration of pride in the work—on an individual level and as a member of the restaurant team. A solid team is needed to assist in achieving the goal of a restaurant. The work of each and every staff member plays a role in the final product. Thus, it is important that each team member takes pride in their part of the meal to ensure a final product that reflects the best of the team's ability.

As the adage goes, "two heads are better than one". Team members support each other in decision making, staff management, purchasing, selecting menu items—to name a few duties. For example, Chef Fortunato was excited to add beef-cheeks to his menu. After many trials, he was unable to find a suitable vegetable to accompany this meat dish. Chef Lara was happy to make the suggestion of serving the meat with grilled spring onions. Although this concept of helping one another seems simple, support is an important feature of any team. This type of collaboration is sadly too often stymied by egos, personality clashes, or by people not valuing the ideas of their colleagues.

Another proverb promises that "many hands make light work." Often, an extra set of hands can be extremely useful in the kitchen. Chef Fortunato and Chef Lara recounted a story when the Felidia kitchen staff was busy preparing a spring salad with asparagus and poached eggs and the poached eggs did not turn out. Chef Lara and her pastry team were not terribly busy at that moment; they put down their duties and made the poached eggs for the line. This teamwork and interaction between the culinary and the pastry staffs enabled service to go uninterrupted.

Chef Fortunato and Chef Lara emphasize the importance of the group dynamic at Felidia. They encourage their staff to grow their positions by taking on new and greater responsibilities within the team. Chef Lara shared an example of a man who worked his way from a dishwashing position to become bread baker for the restaurant. During the job search for the bread baker position, Chef Lara noticed that during free time at the restaurant, this employee took it upon himself to watch how the bread was made and practice baking. Chef Lara and Chef Fortunato knew that this man understood the needs of the position and was familiar with the time and effort necessary for this job since he had thoroughly observed the role. He understood the commitment and took

pride in the products of Felidia. These qualities allowed Chef Lara and Chef Fortunato to confidently hire him for this position within their team.

Lack of teamwork and leadership is often more noticeable in a group environment. When these skills are not present in a restaurant the entire energy of the staff, the food, and even the guests are affected.

Chef Lara and Chef Fortunato recounted an episode in which lack of leadership and confusion amongst the team caused a near disaster when they traveled to Detroit to cook for 250 people at a special event.

Fortunato's Misfortune:

Only 4 people from the New York restaurant were at the site to assist with the cooking. The Felidia team was working in an unfamiliar kitchen with 15 other cooks with whom they had never worked before. The Felidia team started the soup for the dinner. Chef Fortunato told one of the cooks from the local Detroit kitchen to check on the soup every fifteen minutes. The cook checking the soup mistook the dish for a pot of steamed vegetables and, once he ascertained that the vegetables were tender, strained the liquid out of the pot. Thankfully, someone from the Felidia team thought to check on the soup, recognized the mishap and was able to correct the mistake by improvising another broth and saving the dish. Had he not, the dinner would have been missing its first course!

Lara's Dilemma:

Lara was making a Limoncello Tiramisu for dessert. Like Chef Fortunato, she was not in her own kitchen, and did not have the equipment she was accustomed to working with. Instead of cooking with her equipment, which would involve making each dessert in an individual ramekin, she was forced to make the dessert in hotel pans, using 3 ½ inch round cutters to carve the dessert into servings. Lara was extremely displeased by the appearance of the final product, which didn't cut cleanly and looked saggy. In a very short amount of time, with the assistance of a fellow team member, Chef Lara searched the limited kitchen and found a solution to the problem. Using leftover ladyfingers and some almond slivers, Chef Lara masked the unattractive sides of the desserts. This adaptation not only disguised the problematic appearance of the dessert but also added an additional crunchy texture to the dish. All of the guests and restaurant owner Lydia Bastianich were impressed by the taste and appearance of the dessert created by Chef Lara and her teammate.

Because of the long and intense hours a restaurant staff spends together, it is important that every player works for the team. The dynamics are often like those of a large family: sometimes everyone gets along and sometimes you're stuck together and have to deal with the group. With this in mind, it is important that every member of the staff understands the importance of this dynamic and finds a way to be a productive, considerate, and supportive part of the team.

Also, keep in mind that a strong team is necessary to the sustainability of a business. The shared goal of every team member is the health and success of the restaurant. With everyone working toward that goal, there's a real shared sense of accomplishment in every success. Team members not only rely on each other—they can back each other up in times of need, as demonstrated in examples throughout this book (think poached eggs). Teamwork is built on many of the skills we encourage you to develop, especially good communication.

Case Study Questions

❶ Were you surprised at the examples in this case of how closely an executive chef and executive pastry chef work together? Why or why not?

_____

_____

_____

❷ Give an example from your work, school or personal life where a team fell apart. What happened? What could have prevented the breakdown?

_____

_____

_____

_____

❸ Give an example from your work, school or personal life where a team came together and worked effectively. What happened? What were the key factors in your team's success?

_____

_____

_____

_____

❹ This chapter is devoted to team-building games. Without knowing the specifics of the games that follow, based on this case study, what are some things your team can do to ensure success?

_____

_____

_____

_____

Game: Team Cooks

Menus are complicated things. Many hands are involved in making even one completed dish, from menu development and cost control, ordering, receiving, butchery, vegetable prep, sauces, line cooks, expediter, server, and steward. As was previously discussed, a breakdown in any one of these areas leads to chaos.

Describe what would happen if you removed any one of these elements from the equation:

_____

_____

_____

_____

_____

It is important that everyone on the team has their mind on the end goal: the finished dish reaching the customer. Keeping the final product in mind helps to ensure that at each step along the way, every team member who touches it ensures that the dish makes sense when it comes together, using quality ingredients, appropriate portions, properly cooked and seasoned components, and an eye for visual appeal. Of course the front-of-the-house ambiance and order must be in place as well, and the waitstaff must be able to explain and sell your dish!

A common problem in commercial kitchens is that staff members do not consistently have their eyes set on the end goal. For example, the chef may order twelve-ounce whole trout for a particular grilled fish preparation. If twenty-ounce fish of high quality arrive instead, the receiving clerk or butcher may be tempted to receive them. But at nearly double the size, the fish may be too large to be used per the chef's original intent.

In this game your team is challenged to cook in a way where only one person—the team leader—has the end goal in mind, and suffer the struggles related to that challenge. For the leader, there is an additional challenge of dividing the steps for the dish among many hands in a way that is expeditious, fairly balanced, and speaking toward the individual strengths of the team members.

Game Details

This game is for a student with basic to advanced skills. You should be comfortable in a kitchen and be familiar with basic preparations and applications, at minimum. There is no maximum skill level. Even professional chefs have fun with and are challenged by this game.

In this game you should form a team of three or four students. Your instructor may divide you or allow you to select.

First, determine who will be the leader of the team by completing the following worksheet individually and then comparing notes as a team.

Specifications for Game

ANTICIPATED TIME:	THREE HOUR LAB
Concept Presentation	20 minutes
Team Leader Meeting and Station Set-up	10 minutes
Cooking	100 minutes
Tasting, Discussion and Debriefing	30 minutes
Clean-up	20 minutes

Student Guidelines

- **Safety First.** Put knife safety and safe food handling at the fore.
- Think as you go. While doing your work, think of the questions posed above.
- Follow the rules!

Team Leader Worksheet

What characteristics do you look for in a leader in the kitchen?

1. _____

2. _____

3. _____

Compare your responses with those of your teammates. Choose the five characteristics that are most important to you as a team.

1. _____

2. _____

3. _____

4. _____

5. _____

- Next, circle the two characteristics you feel are most important.
- Select a member of your team who you feel possesses some of those five characteristics. Elect that person your team leader.
- Your instructor will meet privately with all of the team leaders. Team leaders will be given a recipe that the team is to prepare. Each team will prepare the same recipe. For reasons important to the game, the recipe is not printed here. The recipe is in the instructor guide or your instructor may choose a different one.
- In the mean time, the team members should set up work stations with cutting boards, knives, waste bowls and sanitizing buckets.
- Your team leader will return and will guide you through the recipe preparation. But here is the challenge: Your team leader may not tell you anything about the final dish as a whole and you many not ask any clarifying questions.
- The team leader will tell you to do specific tasks that will contribute to the finished dish such as: "Julienne a carrot," "Caramelize three shallots," or, "Cut this into half-inch slices." Team members may not ask any questions but must do as they are told. The team leader can, however, offer feedback along the way, such as, "That's good," or "Please cut the next ones a little thinner."

Supporting Activities

As you cook the entire dish, make some notes on the following questions:

Did the qualities of the team leader you listed help in the process? If so, how? If not, why not?

_____

_____

_____

_____

How might you do this differently if you knew what the finished product was to be?

_____

_____

_____

_____

What are your frustrations?

_____

_____

_____

_____

What is going well?

_____

_____

_____

_____

Reflection Questions

When you taste your completed dish, answer the following questions:

Team Members:

❶ Did the qualities of the team leader help in the process?

_____

_____

_____

_____

❷ How might you have done things differently if you knew what the finished product was to be?

_____

_____

_____

_____

❸ What were your frustrations?

_____

_____

_____

_____

❹ What went well?

_____

_____

_____

❺ How did you do as a team?

_____

_____

_____

_____

❻ What would have improved the team's process?

_____

_____

_____

_____

❼ How did your team leader do?

_____

_____

_____

_____

❽ How could your team leader have been more helpful to you without breaking the rules of the game?

_____

_____

_____

_____

_____

Team Leader:

❶ What went well?

_____

_____

_____

_____

❷ What were your frustrations?

_____

_____

_____

_____

❸ How did knowing what the finished product was to be affect how you tried to communicate the tasks?

_____

_____

_____

_____

❹ How did you divide the tasks?

_____

_____

_____

_____

_____

❺ How did the team do?

_____

_____

_____

❻ What would have improved the team's process?

_____

_____

_____

❼ How did you do as a leader?

_____

_____

_____

❽ How could you have led better?

_____

_____

_____

_____

Variations to Game
This game can be adapted for any number of recipes. Entrée plates with multiple components and some unusual flavor combinations and garnishes work well.

Game: Sensory Perception

This game has you working creatively as a team while testing your flavor and palate skills. It's a lot of fun and if you work well as a team you will be amazed at the results.

In this game, each member of a three-person team will be allowed to use a different sense:

- Taste
- Smell
- Touch

to evaluate a soup or stew prepared by the instructor or a student assistant in advance. Then the team will be challenged to reconstruct the dish, combining their sensory perceptions.

Game Details

This game is for a student with medium to advanced skills. You should be comfortable in a kitchen and be familiar with basic preparations and applications, at minimum. You should have done at least one game from the flavor and palate development chapter.

- Students should form teams of three. Instructor can form teams or students can self-select.
- Each team should designate a taster, a smeller and a toucher. Each student should blindfold him/herself (side towels work well). No peeking!
- The instructor should distribute cups of a warm (not too hot) previously prepared soup or stew (a recommended recipe is provided in the instructor guide). Tasters should taste, smellers should smell and touchers should touch. It is helpful for the touchers to also have a plate so that they may pour the soup out and palpate the particulates.
- The instructor should collect the leftovers while all students remain blindfolded, touchers should wash their hands and the team members should complete their portion of the following worksheet:
- Note: if some groups have more than three members, more than one student could be assigned to the same sense.
- Cook! The instructor will provide a variety of ingredients from which to choose. All ingredients necessary to prepare the soup as well as a number of distracter ingredients should be made available.
- As you cook use **all** of your senses and the tasting notes of each group member to try to get as close as possible to the original.
- Once you have a finished product, conduct a comparison tasting with the original provided (again) by the instructor.

Specifications for Game

ANTICIPATED TIME: THREE HOUR LAB
Concept Presentation . . . . 20 minutes
Student Sensory Evaluation,
Planning and Station Set-up. . 20 minutes
Cooking. . . . . 90 minutes
Tasting, Discussion
and Debriefing. . . . . 30 minutes
Clean-up . . . . 20 minutes

Ingredients Needed
(per team of 2-3)

If using recipe in the instructor guide, a finished batch is needed as well as ingredients to make ¼ batch per team. In addition, some decoy and extra ingredients are needed. A variety of spices and seasonings should be made available.

Student Guidelines

- **Safety First.** Put knife safety and safe food handling at the fore.
- Use the tools in the flavor chapter to help you with your sensory evaluation.
- Write a plan for recipe execution. Do not be afraid to alter the design as you go.
- Taste as you go. When making an adjustment, try a small amount before proceeding with the whole batch wherever possible.
- Divide the prep work among the team.
- Maintain constant communication

Tasting Notes Worksheet

As you sample the product, whether by taste, smell or touch, describe your impressions
as richly as possible:

_____

_____

_____

_____

Next, guess what ingredients are included in the dish and list them below:

_____

_____

_____

_____

Finally, compare notes with your teammates and circle areas of agreement, adding
additional impressions and ideas below:

_____

_____

_____

_____

Tasting Notes Worksheet, continued

Next, as a group, devise a list of ingredients you think you will need to make this dish:

_____

_____

_____

_____

_____

_____

And a method and division of labor:

_____

_____

_____

_____

_____

_____

_____

Reflection Questions

❶ How was the process?

_____

_____

_____

_____

❷ How did the team need to work together and rely on one another?

_____

_____

_____

_____

❸ Where did things go well?

_____

_____

_____

_____

❹ Where did things break down?

_____

_____

_____

_____

❺ How did the product replication go? How close was your team to the original?

_____

_____

_____

_____

❻ Which sensory test was most helpful?

_____

_____

_____

_____

❼ At the conclusion of the game, your instructor shared the recipe. What surprised you about this recipe?

_____

_____

_____

_____

❽ What did you miss in your attempt?

_____

_____

_____

_____

Variations to Game
Instructors can use the recipe in the instructor guide or can create their own. Where pre-preparation is not possible, store-bought product could be used, preferably a quality product where instructor has access to the ingredient list. Or, if time allows, teams can create recipes and challenge the other teams to replicate their creations.

Game: Find Your Match

In the previous game, Sensory Perception, your team was challenged to replicate an existing recipe. In many team situations, you have the luxury of choosing your team and can select people with whom you get along, have similar vision, or have complementary skills. In this game, Find Your Match, you will be challenged to form your own team, based not by personality, work-style or friendship, but by desired flavor combination.

In this mystery basket-style game, culinary improvisation and creative cooking are at the fore. The key factor is how you ally yourself to create winning flavor combinations.

Special Rule:

The flavors you've selected must feature prominently in the finished dish.

Game Details

This game is for a student with basic to advanced skills. You should be comfortable in a kitchen and be familiar with basic preparations and applications, at minimum.

The instructor will provide an assortment of brown paper bags with the number of bags corresponding to the number of students participating in the game. Each bag will contain a different ingredient, which may be a fruit, vegetable, grain, protein item or dry good. Instructors might select their own foods based on desired learning outcome and availability or may select from the following list:

Specifications for Game

ANTICIPATED TIME:	THREE HOUR LAB
Concept Presentation	20 minutes
Student Planning and Station Set-up	20 minutes
Cooking	90 minutes
Tasting, Discussion and Debriefing	30 minutes
Clean-up	20 minutes

White Elephant

- Each student should draw a number from 1 to the total number of students in the class.
- Beginning with number 1, students should select a bag from the front of the room and show the product inside. Beginning with number 2, students may select another bag or may steal the ingredient that someone with a lower number has chosen. If someone's item is taken, that person selects another bag. Students should pay attention to who has each ingredient.
- At the end of this activity, every student will have an ingredient.
- Next, form a team of three based, *not on who you want to work with but on which flavors you think will work together in an interesting way to form a dish.* Some pairings will seem like naturals; others may be more challenging and will take a good measure of creativity and improvisation on your part in order to achieve a good result.
- Next develop a plan for your dish based on the following worksheet and cook! Prepare an appetizer, entrée, or dessert featuring all of your group's ingredients and using available pantry items as well.

Ingredients Needed (per team of 2-3)

Obviously, the featured items will need to be purchased in small quantities. These should be bagged before the start of class. Instructor should choose one item per student.

Pantry staples such as flour, butter, sugar, eggs, grains, stock and sauces should be available as always.

½ lb. Salmon	2 Pork Chops	½ lb. Italian Sausage
1 bu. Arugula	1 bu. Leeks	1 c. Quinoa
1 small package Tea Leaves	½ lb. Scallops	1 lb. Pumpkin
1 Eggplant	¾ c. Amaranth	4 oz. Chocolate
1 nub Ginger	2 bu. Spinach	½ lb. Mushrooms
5 oz. Bleu Cheese	1 bu. Cilantro	1 lb. Pork Belly
2 Turkey Thighs	1 package Tofu	1 Nutmeg
1 jar Chili Oil	1 package Crackers	3 Turnips
3 Apples	3 Pears	1 bu. Grapes
4 Peaches	4 Kiwi	1 lb. Cherries
Other...	Other...	Other...

✂

Page intentionally
left blank, back side
of cutout cards

Student Guidelines

- **Safety First.** Put knife safety and safe food handling at the fore.
- Use the tools in the flavor chapter to help you brainstorm initial ideas and guide you through the game. Discuss merits of all suggestions and reach consensus on leading concepts.
- Write a plan for recipe execution. Do not be afraid to alter the design as you go.
- Taste as you go. For unusual combination experiments, try a small amount before proceeding with the whole batch wherever possible.
- Divide the prep work among the team.
- Maintain constant communication.
- Present finished product in a way that is visually appealing and is served at the appropriate temperature. Use the plating template in the resource section as a guide.

Supporting Activities

What are the primary ingredients you are working with?

1. _____

2. _____

3. _____

What about these ingredients made you want to work together? What do you think will work well?

_____

_____

_____

_____

What pantry items will you add to make this dish?

_____

_____

_____

_____

Do you anticipate any potential pitfalls or challenges?

_____

_____

_____

_____

Sketch out some menu concepts using these ingredients.

Refine your ideas.

Create a work plan and division of labor for this menu item. (Don't be afraid to alter as you go).

_____

_____

_____

_____

Diagram a possible plate presentation for this menu item. (Don't be afraid to alter as you go).

Reflection Questions

❶ How was the process of forming a team not based on personality or skills but on resource availability?

_____

_____

_____

_____

❷ Would you have worked with these teammates if you hadn't needed their ingredients? Why or why not?

_____

_____

_____

_____

❸ What worked well with regard to flavor and cooking process?

_____

_____

_____

_____

❹ What worked well with regard to team process?

_____

_____

_____

_____

❺ What was a struggle with regard to flavor and cooking process?

_____

_____

_____

❻ What was a struggle with regard to team process?

_____

_____

_____

_____

Variations to Game

This game is an especially good opportunity for you or your instructor to adjust the focus to specific and/or seasonal ingredients, whether those listed or those from the "other" category. Students can also create their own technique and ingredient cards (though ingredient cards need to be written and vetted well in advance to allow for purchasing). For a more challenging version of this game, use stronger or more unusual ingredients and form larger groups, necessitating that more flavors be incorporated. This game also represents a good opportunity to focus on ethnic or regional flavors by selecting relevant ingredients.

Game: Ingredient Trade

In the previous game, Find Your Match, you were challenged to form a team based on the compatible flavors held by you and your classmates. This game is very nearly the reverse of that. This is a mystery basket game of a different order.

Your team will be given a mystery basket, as will the other teams. But your ingredients may not work well together at all. Neither will theirs.

The challenge in this teamwork game is to trade ingredients with neighboring teams to create combinations that work—with a twist.

....

Game Details

This game is for a student with medium to advanced skills. You should be comfortable in a kitchen and be familiar with basic preparations/applications, at minimum. There is no maximum skill level.

Students should form teams of 3–4. Students should be given a mystery basket to include:

- A starch (potato, pasta, rice, grain)
- A protein item (fish, poultry, meat or meat substitute)
- A vegetable
- A **strong** seasoning of distinctive flavor such as mustard, chocolate, chili oil, vinegar, or an herb or spice

Once your team receives your basket, complete the following worksheet.

....

Ingredients Needed (per team of 3–4)

The instructor can compose mystery baskets based on product availability and intended learning outcomes. In addition, pantry items and staples should be made available. Each team needs approximately ½ lb. of protein item, 1 lb. of starch item after cooking, ½ lb. of vegetable, and a small amount of main seasoning item.

Student Guidelines

- **Safety First.** Put knife safety and safe food handling at the fore.
- Use the tools in the flavor chapter to help you brainstorm initial ideas and guide you through the game. Discuss merits of all suggestions and reach consensus on leading concepts.
- Write a plan for recipe execution. Do not be afraid to alter the design as you go.
- Taste as you go. For unusual combination experiments, try a small amount before proceeding with the whole batch wherever possible.
- Divide the prep work among the team.
- Maintain constant communication.
- Present finished product in a way that is visually appealing and is served at the appropriate temperature. Use the plating template in the resource section as a guide.

Supporting Activity

List the ingredients in your mystery basket:

Starch: _____

Protein: _____

Vegetable:_____

Seasoning:_____

Which work well together?

_____

Which do not?

_____

Next, select one ingredient that you feel does not work well with the others. Elect a team member to bring that ingredient to the instructor.

The instructor will then have one team member and one ingredient contributed from each group. Based on their knowledge of the team and the other ingredients, that team member's job is to replace her- or himself with both a person and an ingredient contributed by another team. So you're swapping out both an ingredient and a team member.

Now with your new team formed, complete the following worksheet and cook an appetizer, entrée and dessert improvisationally that you feel best make use of your team's strengths and your available products:

What are the ingredients you are working with?

Starch: _____   Other new addition:_____

Protein: _____

Vegetable:_____

Seasoning:_____

Group strength analysis: What things can our team members do well together?
What strengths does each individual bring?

_____

_____

_____

_____

What about these ingredients work together? What do you think will work well?

_____

_____

_____

_____

Do you anticipate any potential pitfalls or challenges?

_____

_____

_____

_____

How can your skills merge with these ingredients to create something extraordinary?

_____

_____

_____

_____

_____

Sketch out some menu concepts using these ingredients.

_____

_____

_____

_____

Create a work plan and division of labor for this menu item. (Don't be afraid to alter as you go).

_____

_____

_____

_____

Diagram a possible plate presentation for this menu item. (Don't be afraid to alter as you go).

Reflection Questions

❶ Did the strengths of your team and teammates show themselves in the completed dish? Why or why not? Cite specific examples.

_____

_____

_____

_____

❷ How did you feel about the addition to your team? Did it work in the end? Why or why not?

_____

_____

_____

_____

❸ What worked well with regard to flavor and cooking process?

_____

_____

_____

_____

❹ What worked well with regard to team process?

_____

_____

_____

_____

_____

❺ What was a struggle with regard to flavor and cooking process?

_____

_____

_____

_____

_____

❻ What was a struggle with regard to team process?

_____

_____

_____

_____

_____

Game: Kitchen Entrepreneur

This game puts your team in an entrepreneurial environment. The challenge is to create a menu item based on a basic dough, and market and price it competitively. In this game the instructor can be the judge of success or you could test your products in the marketplace at your school.

In playing this game, the competitive environment will introduce some real questions and challenges to your team.

....

Game Details

This game is for a student with medium to advanced skills. You should be comfortable in a kitchen and be familiar with basic preparations/applications, at minimum. There is no maximum skill level.

This game challenges your team to produce a cost-effective and appealing crust-based menu item. The size, shape, flavorings and branding of the items are your items are up to you but you must observe the following limitations:

- Only pantry items provided by the instructor can be used.
- Excluding basic seasonings, only three pantry items may be incorporated in your dish.
- You must produce at least sixteen portions, displaying ten for "sale".
- Students should form teams of 3–4. Each team should prepare two pounds of pizza dough using a standard recipe from a culinary text.

While the dough is proofing, students should complete the following worksheet.

....

Ingredients Needed (per team of 3–4)

A variety of meats, cheeses, fruits and vegetables can be made available in addition to pantry items.

Student Guidelines

- **Safety First.** Put knife safety and safe food handling at the fore.
- Use the tools in the flavor chapter to help you brainstorm initial ideas and guide you through the game. Discuss merits of all suggestions and reach consensus on leading concepts.
- Write a plan for recipe execution. Do not be afraid to alter the design as you go.
- Taste as you go. For unusual combination experiments, try a small amount before proceeding with the whole batch wherever possible.
- Divide the prep work among the team.
- Maintain constant communication.
- Present finished product in a way that is visually appealing and is served at the appropriate temperature.

Supporting Activities

What ingredients might be combined with the dough to add value? Brainstorm.

_____

_____

_____

_____

Do you anticipate any potential pitfalls or challenges?

_____

_____

_____

Are you stifled by the restriction on the number of ingredients that may be added? Why or why not?

_____

_____

_____

Sketch out some shapes and concepts using these ingredients.

_____

Create a work plan and division of labor for this menu item. (Don't be afraid to alter as you go).

Diagram a possible plate presentation for this menu item. (Don't be afraid to alter as you go).

Produce sixteen portions of your item, reserving ten for sale or judging.

Reflection Questions

❶ Describe the team process used in this game.

_____

_____

_____

_____

❷ What worked well with regard to team process?

_____

_____

_____

_____

❸ What was a struggle with regard to flavor and cooking process?

_____

_____

_____

❹ What was a struggle with regard to team process?

_____

_____

_____

_____

Variations to Game

Cost restrictions rather than or in addition to ingredient limitations could be imposed for each item. Rather than pizza dough, phyllo, enriched bread dough, puff pastry or another platform could be used. This game is a good opportunity to focus on certain international cuisines depending on restrictions given and pantry items made available.

Chapter Summary

In this chapter you experienced a variety of team scenarios that challenged you to think and work creatively as a team, often in new ways, while simultaneously refining your culinary and flavor skills.

Chapter 8 Assessment Questions

❶ Describe a team you worked with that worked especially well. Why did it work?

_____

_____

_____

_____

❷ Describe a team you worked with that didn't work well. Why not?

_____

_____

_____

_____

❸ Describe a leader (whether natural or chosen) that was effective on one of your teams. What did she or he do that made that person an effective leader?

_____

_____

_____

_____

❹ What did you learn about the team process from these games? How might that help you in the future?

_____

_____

_____

_____

❺ Describe the cooking process you used for each game. What worked well? What would you have done differently?

_____

_____

_____

_____

❻ Assess your final outcome. What worked in your concepts? What didn't? What would you do differently in the future?

_____

_____

_____

_____

To Summarize...

This chapter is about working in harmony as part of a team. Teamwork is not only crucial in sports; it's a guiding principal of our modern working world as well. In a busy kitchen, teamwork is crucial, because it is a system build on many moving parts, and there can be no weak links in the chain of workers required to get the food on the plate to the guest. All strive toward similar goals, and a lesson of this chapter is how to set these goals and get team members to work toward them together. Building teams not from personal preference but for a match of skills or flavors teaches how to be an improvisational professional.

Assessment Rubric for Teamwork Games

CRITERIA	PROFESSIONAL	DEVELOPING	NOVICE
Cooking Advanced Culinary Techniques	Student demonstrated professional-level knife skills and cooking techniques, needing little support. Student worked neatly, observing all safety and sanitation guidelines.	Student demonstrated some professional-level knife skills and cooking techniques, needing support or correction. Student did not neatly maintain station or did not observe some important safety and sanitation guidelines.	Student demonstrated developing skills and cooking techniques, needing help. Student did not maintain station or failed to observe critical safety and sanitation guidelines.**
Teamwork	Student was an active and engaged participant in the team and team members could clearly point to student's contribution. Student fully understood scenario and quickly adapted to situation, helping other students along.	Student worked with team but was not a key contributor to the final result. Student understood scenario and took direction from classmates in order to adapt to the situation.	Student did not show evidence of engagement with team and did not significantly contribute to the result. Student misunderstood scenario or did not adapt to situation.
Adaptive skills Working in groups	Student was an active and engaged participant in the team and team members could clearly point to student's contribution. Student fully understood scenario and quickly adapted to situation, helping other students along.	Student worked with team but was not a key contributor to the final result. Student understood scenario and took direction from classmates in order to adapt to the situation.	Student did not show evidence of engagement with team and did not significantly contribute to the result. Student misunderstood scenario or did not adapt to situation.
Written Communication Informal writing and reflection	Student work exhibited thoughtful reflection on process and included concrete and significant conclusions.	Student work exhibited reflection on process and awareness of issues.	Student work lacked reflection on process or awareness of issues.
Style and Creativity Professional presentation	Student brought innovative and creative ideas: dish was attractive and restaurant quality.	Student did some innovative or creative things: dish was acceptable but unremarkable.	Student did not show evidence of creativity or innovation: dish was only attention-getting due to inadequacies.

*Note: Criteria could be given equal or various weights at instructor's discretion and tied to letter or number grades as desired.

**Note: Critical Safety and Sanitation Violations include: Cross-Contamination, Time/Temperature Violations, and knife handling hazardous to self or others.

9/
Communication Games

In Chapter 6 we discussed problems and problem solving. Problems, you remember, are what happens when there is a negative difference between what is expected and what occurs. So if the expectation is that the pizza you order will arrive hot, within thirty minutes, and it arrives cold after two hours, that's a problem—a negative difference between what is expected and what occurs.

CHAPTER OBJECTIVES

By the end of these games you should be able to:

① Demonstrate effective interpersonal communication in the kitchen.

② Overcome communication challenges in the kitchen

③ List and explain some challenges in communication and how they might be overcome.

While:

❹ Demonstrating appropriate knife skills.

❺ Demonstrating appropriate cooking techniques.

❻ Demonstrating appropriate kitchen sanitation and safety procedures.

❼ Cultivating advanced culinary technique.

❽ Working as an effective team member.

While problems are inevitable, in the kitchen and in life, effective communication skills are a key factor in preventing problems before they occur and dealing with them deftly when they do arrive.

Consider our pizza example. If you were told when you ordered that a delivery would take two hours and that it may not arrive hot, you may be frustrated but you don't have a problem. The reality of the situation is clearly communicated and you can deal with it—by ordering from another pizza shop, by cooking a grilled cheese sandwich instead, by picking the pizza up yourself or even by waiting two hours and being pleasantly surprised if the pizza arrives after only 100 minutes. The key message is that by communicating effectively, the reality remains unchanged but your perception of a problem is eliminated.

Chefs tell us that while they can teach culinary skills, they are always in search of good communicators on their team. A good cook is useless if she neglects to call in sick when she can't come to work, doesn't let her supervisor know about a delivery of suspicious-smelling product that came in early in the morning or doesn't let the front-of-house staff know that she's down to one remaining veal chop before that item is 86'd from the menu. In these examples, effective communication allows a problem to be prevented—a substitute cook can be called in, the dubious item can be replaced or taken off the menu before service and the guests can be warned before they order that the veal chop entrée is not an option. Left to itself, and these issues result in problems ultimately impacting on the guest's experience.

Communication in the professional kitchen need not be limited to speaking with colleagues. Writing is an important form of communication. A clearly written menu, clearly written purchasing specifications for vendors, clearly written prep lists for cooks and plating diagrams for line cooks are all communicating critical information to key constituencies. Similarly, cooks need to communicate verbally with guests, vendors, contractors and other staff. A miscommunication about a guest's food allergy or a food product unfit for consumption can truly be a life-or-death error.

Finally, in the physical performance of cooking, much is communicated without words at all. If you enter the kitchen and notice the chef storming around the range, tasting a sauce and then throwing the pan in the sink, what do you think has happened? Do you think it's a good time to ask her for a signature on an externship form? Or consider a couple in the dining room, gazing into one another's eyes, with their heads a few inches apart. Is it a good time to approach and ask if they were satisfied with their meal?

Imagine being invited to a new acquaintance's home for a meal. Whether you are served raw oysters and champagne, spaghetti with canned tomato sauce, or slow-cooked barbecue ribs may say more about your new friend's feelings toward you than words could. It also may speak volumes about your friend—values, cultural heritage, economic status, amount of leisure time, or even her or his aesthetic taste.

In this chapter you will be challenged by some games that rely on your team's effective written, verbal and even non-verbal communication. You will find yourself not only communicating *about* food, but also communicating *with* food.

From the Line: Case Study

CHEF NATE FELDMILLER, CHEF-OWNER OF CIRCE, KANSAS CITY, MISSOURI

Communications in a restaurant start with serious decisions about what food items are offered and how these items are communicated to the guests. The necessary ingredients to prepare the menu items are ordered via phone, fax, e-mail, or face-to-face and the delivery times are constantly communicated between the vendors and the restaurant staff. The restaurant manager communicates staffing and venue needs, as well as a host of other issues, to a chain of personnel in the front and back of the house.

The menu offerings are communicated from the kitchen to the wait staff and in turn to the guest. The guest communicates their preference to the server, who in turn relays the information back to the kitchen. The cooks communicate with each other to prepare the order for the guest. The cooks communicate with the wait staff to alert them that the order is complete and that the plate needs to be delivered to the guest. Did we mention dessert? The pastry chef has his / her own set of communications and timing that are necessary as well. The circle of staff communications also includes bussers and dishwashers who need to know what work is coming and when because it directly affects their work and pace. At the

close of the evening, someone has to communicate with each team of the restaurant about closing duties and time-sensitive material for the next day of business. And wouldn't you like to know how much revenue was generated that night? That's a lot of communications, and one tiny lapse in this circle of communication can cause large problems in an operation.

Nate Feldmiller, chef-owner of Circe restaurant in Kansas City, shared his experiences of how communications skills—and sometimes the lack thereof— influenced his daily work environment as well as the daily operations of Circe.

On a daily basis, Chef Nate speaks with his staff about what happened at the restaurant during service the previous night, what is expected to take place that day, what deliveries are coming, outstanding accounting, special items on both the lunch and dinner menus, staff for each shift, and much more. Without conversations, updates, and general communications about such issues, Circe would struggle to operate.

At Circe, the menu changes often. With each change, a series of communications is necessary. The wait staff needs to know what starch, sauce and vegetable is served with the halibut to sell the dish effectively. If a guest has a food allergy, it is important for the wait staff to know what ingredients are in each dish. Certain guests may have special dietary needs that need to be understood by the server and relayed to the kitchen.

Chef Nate believes in clear and efficient communications when cooking. For example, he pointed out that, "The man cooking the vegetables needs to be working with the same timing as the woman preparing the fish. All of the foods that are served together on a plate need to come up for service at the same time." This process requires constant communication amongst the kitchen team.

Chef Nate admits that accidents happen. Occasionally he forgets to mention to the purchaser that he needs something for the kitchen. Chef Nate simply chuckled to himself when he mentioned this fact and said, "It's bound to happen." He recalls how his lack of communications put Circe in a difficult position on opening weekend. "Circe opened and lots of people arrived at once and for whatever reason they all ordered the tuna entrée. I was so busy cooking that I forgot to tell the general manager that I needed more tuna. Before I knew it, four more tuna orders came into the kitchen! The General Manager had to run to the store to buy more tuna, leaving the restaurant temporarily understaffed. Had I simply told him earlier in the night, we could have handled the situation and there would not have been any delay in service and gap in staff."

The implementation of thorough and clear communication skills is a necessity for all aspects of the restaurant industry. Lack of communications has repercussions that reverberate from the kitchen to the guest. Critical thinking, consideration, and communication directly impact the daily and long term operations of restaurant.

Case Study Questions

❶ What communications steps would need to be taken to change an item on the menu at Circe?

_____

_____

_____

_____

❷ Give an example from your work, school or personal life where communications fell apart. What happened? What could have prevented the breakdown?

_____

_____

_____

_____

_____

❸ Give an example from your work, school or personal life where you communicated effectively. What happened? What were the key factors in your team's success?

_____

_____

_____

_____

_____

Game: Mood Food

In the introduction to this chapter we discussed that food is not only something that you could communicate about, it is something you can communicate with.

Mood Food is a menu design game that has you developing menus to communicate different emotions or situations that you draw from a hat or create on your own.

Depending on the instructor's goals and available time, this game could be a design-only game with no actual cooking, or you could execute the full meal you've designed.

Developing a menu to match a specific mood or situation is an advanced culinary skill that could serve you well in a variety of situations.

Specifications for Game

ANTICIPATED TIME: FOUR HOUR LAB IN TWO PARTS—ONE HOUR INITIAL TASTING AND PLANNING SEPARATED BY TIME FOR PURCHASING. THREE-HOUR LAB TO FOLLOW.

PART I

Concept Presentation	10 minutes
Student Tasting and Notes	10 minutes
Menu Concept Planning and Formulation	25 minutes
Ingredient and Shopping Lists and Game Plan	15 minutes

Students will generate desired shopping lists after Part I.
In addition, pantry items should be made available as usual.

PART II

Review of Concept and Game Plan	10 Minutes
Station Set-up and Mise en Place	15 Minutes
Cooking	95 Minutes
Tasting and Comments	30 Minutes
Clean-Up and Debriefing	30 Minutes

Game Details

This game is for a student with basic to advanced skills. You should be comfortable in a kitchen and be familiar with basic preparations and applications.

- In this game you should form a team of three students. Your instructor may divide you or allow you to select.

- For this game, you will need to develop a menu that communicates a mood or situation provided by the instructor from the tables below. Don't share your project with the other teams—allow them to guess what mood or situation you are working on.

- This could be a design-only game or the game could be conducted in sections—the design in one section with lead time for ordering food and supplies, and the cooking during a separate time.

- First, the instructor will provide you a mood and situation or ask you to develop your own (see cutout cards on page 251 & 223).

Once you've selected your mood and situation, complete the following worksheet activities.

Student Guidelines

- **Safety First.** Put knife safety and safe food handling at the fore.
- Use the tools in the flavor chapter to help you brainstorm initial ideas and guide you through the game. Discuss merits of all suggestions and reach consensus on leading concepts.
- Write a plan for recipe execution. Do not be afraid to alter the design as you go.
- Taste as you go. For unusual combination experiments, try a small amount before proceeding with the whole batch wherever possible.
- Divide the prep work among the team.
- Maintain constant communication.
- Present finished product in a way that is visually appealing and is served at the appropriate temperature. Use the plating template in the resource section as a guide.
- Guide classmates through tasting process.

Supporting Activity

What do you associate with that mood/situation?
What do you picture?

_____

_____

_____

_____

_____

How could you communicate your mood/situation through food? What sort of flavors/textures/colors/shapes/cooking methods would be effective in communicating the goal?

_____

_____

_____

_____

_____

How might the appearance of the finished product communicate the mood or situation? Sketch a design:

Refine your ideas.

Create a work plan for creating the dish.

_____

_____

_____

_____

_____

_____

Create an ingredient (shopping) list and prep list.

_____

_____

_____

_____

_____

_____

_____

MOOD:

Angry

MOOD:

Happy

MOOD:

Sad

MOOD:

Bored

MOOD:

Excited

MOOD:

Frustrated

MOOD:

Confused

MOOD:

Mellow

MOOD:

Contented

MOOD:

Other

MOOD:

Other

MOOD:

Other

✂

Page intentionally
left blank, back side
of cutout cards

Situation

A la minute	Airplane	Bar mitzvah
Batch cooking	Breakfast	Brunch
Cruise	Festival	Formal
Formal reception	Funeral	Graduation
High volume	Hospital	Kids
Limited equipment	Low budget	Nursing Home
Pub	Romantic	School cafeteria
Small kitchen	Snack	Take out
Wedding	Dairy Allergy	Nut Allergy
Sustainable (Green)	Loss of Electricity	Loss of Gas
Loss of Running Water	Other	Other

✂

Page intentionally
left blank, back side
of cutout cards

Reflection Questions

❶ In what ways did your food communicate?

_____

_____

_____

_____

❷ Did the situation you incorporated attract or detract from communicating the mood. Explain.

_____

_____

_____

_____

❸ Describe a real world application of this exercise.

_____

_____

_____

_____

❹ Describe a situation where you wanted to communicate something through food. What did you prepare and why? What was communicated? Was it effective?

_____

_____

_____

_____

_____

❺ How was the process for this game? What were the obstacles?

_____

_____

_____

_____

_____

Variations to Game

This game can be adapted in a number of ways. Menus could consist of one to five courses depending on desired learning outcomes. Students could generate their own moods and situations and exchange with one another. Students could be challenged to guess at the mood or situation being presented. Depending on product availability and instructional goals the instructor could restrict menu options to specific ingredients or techniques.

Game: Scrambled Recipe

Where the last game, Mood Food, dealt with how food communicates, in this game, Scrambled Recipe, your challenge is to assemble the steps of a recipe to cook something in a way that you think will work.

The main twist in this exercise is that you have to unscramble the steps and improvise at the same time, since the steps themselves are verbs that are vague, intuiting a lot from a basic communication.

Game Details

This game is for a student with advanced skills. You should be comfortable in a kitchen and be familiar with basic preparations and applications. You should have done at least one game from the flavor and palate development chapter.

- Students should form teams of three. Instructor can form teams or students can self-select.
- In this game you are to prepare a three-component entrée from the following ingredients:

Protein Item (Poultry, Fish, Meat) / Rice / Green Vegetable

- Using *all* of the scrambled verbs below, organize them so that you can prepare the menu above in a way that is flavorful and appealing. Visualize a finished dish that manages to incorporate each of the action verbs that you have to work with. You must use each word and can add but cannot remove. On the right hand column, rearrange the terms and write the full sentence.
- For example, if on the left it says, "Chop," your first task on the right might indicate, "Chop one small onion." You can use your words in any order, but list them in recipe format to follow them one-by-one.
- Then, trade recipes with other teams and see how well the written instructions communicate the execution you envisioned.

Specifications for Game

ANTICIPATED TIME: . . . .THREE HOUR LAB

Concept Presentation . . . . .20 minutes

Planning, Descrambling
and Station Set-up . . . . .20 minutes

Cooking. . . . . .90 minutes

Tasting, Discussion
and Debriefing. . . . . .30 minutes

Clean-up . . . . .20 minutes

Ingredients Needed
(per team of 2–3)

Each team should be given two items such as poultry, fish or meat, ½ cup of rice and about ½ pound of a green vegetable. Pantry items should be made available.

Student Guidelines

- **Safety First.** Put knife safety and safe food handling at the fore.
- Use the tools in the flavor chapter to help you plan.
- Write a plan for recipe execution.
- Taste as you go.
- Divide the prep work among the team.
- Maintain constant communication

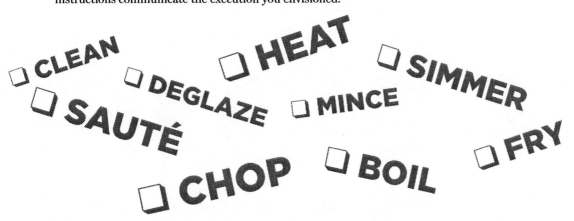

REMEMBER YOU MUST USE ALL OF THE VERBS BELOW YOU CAN ADD BUT YOU CANNOT REMOVE!

- ❏ Clean
- ❏ Sauté
- ❏ Deglaze
- ❏ Chop
- ❏ Mince
- ❏ Heat
- ❏ Simmer
- ❏ Boil
- ❏ Fry

ACTION VERBS	WRITE THE FULL SENTENCE. For example, if on the left it says, "Chop," your first task on the right might indicate, "Chop one small onion." You can use your words in any order, but list them in recipe format to follow them one-by-one.

Reflection Questions

❶ How well did you understand the instructions as they were communicated to you? What would have made them clearer?

_____

_____

_____

❷ How well did the other team understand the instructions as you communicated them? What could have made them clearer?

_____

_____

_____

❸ How did the process for the game work? What worked well? What didn't?

_____

_____

_____

❹ Describe a real world application of the communication skills you developed in this game.

_____

_____

_____

Variations to Game

Instructors can use the recipe in the instructor guide or can create their own. Teams can also create their own scrambled recipes and challenge other teams to unscramble them.

_____

Game: Shift's Over

A kitchen under control, where everyone works well together and knows their role is a quiet place. People are busy cooking. Conversations are muted and polite—asking for feedback or advice, but never a mad scramble. To achieve this kind of work environment, cooks need to be skilled at their craft, skilled at working as a team and comfortable with the menu and with one another.

The previous games in this communication chapter focused on using food to communicate and communicating how to cook through a written recipe. This game challenges you to communicate with your teammates on the fly.

It tests your knowledge of classic preparations as well as how well you communicate steps in the cooking process.

....

Game Details

This game is for a student with advanced skills. You should be comfortable in a kitchen and be very familiar with basic preparations and applications. There is no maximum skill level. Even professional chefs have fun with and are challenged by this game.

- Students should be in teams of 2–3. Each team should be told in advance that they will be preparing a classic recipe from a major culinary textbook. Students may choose their own or can be assigned a recipe. Possibilities include:
  - Lamb couscous
  - Bouillabaisse
  - Chicken Cacciatore
  - Fresh Pasta with Garlic Alfredo
  - Pissaladiere
  - And many more that can be completed within the available time.
- Each team should begin their mise en place and cooking of their classic recipe. Then the game starts!
- Every 10 minutes, and the instructor's indication, there is a shift change and each team must rotate to the neighboring team's recipe.
- With each shift change there is a 30 second maximum briefing allowed. One team member should stay behind to brief the new team on progress and the recipe and at least one team member should be briefed on the new recipe.
- The rotation should end with the original teams finishing the recipe that they started.

- Along the way consider the following reflection questions to be discussed at the end:
  - Which briefings went smoothly? Why?
  - Which did not? Why not?
  - Was it challenging to pick up where someone left off? Why or why not?
  - How did the work habits of the other teams influence the transitions?
  - What forms of communication were in evidence?
  - Did the finished product come out as hoped? Why or why not?

....

Specifications for Game

ANTICIPATED TIME: .... THREE HOUR LAB

Concept Presentation . . . . .10 minutes

Student Planning and
Station Set-up . . . . 15 minutes

Cooking. . . . . .110 minutes

Tasting, Discussion
and Debriefing. . . . . .25 minutes

Clean-up. . . . . 20 minutes

....

Ingredients Needed
(per team of 2–3)

Depending on what recipes are chosen, enough for a few portions should be made available as for any culinary class.

Student Guidelines

- **Safety First.** Put knife safety and safe food handling at the fore.
- Write a plan for recipe execution.
- Divide the prep work among the team.
- Present finished product in a way that is visually appealing and is served at the appropriate temperature. Use the plating template in the resource section as a guide.

Reflection Questions

❶ Which briefings went smoothly? Why? Which did not? Why not?

_____

_____

_____

_____

❷ Was it challenging to pick up where someone left off? Why or why not?

_____

_____

_____

_____

❸ How did the work habits of the other teams influence the transitions?

_____

_____

_____

_____

❹ What forms of communication were in evidence?

_____

_____

_____

_____

_____

_____

❺ Did the finished product come out as hoped? Why or why not?

_____

_____

_____

_____

_____

_____

Variations to Game

This game is an especially good opportunity for you or your instructor to adjust the focus to specific classic or advanced culinary skills as well as specific styles of cuisine or featured ingredients. Since everyone will work on every recipe over the course of the game, it is a good opportunity to test knowledge of classic recipes and preparations.

Game: Welcome Aboard

In the previous game, Shift's Over, you worked on your communication skills by taking over someone's station with only a short briefing, relying heavily on communication and your knowledge of the repertoire of cuisine to make the transitions smoothly.

This game is a variation of Shift's Over, but one worthy of its own category.

In Welcome Aboard, the entire team doesn't move from station to station but rather at each shift change you select one team member to rotate to the next station. The result is that at all times you have a mixture of old and new on your team, experienced at that station and novice, much like life in a busy foodservice operation.

This game challenges you to get a new team member up to speed so that that team member can quickly contribute to your team's success. The other wrinkle in this game is that you have less time to make the same products, so allowing your new team member to stand to the side and observe will not be an efficient strategy! To succeed you'll need to quickly train your team's new addition.

One important rule: The new team member must stay on the team through at least one more rotation.

Game Details

This game is for a student with advanced skills. You should be comfortable in a kitchen and be very familiar with basic preparations and applications.

- Students should be in teams of 2–3. Each team should be told in advance that they will be preparing a classic recipe from a major culinary textbook. Possibilities include:
  - Lamb couscous
  - Bouillabaisse
  - Chicken Cacciatore
  - Fresh Pasta with Garlic Alfredo
  - Pissaladiere
  - And many more that can be completed within the available time.
- Each team should begin their mise en place and cooking of their classic recipe. Then the game starts!
- Every 10 minutes, at the instructor's indication, there is a shift change and each team must *choose one team member* to rotate to the neighboring team's recipe. By the third shift change, all team members need to have rotated at least once.
- With each shift change there is a 30 second maximum briefing allowed. One team member should stay behind to brief the new team on progress and the recipe and at least one team member should be briefed on the new recipe.

- The rotation should end with the original teams finishing the recipe that they started.
- Along the way consider the following reflection questions to be discussed at the end:
  - Which team members were chosen to move on? Why?
  - Which team members chose to move on themselves? Why?
  - How do these decisions relate to your experiences in the Teamwork chapter?
  - Which briefings went smoothly? Why?
  - Which did not? Why not?
  - Was it challenging to pick up where someone left off? Why or why not?
  - How did the work habits of the other teams influence the transitions?
  - What forms of communication were in evidence?
  - Did the finished product come out as hoped? Why or why not?
  - If you also played Shift's Over, how did this game compare?

Specifications for Game

ANTICIPATED TIME: . . . . THREE HOUR LAB

Concept Presentation . . . . 15 minutes

Student Planning and

Station Set-up . . . . 15 minutes

Cooking . . . . 90 minutes

Tasting, Discussion

and Debriefing . . . . 30 minutes

Clean-up . . . . 30 minutes

Ingredients Needed
(per team of 2–3)

Depending on what recipes are chosen, enough for a few portions should be made available as for any culinary class.

....

Student Guidelines

- **Safety First.** Put knife safety and safe food handling at the fore.
- Write a plan for recipe execution.
- Divide the prep work among the team.
- Present finished product in a way that is visually appealing and is served at the appropriate temperature. Use the plating template in the resource section as a guide.

Reflection Questions

❶ Which team members were chosen to move on? Why?

_____

_____

_____

❷ Which team members chose to move on themselves? Why?

_____

_____

_____

❸ How do these decisions relate to your experiences in the Teamwork chapter?

_____

_____

_____

❹ Which briefings went smoothly? Why?

_____

_____

_____

❺ Which did not? Why not?

_____

_____

_____

_____

_____

❻ Was it challenging to pick up where someone left off? Why or why not?

_____

_____

_____

_____

_____

❼ How did the work habits of the other teams influence the transitions?

_____

_____

_____

_____

_____

_____

❽ What forms of communication were in evidence?

_____

_____

_____

_____

_____

❾ Did the finished product come out as hoped? Why or why not?

_____

_____

_____

_____

_____

❿ If you also played Shift's Over, how did this game compare?

_____

_____

_____

_____

_____

Variations to Game

This game is an especially good opportunity for you or your instructor to adjust the focus to specific classic or advanced culinary skills or specific world cuisines or featured ingredients. Since everyone will work on every recipe over the course of the game, it is a good opportunity to test knowledge of classic recipes and preparations.

Game: Teaching's Not as Easy as it Looks!

To this point in the chapter we have looked at communication in three ways:

- How food communicates.
- Written communication about food.
- Interpersonal verbal communication about food.

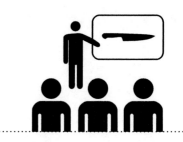

This game ties all of these elements together by having you do the challenging job your instructor does every day—teaching.

Teaching is a complicated and high-level form of communication because communicated items need not only to be understood, but to be internalized by the learner in such a way that they're incorporated into the learner's practice. For example, when your culinary instructor demonstrated a new knife cut such as a tourner to you, you had to do more than just listen or look at the demonstration. You had to envision yourself making those cuts, practice and then do it for real.

In this game, Teaching's Not as Easy as it Looks, you're challenged to use multiple forms of communication to teach your classmates an advanced culinary skill such as a knife cut or garnish, food or preparation of another culture, pastry technique or culinary technique.

So where does the game come in? Once you've taught your classmates the new skill, they need to apply it in a design for a recipe or menu application so that they can demonstrate their understanding of the skill—in short, how well you communicated to them.

Game Details

This game is for a student with advanced skills. You should be comfortable in a kitchen and be very familiar with basic preparations and applications.

- Students should be in teams of 2–3. Each team should be told in advance that they will be teaching their teammates an advanced culinary technique or skill in a lesson of approximately 10 minutes. Be sure the teaching of the lesson includes both auditory and visual communication methods.
- Then the game starts!
- Based on the team's understanding of the new techniques and applications learned, design a menu item or menu incorporating the new skills.
- If time allows, these items can be executed in another session.

Specifications for Game

ANTICIPATED TIME: THREE HOUR LAB

Concept Presentation . . . . 15 minutes
Student Planning and
Station Set-up . . . . 15 minutes
Cooking. . . . . 90 minutes
Tasting, Discussion
and Debriefing. . . . . 30 minutes
Clean-up. . . . . 30 minutes

Ingredients Needed
(per team of 2-3)

Depending on what techniques or applications are chosen, enough for a few portions should be made available as for any culinary class.

Student Guidelines

- **Safety First.** Put knife safety and safe food handling at the fore.

Supporting Activities

List and describe the new advanced skills/techniques taught in your group:

What were the challenges you had in teaching these skills?
What were the challenges you had in learning them?

What modes of communication were incorporated in your teaching and learning?

Brainstorm ideas for a menu item that would incorporate the new skills you learned:

_____

_____

_____

_____

Sketch out some thoughts:

Refine your ideas.

Create a prep list and work plan for execution.

_____

_____

_____

_____

If executing, prepare a shopping list.

_____

_____

_____

_____

Reflection Questions

❶ How did teaching compare to your preconceptions of how it would be to do it?

_____

_____

_____

_____

❷ What modes of communication are most comfortable for you?

_____

_____

_____

_____

❸ What were the biggest challenges in teaching?

_____

_____

_____

_____

❹ Would you choose a different skill to teach if you were doing this again?

_____

_____

_____

_____

_____

_____

Chapter Summary

In this chapter you experienced a variety of scenarios that challenged you to communicate in a variety of ways You played a game where you used food itself to communicate and also played games where good interpersonal verbal and written communication was a key to success.

These games assess written, verbal and nonverbal communication. A restaurant cannot operate without good communication between staff members, from guests to kitchen. Beyond running the restaurant, communicating is crucial to the experience of your guest, and establishing what your restaurant is about. Communicating with food is a way of communicating with customers at a time when diners are seeking that connection to people and places, in what they eat. You should now understand how food communicates, written communication about food, and interpersonal verbal communication about food.

Chapter 9 Assessment Questions

❶ Describe a team you worked with that worked especially well Why did it work?

_____

_____

_____

_____

_____

❷ Describe a team you worked with that didn't work well. Why not?

_____

_____

_____

_____

_____

_____

❸ Describe a communicator that was effective on one of your teams.
   What did she or he do that made that person an effective communicator?

_____

_____

_____

_____

_____

❹ What did you learn about communication from these games? How might that help you in the future?

_____

_____

_____

_____

_____

❺ Describe the cooking process you used for each game.
   What worked well? What would you have done differently?

_____

_____

_____

_____

_____

❻ Assess your final outcome.

What worked in your concepts? What didn't? What would you do differently in the future?

Assessment Rubric for Communication Games

CRITERIA	PROFESSIONAL	DEVELOPING	NOVICE
Cooking Advanced Culinary Techniques	Student demonstrated professional-level knife skills and cooking techniques, needing little support. Student worked neatly, observing all safety and sanitation guidelines.	Student demonstrated some professional-level knife skills and cooking techniques, needing support or correction. Student did not neatly maintain station or did not observe some important safety and sanitation guidelines.	Student demonstrated developing skills and cooking techniques, needing help. Student did not maintain station or failed to observe critical safety and sanitation guidelines.**
Teamwork	Student was an active and engaged participant in the team and team members could clearly point to student's contribution. Student fully understood scenario and quickly adapted to situation, helping other students along.	Student worked with team but was not a key contributor to the final result. Student understood scenario and took direction from classmates in order to adapt to the situation.	Student did not show evidence of engagement with team and did not significantly contribute to the result. Student misunderstood scenario or did not adapt to situation.
Oral and Written Communication	Student work exhibited thoughtful reflection on process and included concrete and significant conclusions. Student communicated clearly and concisely to teammates.	Student work exhibited reflection on process and awareness of issues. Student mostly communicated clearly to teammates.	Student work lacked reflection on process or awareness of issues. Student was unable to communicate effectively to teammates.
Style and Creativity Professional presentation	Student brought innovative and creative ideas: dish was attractive and restaurant quality.	Student did some innovative or creative things: dish was acceptable but unremarkable.	Student did not show evidence of creativity or innovation: dish was only attention-getting due to inadequacies.

*Note: Criteria could be given equal or various weights at instructor's discretion and tied to letter or number grades as desired.

**Note: Critical Safety and Sanitation Violations include: Cross-Contamination, Time/Temperature Violations, and knife handling hazardous to self or others.

10/
Creating Your Own Games and Continuous Improvement

If you have worked through this book in sequence you have come a long way. You have worked through some basic tools to help you in your career—a review of the basics, platforms, flavor tools and seasonality and the food system.

You have read about competencies that chefs think are critical to your success—problem solving, flavor and palate development, teamwork and communication—and have read real-world situations in which a mastery of these competencies have saved the day for several accomplished chefs. You have played a series of culinary games that work to develop your culinary and competency-based skills in fun, realistic, challenging, or unusual ways.

And if we've succeeded as authors, you are a better cook in one or more ways. Perhaps you're more comfortable cooking from a platform now rather than a traditional recipe. Perhaps you feel a new confidence when given ingredients without cooking instructions. Perhaps you've led your team to an unanticipated success. Perhaps you've developed new skills in combining flavors that work together in innovative ways.

Now, drawing on all you have learned and done, you have two important challenges to tackle:

- Creating your own games
- Continuous improvement

Creating Your Own Games

As a player of many of these games you know which features you like and which you do not. This chapter leaves you with an opportunity to teach us a few things as you develop and pilot your own game. We begin with identifying some guidelines for creating your games, we provide the same template we used in constructing games, and we encourage you to share your games with us via our culinary website, *culinaryimprovisation.com*. You can even have your games included in the next edition of this book.

When you share your improvisational ideas and food concepts, you're not only sharing with us, but with a community of improvisational cooks like you. They will read your thoughts and respond, forming a critical

CHAPTER OBJECTIVES

By the end of these games you should be able to:

① Explain guidelines for creating improvisational games.

② Create a game

③ Explain criteria for assessment of game performance.

community; you have the opportunity to try out your ideas in psychic space before you prepare them with your hands in the kitchen.

This process is used in many crafts, and referred to as workshopping. "Workshop" has many meanings, all of which apply to the development of culinary concepts. A workshop is a place where things are designed, built or finished, with the tools or machines that are stored there—in your case, the kitchen, with its stoves, pots, utensils and ingredients. A workshop is a gathering of people for instruction, like a training session—exactly what you have participated in while completing the games in this book, receiving instruction about various competencies. Creating your own games and playing them with other students continues the culinary workshopping you have begun here.

Your work and participation in the games has most likely been critiqued by the instructor and by your classmates. In theater, a play is workshopped when actors read the lines aloud with the playwright in attendance, and criticism and commentary is offered by those involved in the production of the play and an audience. In writing, a workshop is a group who gather to discuss and critique new work. Both of these notions of workshopping are at play when you develop a network of chefs and informed tasters—online, in person—to share culinary concepts and ideas.

Workshopping gets your creative juices flowing, by feeling the pressure of sharing your ideas, and by hearing the ideas of others and building on them. Participating in a workshop keeps you thinking creatively about food and technique. Workshopping

is constructive criticism: shared ideas, responses and discussion. You post or voice your ideas; others post or voice theirs, and everyone, respectfully, honestly and in turn, comments on them.

Respect is the key factor in workshopping. Respect your fellow chefs and the courage it takes to offer up your ideas for criticism. Everyone who is participating is interested in the work being as good as possible, and comments and critiques are restricted to the food or menu concepts. Do not make personal critiques.

Also remember that specific responses are most useful. Rather than simply saying, "I like this," tell why. "I like that the spiciness of the fresh ginger is gentled by the reduced heavy cream" is a very informative comment. "Cooking matzo balls with a butane torch causes them to lose their nubby texture and taste like burnt paper" could provoke a flurry of experimentation. Specific comments make it easy to alter the concept, and trigger other ideas. Specificity generates action. This cycle of constructive criticism and revision of your concepts can result in amazing, unique foods, and makes you a more knowledgeable and creative chef!

Here are some suggestions to consider as you create your own game:

1. Start from a problem or situation that needs improvement. In writing this book, the first step was not to come up with cool games, but rather to identify the characteristics or competencies that chefs felt were lacking in their employees. We sat down with chefs and food service managers, individually and in small groups, and spent a lot of time on the phone simply asking them to, "Describe what you're looking for in a new kitchen employee" and, "What skills or competencies do you think are lacking in your new employees and why?"

Perhaps you experienced a problem at work or in school that could have been prevented or more easily solved with the right skills—that's a perfect starting point for an improvisation game.

2. Balance creativity with structure. It's great to come up with games that really push you to your creative limits. That said, at what point does creative cooking cease to become innovative and just end up weird? Balance game ideas that challenge you to be creative with those that set limitations on the finished product—that it need to be salable, appeal to the customer, or be reproducible.

3. Think time and limitations. Keep in mind the typical structure of your class or lab. These games have to fit into that structure. Supplies and equipment need to be available. For instance, it would be a great challenge to design a game around regional food and improvisation: all ingredients must be sourced from within 100 miles of your school's kitchen. But how would a student—or an instructor—be able to work within those restrictions? A chef 100 percent in charge of their own kitchen can source 100 percent whatever they want, but most of us have stricter limitations.

4. Don't try to do everything. Decide the main objective that you want your game to achieve. Is it to reinforce one of the competencies focused on in this book—problem solving, flavor and palate development, teamwork or communication? Is it simply to be a better improviser? Is it a specific culinary skill like knife work, cooking en papillote, or charcuterie? Or does it challenge you to work with a specific ingredient such as a whole fish or a special miso? Try to keep the key objective at the fore. Many of the games naturally touch on other competencies as well—nearly all challenge you to incorporate proper culinary technique, good seasoning, and good plate presentation skills, for example. But don't try to incorporate everything in a single game.

5. Be clear with the rules. The toughest part of designing a game is writing the rules clearly so that they can be understood by all of the players. If the rule isn't clear there's really no game at all. As you write them envision yourself as a player and think about what you would need to know. Test their clarity by giving them to someone else and asking them to explain to you, in their own words, how the game is played.

6. Try it out. The best way to know whether these games work is to try them! All of the games in this book have been tested by student teams. Test your game with a few students before scaling it up. As you test it, make some notes on what works and what doesn't and fix the tricky parts. This may be a simple matter of clarifying one of the rules or the game may not work and you'll need to scrap it completely.

7. Scale it up. Once you are confident your game works on a small scale, work out the problems, clarify the language and scale it up!

Game Template

Now that you have some guidelines for your game development, complete the following template to develop your new game.

Critical Competency

What desired competency are you addressing?

_____

_____

_____

_____

Introduction to Game

How will this game address the competency? Why is it important?
What's great about this game?

_____

_____

_____

_____

Objectives for Game

What is the object of the game and what will the players learn by playing
this game?

_____

_____

_____

_____

The Rules of the Game

How is the game played? Outline the rules step by step.

1. _____

2. _____

3. _____

4. _____

5. _____

6. _____

7. _____

8. _____

9. _____

10. _____

11. _____

12. _____

Timing

How long should this game take to play? What are the steps?

_____

_____

_____

_____

Specifications for Game

What food, equipment and other supplies are required to play this game?

_____

_____

_____

_____

_____

Student Guidelines

What should the players keep in mind in order to succeed in this game?

1. _____

2. _____

3. _____

4. _____

5. _____

6. _____

7. _____

8. _____

9. _____

10. _____

Instructor/Facilitator Guidelines

What should the instructor or facilitator keep in mind in order for the game to be played?

1. _____

2. _____

3. _____

4. _____

5. _____

Success

How is the winner decided? What are you looking for in the results?

_____

_____

_____

_____

_____

_____

Assessment and Continuous Improvement

In a traditional culinary class, assessment guidelines are fairly clear. For example, the instructor may prepare a hollandaise sauce as a demonstration. Then you, as a student, would try to make a hollandaise sauce similar to your instructor's. If it looks and tastes like hers or his, good job! "A"! If it doesn't, you've done something wrong and you either need to redo it or take a lesser grade.

But in culinary improvisation we want your finished product to be different and creative. We want you to use proper culinary technique, work neatly and safely, and serve palatable food, of course, but what if you make something really weird? Should that be given an especially good or poor grade? What if you try something and it simply fails from a culinary perspective. Do you fail the exercise?

No. You shouldn't.

A variety of assessment suggestions are given in the instructor's guide that accompanies this book. The following assessment rubric will be helpful in working through your games. You'll notice that we don't recommend you be graded on how delicious your food is, but rather a host of factors—how professionally you work, how creative you can be while observing the rules of a game, how well you work as a team and how well you communicate with others. Of course we want your final product to be presented proudly and professionally as well. But if it's really off-the-wall, we know as well as you do!—it's part of the game.

Chapter Summary

The culmination of all your learnings about problem solving, communication, teamwork, flavors and techniques is to create games of your own, that teach the values and concepts you look for in a culinary partner. Experimenting, constantly assessing your own improvement, developing your own ideas for games, and interacting with others to share knowledge and ideas put you on the path to culinary mastery! Best of luck!

CRITERIA	PROFESSIONAL	EXPERIENCED	DEVELOPING	NOVICE
Culinary Improvisation Advanced cooking 40 points	Student demonstrated professional-level knife skills and cooking techniques, needing little support. Student worked neatly, observing all safety and sanitation guidelines.	Student demonstrated professional-level knife skills and cooking techniques, needing some support. Student worked neatly, observing most safety and sanitation guidelines.	Student demonstrated some professional-level knife skills and cooking techniques, needing support or correction. Student did not neatly maintain station or did not observe some important safety and sanitation guidelines.	Student demonstrated developing skills and cooking techniques, needing help. Student did not maintain station or failed to observe critical safety and sanitation guidelines.
Adaptive skills Working in groups 20 points	Student was an active and engaged participant in the team and team members could clearly point to student's contribution. Student fully understood scenario and quickly adapted to situation, helping other students along.	Student was an active and engaged participant in the team and student's contribution could be discerned. Student understood scenario and adapted to situation.	Student worked with team but did not show evidence of engagement with the team and did contribute to the result. Student understood scenario and took direction from classmates in order to adapt to the situation.	Student did not show evidence of engagement with team and did not significantly contribute to the result. Student misunderstood scenario or did not adapt to situation.
Written Communication Informal writing and reflection 20 points	Student work exhibited thoughtful reflection on process and included concrete and significant conclusions.	Student work exhibited thoughtful reflection on process and included concrete conclusions.	Student work exhibited reflection on process and awareness of issues.	Student work lacked reflection on process or awareness of issues.
Style and Creativity Professional presentation 20 points	Student used an innovative approach and brought creative ideas: dish was innovative and restaurant quality.	Student used an innovative approach or brought creative ideas: dish caused one to take notice.	Student did some innovative or creative things: dish was acceptable but unremarkable.	Student did not show evidence of creativity or innovation: dish was only attention-getting due to inadequacies.

Your instructor may adopt this rubric to assess your performance, may adapt it to meet her or his needs or may use entirely different assessment criteria. Regardless, the rubric above can be helpful in improving your game and workplace performance in the process of continuous improvement.

To use the rubric, read each row across and indicate how you think you performed in a particular game. You may decide you're somewhere in between two categories which is fine. Mark an "X" in each box that you think describes you. Now mark a star on where you hope to be. While your instructor may provide you with a grade important to your ego, graduation, or competitive spirit, it is a valuable exercise to assess yourself and make sure that you are moving along the scale from novice to professional. Remember, the primary force grading you when you finish with school will be yourself!